A **NAOMI SCHNEIDER** BOOK

Highlighting the lives and experiences of marginalized communities, the select titles of this imprint draw from sociology, anthropology, law, and history, as well as from the traditions of journalism and advocacy, to reassess mainstream history and promote unconventional thinking about contemporary social and political issues. Their authors share the passion, commitment, and creativity of Executive Editor Naomi Schneider.

The publisher and the University of California Press Foundation gratefully acknowledge the generous support of the Anne G. Lipow Endowment Fund in Social Justice and Human Rights.

Healing from Hate

Healing from Hate

HOW YOUNG MEN GET INTO—AND
OUT OF—VIOLENT EXTREMISM

Michael Kimmel

UNIVERSITY OF CALIFORNIA PRESS

University of California Press, one of the most distinguished university presses in the United States, enriches lives around the world by advancing scholarship in the humanities, social sciences, and natural sciences. Its activities are supported by the UC Press Foundation and by philanthropic contributions from individuals and institutions. For more information, visit www.ucpress.edu.

University of California Press
Oakland, California

© 2018 by Michael Kimmel

Library of Congress Cataloging-in-Publication Data

Names: Kimmel, Michael S., author.
Title: Healing from hate : how young men get into-and out of-violent
    extremism / Michael Kimmel.
Description: Oakland, California : University of California Press, [2018] |
    Includes bibliographical references and index. |
Identifiers: LCCN 2017038789 (print) | LCCN 2017044327 (ebook) |
    ISBN 9780520966086 () | ISBN 9780520292635 (cloth : alk. paper)
Subjects: LCSH: Right-wing extremists—Case studies. | Masculinity—
    Psychological aspects. | White supremacy movements.
Classification: LCC HN49.R33 (ebook) | LCC HN49.R33 .K56 2018 (print) |
    DDC 320.53/3—dc23
LC record available at https://lccn.loc.gov/2017038789

Manufactured in the United States of America

25   24   23   22   21   20   19   18
10   9   8   7   6   5   4   3   2   1

To the memory of my grandmother, Beryl Michtom
And to the memory of my father, Edwin Kimmel

Hate between men comes from cutting ourselves off from one another. Because we don't want anyone to look inside us, since it's not a pretty sight in there.

Ludwig Wittgenstein

Contents

Preface

Domestic terrorism may be the single greatest threat to America's national security. A 2009 Department of Homeland Security report titled "Rightwing Extremism" concluded that "rightwing extremists may be gaining new recruits by playing on their fears about several emergent issues," including, at the time, the election of the nation's first African American president and the economic downturn. Currently, the Southern Poverty Law Center counts 917 active hate groups in the United States alone. These groups range from the neo-Nazis and the Ku Klux Klan to militias, Aryan survivalists, white supremacist youth groups, and violent religious cults. (The largest increase in 2016 was among anti-immigrant and anti-Muslim groups.[1])

You'd think that the current administration would be eager to distance itself from these groups, to establish its populist legitimacy on bases other than racism, xenophobic nativism, and anti-Semitism. You'd be wrong. The Trump administration has embraced what is now being relabeled and nearly legitimated as the alt-right, and even bringing its members into the administration. Ironically, this newfound proximity to political power may decrease the number of hate groups, since their organization rests on opposition to the government. When you have a friend in the White

House, why organize against it? Watch for the Trump administration to herald its success at bringing down the number of oppositional hate groups!

According to a report from the New America Foundation, "Since the attacks on September 11, 2001, nearly twice as many Americans have been killed by non-Muslim extremists than by jihadists."[2] The Trump administration's response was to insist that all references to "terrorism" have the words "radical Islamist" in front of it, and that all programs and projects designed to address domestic terrorism be scrapped.

Sadly, one of the organizations I discuss in this book was actually defunded by this new administration. Life After Hate, a North American organization dedicated to helping violent right-wing extremists get out of the movement, had been awarded a substantial grant over two years to develop a deradicalization program in the United States modeled on EXIT in Sweden. In late June, the Trump administration approved the funding of all the successful grant recipients—except those that addressed right-wing extremism or worked in Muslim communities.[3]

Yes, these are dangerous times, when the voices of hate seem to drown out all hope of dialogue, respect, and reconciliation. Nevertheless, I remain optimistic. Completing this book leaves me hopeful because this research has taken me into some of the darkest crevices of intolerance and rage, yet the people I discuss here have found a way to return to the light. This is a book about how young men (and some women) get into violent extremist movements, and how they can get out—or, more accurately, how many of them *got themselves out*—and now need our help to turn around and help others do the same.

In my previous book, *Angry White Men: American Masculinity at the End of an Era* (2013; revised edition, 2017), I took the temperature of a significant swath of American citizens: disgruntled, angry white men. Whether discussing angry white boys (rampage school shooters); or scions of hate radio, Tea Partiers, and pre-Trump supporters; or men who murder or assault women; or the misogynist Men's Rights Activists, I kept hearing a voice of what I came to call "aggrieved entitlement," a sense of righteous indignation, of undeserved victimhood in a world suddenly dominated by political correctness. The rewards that these white men felt had been promised for a lifetime of, as they saw it, playing by the rules that someone else had established had suddenly dried up—or, as they saw it, the water had been diverted to far less deserving "others."

These men were angry, but they all looked back nostalgically to a time when their sense of masculine entitlement went unchallenged. They wanted to reclaim their country, restore their rightful place in it, and retrieve their manhood in the process. They wanted, in the words of the Tea Party, to "take our country back," and in the last election's most potent slogan, "make American great again."

The last chapter of *Angry White Men* discusses the use of masculinity on the extreme right. Interviews with nearly fifty young, current white nationalists had left me both feeling empathic for these guys' pain and despairing over whether or not anything could enable them to find a place with some dignity in this new, multicultural, and more egalitarian world. I heard them express their distress that the respect and obedience they felt was theirs by birthright actually had been upended, leaving them both bereft and enraged. I saw how they felt emasculated—humiliated as men—by preparing to be breadwinners, family providers, in a world that no longer seemed to need the skills they possessed. I explored how they used gender, in particular masculinity, to "problematize" the Other, to claim that racial or ethnic or religious sexual minorities were not worthy of the rewards they were now reaping, because "they" were not "real men." And I saw how the organizations on the extreme right used masculinity to manipulate these guys' pain and despair into white supremacist and neo-Nazi hatred as a way to "take their manhood back." Was there a way to reach them, to help them get out of such a downward spiral?

It turns out that it was already happening. I began hearing about projects to help neo-Nazi skinheads, white nationalists, Islamist jihadists, and others get out of the movements they'd joined. It was the former members themselves who were doing it, one skinhead at a time, providing the support they needed—material and emotional—to break with a movement that had no future. And they were doing it precisely by addressing what the active members believed they were getting out of their participation. The world of "formers" was a world of building an alternative community, of offering solidarity, friendship, camaraderie, and compassion. Sometimes these formers offered material support, such as safe houses, job training, or job placement. Sometimes they just offered support without judgment, since so many guys feel tremendous shame about what they did while they were in the movement. (In fact, as I came to understand, some guys stay in the movement just because they cannot face the shame of honestly confronting their pasts.)

As I watched groups like EXIT in Stockholm, listened to a leader from Life After Hate recount his story to a throng of entranced Yeshiva students in Brooklyn, or learned how an anti-jihadist imam sits for hours, days even, with young jihadists, I began to see that what they offered these guys getting out was an alternative grounding for their identity, a way to feel like a man without the violence and hatred on which their sense of masculine identity had come to depend. They were putting into practice exactly the sorts of mechanisms I had been imagining as I finished *Angry White Men*. They were giving these guys a way to retrieve a sense of themselves as men, to reassemble an identity from the shards of misplaced rage.

They helped other men, men just like them, untether their sense of masculinity from violence and helped them to reconnect to their loved ones (their wives and girlfriends, their parents, and their children). They gave these "clients" a way to feel like stakeholders in a system they had previously condemned because they had felt so scorned by it. They helped them find new poles—family, work, community, faith—around which this new and fragile sense of masculinity, a masculinity stripped of fraudulent entitlement and enriched by a sense of purpose, could now revolve. And in that way, these organizations, the very organizations I profile in this book—EXIT Sweden, EXIT Deutschland, Life After Hate, and the Quilliam Foundation—offer the one thing that had been so fully drained from these young men's lives: hope.

These young men took many paths into the movement. Yet their stories had one common theme that recurred so continually that the fact it is still so rarely discussed is startling: masculinity. Whether I was talking with ex–neo-Nazi skinheads in Sweden, ex–white supremacists in the United States, or even ex-jihadists in London, the issue of masculinity—of feeling like a real man, proving one's manhood—did not fail to come up. And that isn't because I'm a sociologist, a gender studies scholar, or even a masculinity researcher.

I suspect researchers tend to overlook masculinity because most of the research on extremism focuses on the political and economic sources of participants' discontent, or their psychological and familial backgrounds. That research is vital, necessary—and incomplete. In talking with these guys, I realized that adherence to extremist ideology came rather late in the recruitment process, and that their experiences of camaraderie and community with their brothers, their sense of purpose, of sacred mission, and their sense that their lives, as men, actually mattered in the world were far more salient motivations for both entering the movement and staying in it. The movement was their family, and in their family, the band of the brothers, they felt validated as men.

Let me be clear, as I now write something I will say again and again in the following pages. I am not saying that by exploring the meaning of masculinity for those who engage in extremist politics, we can fully understand and explain these movements. Of course not. I do not offer here a single-variable explanation. We do need to analyze the structural, the political and economic, forces that marginalize so many. We need to hear the stories of childhood abuse, neglect, and violence that traumatize so many children and so badly scar their fragile psyches. And we also need to understand how these forces are experienced as gendered, how so many young guys feel so emasculated by their family lives or their economic marginalization that they seek to retrieve and restore their manhood by joining up. We need to hear and understand their grievances, even if we might suggest that the sense of entitlement from which they spring is undemocratic and illegitimate. We need to understand why so many feel so aggrieved to begin with. That feeling is what brings them in, and it's one of the major reasons why they stay.

What this means is that in helping young men get out of the movement, we must find ways to reintegrate them into society—as men. If we really want to help these guys get out, we have to fully understand why they get in, and why they stay.

Acknowledgments

The initial support for this research was provided by a generous Fellowship from the Carnegie Corporation, and it has been sustained subsequently by grants from the American-Scandinavian Foundation, a President's Distinguished Travel Grant at Stony Brook University, and by Charles Knight.

I am grateful to the many people who were willing to talk with me, the clients to whom I've given pseudonyms and who shared their stories. I'm especially grateful to Jackie Arklöv, Dr. Usama Hasan, Angela King, Tony McAleer, Frankie Meeink, Robert Orell, Christian Picciolini, and Mubin Shaikh.

To Klas Hyllander, who provided my home away from home during all the research trips to Sweden; Daniel Koehler, my initial guide into EXIT Deutschland; to Katja Walstrom and Robert Orell, who arranged my visits to Swedish prisons to speak with Jackie Arlov and facilitated all the interviews with clients at EXIT, my gratitude always.

My agent, Gail Ross, is calming when I need her to be, and an enthusiastic booster when I need that. One couldn't ask for a better editor than Naomi Schneider, and I'm grateful to Steven Baker, Tamie Parker Song, and Benjy Mailings for the help with both prose and pictures.

My family and friends have borne my obsession with the extreme right with just the right mixture of forbearance and fascination, and offered much support and engaged conversation. I hope that this book answers the question about what a nice Jewish boy from Brooklyn was doing hanging around with ex-neo-Nazis in Germany or with ex-jihadists in London. At times, it wasn't even clear to me. But it is now. It was about finding that hope, that possibility of redemption. I suspect we all need it.

M.S.K.
Brooklyn, New York
August, 2017

1 The Making—and Unmaking— of Violent Men

Nationalism typically springs from masculinized memory, masculinized humiliation and masculinized hope.

Cynthia Enloe (1989)[1]

My grandmother used to keep a small suitcase by the door of her apartment in Brooklyn. An "overnighter," you'd call it. Once she showed me what was in it: a change of clothes, some toiletries, an envelope with about $100 in cash, and a nightgown.

"Why?" I asked her.

"Just in case," she said.

"In case what?" I asked, the naïve eight-year-old.

"In case they ever come again," she said.

The year was 1959. Her apartment was on the fifth floor of an apartment facing the water on Shore Road in Brooklyn. As in, New York City. As in, the United States of America. From her balcony we watched the building of the Verrazano Bridge.

When I was a young child in the 1950s, the Holocaust was not ancient history; it was a distinct memory, a terror that lingered. Both the neighborhood butcher and the shoemaker had numbers tattooed on their forearms. The Holocaust was so present that it was never to be spoken of, lest the fates be tempted to return it and this time bring it to our shores.

It is always difficult to approach a historical event in hindsight. My father lied about his age to enlist in the navy in 1944, and I used to ask him, What was it like to not know the end of the story? To not know that when the war ended, we would have won? To fight in a war is, by definition, to not know the ending; indeed, you feel yourself part of what will create the ending your side wants. You hope.

According to an ever-growing number of young men in Europe and the United States and across the Muslim world, we are at the beginning of just such a war. And no one knows how it will end.

To me, what is interesting in the paragraph you just read is not the indeterminacy of the outcome. All crises are like that. No; it is the fact that "ever-growing number of young men" probably does not seem notable to most readers. The fact that virtually *all* of those mobilizing on all sides of this growing clash are young *men*—whether right-wing extremists, anti-immigrant zealots, anti-Muslim skinheads and neo-Nazis, or young Muslims readying for jihad. It's so obvious, it barely needs noting.

And so it isn't noted. When then-president Barack Obama and Secretary of State John Kerry convened a three-day conference titled "Combating Violent Extremism" at the White House in February 2015, hundreds of experts from the diverse fields of law enforcement, security personnel, psychology, international relations, and criminology discussed how young people are recruited into these extremist groups, including scrutiny of recruits' backgrounds, mental health statuses, and religious beliefs. Legal and penal experts discussed court proceedings and incarceration issues. During the entire conference, participants heard not one word about "masculinity." (Indeed, the big controversy was whether President Obama sufficiently and specifically addressed *Islamic* terrorists.)

"We have to confront squarely and honestly the twisted ideologies that these terrorist groups use to incite people to violence," Mr. Obama told the audience. A year earlier, Secretary Kerry had argued that countering terrorism should involve "better alternatives for a whole bunch of young people" and greater "opportunity for marginalized youth." "People." "Youth."[2]

But which "people" exactly? What "youth?" If we close our eyes and imagine those people, those young people, whom do we see? And what is their gender?

If we imagine for a moment that all those amassing on all the different sides of this looming cataclysm, all those drifting to the edges of the political spectrum and toward violent extremism, were female, would there be any other story? Would not magazines be filled with individual profiles, TV news shows highlighting the relationship between femininity and violence, bookshelves sagging from the weight of the "gender" analysis? Yet the fact that virtually every single violent extremist is male creates hardly a ripple.

It can be easy to think, "But wait, what about those female suicide bombers? What about those skinhead girls? Those women of the Klan?" This proves my point. We notice the minuscule percentage of female activists. We overnotice them precisely because they are so counterintuitive. Man bites dog.

To be sure, there *are* plenty of women attracted to extreme politics. Some are comrades in arms, and many more are involved as wives and mothers. About 10 percent of jihadist recruits from the United States are female—in France it's about double that percentage—and many more visit their partners and sons and brothers in prison, even if they are not as often the inmates. Women drink and party at the White Power festivals, but they rarely venture into the mosh pit. Women are definitely part of the movement, but they are underrepresented as activists; they rarely train for war or engage in terrorist activities. It's what makes them interesting to study, of course, and we will meet a few in this book.

When others have examined the women who are attracted to extremism, gender has been front and center in the analysis.[3] When we look at female skinheads or suicide bombers, female neo-Nazis or women of the Klan, we ask about gender, about how their ideas and actions are shaped by, through, and often against their notions of femininity. Gender is visible. In fact, sometimes gender might be overemphasized at the expense of other aspects of women's experience. That's how evident it is.

It can be easy to shrug off this remarkably skewed gender difference with a bemused eye-rolling nod toward biology. Boys will be boys, right? Man-the-hunter avatars, cavemen in caftans or cargo pants, biologically predisposed toward violent rapacious predation, their eyes glazed over with testosterone-fueled rage. Except that only a tiny fraction of young males, driven by their endocrine systems or their evolutionary imperative, ever remotely consider such extremist violence. Those 99+ percent—are they not men?

If we do acknowledge something about the prevalence of men—as men—we're pretty quick to change the subject. It's psychological trauma. Political disenfranchisement. Downward economic mobility. Gradual irrelevance in a globalizing world. Religion.

I want to start by asking some different questions. Who are these young men? What draws them to violent extremism? What are the ideologies that inspire them, the psychological predispositions that lead some and not others to sign up? What emotional bonds are forged and sustained through membership in violent extremist groups?

An answer cannot be found in popular media analysis. In an otherwise insightful 2015 article in *The New Yorker*, "Journey to Jihad," Ben Taub promises to explain "how *teenagers* are lured into Syria's war," and then focuses entirely on the increasingly myopic Manichean worldview of ISIS clerics, portraying the Belgian and other European boys whom Islamic State has recruited as impressionable naïfs.[4] (The italics above are mine; it's not about "teenagers," after all, but about teenage *boys*. The only girls mentioned are a couple of ex- and current girlfriends.) There's not a word about masculinity, not a word about feeling as though they are finally *doing* something great, for a cause greater than themselves. Not a word about the visceral, quasi-erotic appeal of extremist politics to young men, offering that chance to prove their masculinity, to be a man among men and reap the sexual payoff of women's admiration, either in this or in the next life. Nor even about the terrifying ways that their terrorist beheadings increasingly resemble the video games they are playing constantly in the training camps.

And you won't find the answer in official U.S. policy documents. The official U.S. efforts at "combatting violent extremism" (CVE) focus exclusively on Muslims. Exclusively as in, 100 percent of federal CVE funds are aimed at Muslim communities within the United States. Officially, the administration's strategy states unequivocally that "al-Qa'ida and its affiliates represent the preeminent terrorist threat to our country."[5] An extract from a White House briefing document, "Empowering Local Partners to Prevent Violent Extremism in the United States," discusses solely Islamic extremism and Al Qaeda.[6] (According to studies by the University of

Maryland's Study of Terrorism and Responses to Terrorism [START] pro-gram, the vast majority of attacks in the United States were carried out by non-Islamist extremists.)

Nor will you find it in some of the recent research on deradicalization. Scholars point us in many directions, all useful, and all incomplete. John Horgan, a psychologist and the director of the International Center for the Study of Terrorism at Penn State, sees the appeal of terrorism in group participation and identity formation. While identity formation is a deeply gendered process, Horgan spends scant time on gender; the word does not appear in his index (nor does *masculinity, manhood,* or any other such word). But doesn't "group participation" provide a sort of gendered compensation, an alternate route to experience a successful gender iden-tity, to prove one's manhood? As a result of ignoring gender entirely in his examination of engagement, his model of disengagement stresses only how "individuals" get out.

Anthropologists such as Scott Atran and sociologists such as Marc Sageman successfully refute the immiseration thesis: terrorists are not the poorest of the poor, barely literate and utterly suggestible to groupthink. Indeed, Sageman finds that the majority of the jihadists he interviewed were well educated and reasonably well-off. Atran calls them "patently ordinary people" who simply want to be part of the in-crowd. To him, ter-rorism is transactional: terrorists commit acts of violence as a way of thanking the in-crowd for letting them join the group. This sounds remarkably similar to a fraternity rush.[7]

There is now a periodical called the *Journal for Deradicalization,* coed-ited by Daniel Koehler, which lists among its advisors some of the top names in the field—many of whom are scholars whose work I have relied on for background. But if you're looking for a gender analysis of deradicali-zation, you'd be well advised to look elsewhere. Through ten issues I could find only a handful that might have given any weight to gender. Typical is a "systematic review of the literature" which concludes that one of the pri-mary mechanisms for fostering deradicalization is to "increase social bonds [that] provide individuals a 'stake in conformity' and ease them out of criminal lifestyles." Another article seemed promising, proposing a typol-ogy of "thugs" and "terrorists." It suggests attacking frequencies and differ-ences in perpetrators' strategies and organization, but without discussing how any of this might be related to gender. Yet another article points to "identity crises" as a predictor of entry, without ever considering that they might be linked to questions about proving masculinity.

"Individuals" again. "People." If all these "individuals" were women, we would not be talking about "individuals"; we'd be talking about gender. In the end, I could find not a single article in this new and seemingly authoritative journal that used the word *gender*, let alone *masculinity*. The fish are the last to discover the ocean.[8]

In an intriguing study of terrorist networks, Marc Sageman, a physician and sociologist who also served as a CIA operations officer, notices that the networks he examines are composed exclusively of men. He then examines their age, faith, employment, location, and their experiences of relative deprivation, but does not investigate the gendered emotions or experiences of those factors. If basically no women of identical age, level of employment, experience of faith, and experience of relative deprivation become involved in terrorist networks, it bears investigating why it is only *men* with these backgrounds who become radicalized.[9]

One researcher published in the *Journal for Deradicalization* comes agonizingly close to understanding gender, but then backs away entirely. Charles Mink debriefed hundreds of accused terrorists affiliated with the Islamic State in Iraq and Syria between 2007 and 2008. He expected a bunch of "political outsiders, economic pariahs and religious zealots." Instead, he found detainees who were "fairly well educated, completely uninterested in state politics, gainfully employed in one way or another, and—perhaps most surprising—they were religiously apathetic." They were not, by and large, "angry, impoverished, or especially pious." Instead, Mink argues, those drawn to terrorism were "looking to fill their lives with companionship and significance. They join terrorist groups because they see affiliation with a global phenomenon as the best way to experience intimacy and solidarity with like-minded people." They want intimacy, solidarity, community, connection. Mink makes joining ISIS sound more like pledging a college fraternity than joining a group of religious fanatics bent on death. Well, perhaps, to paraphrase Shakespeare's *Henry V*, "he who sheds *someone else's* blood with me shall be my brother."[10]

Mink echoes the analysis of radicalization and deradicalization offered by Tore Bjørgo, perhaps the foremost researcher in this area. It was Bjørgo's initial insight that the primary motivation for joining extremist groups is not ideology, but rather the offer of a visceral experience of camaraderie and belonging. This insight led to the formation of EXIT, an organization devoted to helping neo-Nazis, skinheads, and other extremists get out of the movement, first in Norway and later in Sweden, Germany, and now, under the auspices of Life After Hate, the United States. But unlike those who see these yearnings for connection and camaraderie as generic psychological needs, Bjørgo recognizes the distinctly gendered route young Scandinavian boys take to meet them.

While several studies of women on the far right consider the relationship between gender and political extremism, no study of neo-Nazi skinheads or other white nationalists considers masculinity in its analysis. The literature on jihadists is far more extensive, but even in that subfield only one book stands out as placing gender at the center of the analysis. Maleeha Aslam's *Gender-Based Explosions* disentangles, as her subtitle promises, "the nexus between Muslim masculinities, jihadist Islamism and terrorism."[11]

Aslam goes way back into Muslim scriptures and images of Mohammad in the Qur'an, and then ties these traditional religious images to the obligations and entitlements that come with being a Muslim man. She comes to understand these men as having "troubled masculinities," embracing traditional religious notions of manhood suffused with deeply cultural understandings of shame and honor, while living in a world in which their capacity to express and experience successful manhood is increasingly tenuous. A man, one of her interviewees told her, is "someone who can take care of family and can afford to keep a wife and certain number of children." When he can't do that, he has to have alternatives. Another interviewee said:

> Men want to take care of their families. If they feel incapable of doing so, in most cases they leave the house and never return. After leaving the house they start acting criminally. Men are vulnerable to external influences. Women remain protected in their house. Men become part of street culture. They opt for drugs. They start abusing people around them. They indulge in physical violence—and they shout, use foul language. They do all this to eliminate the list of demands that their family wants to place on them.[12]

So when men are incapable of living up to the ideals their culture has set for them, they act out, take drugs, act violently, curse, shove—and sometimes they join jihad.

Aslam carefully and thoughtfully explores the doctrinal and cultural links between economic autonomy, financial security, and domestic patriarchy—that is to say, control over women and children. Domestic patriarchy breaks down when economic security breaks down, and men will often use violence to restore the domestic side of their entitlements, as they feel humiliated in failing to meet the obligations that masculinity places on them in the public sphere. The private is compensation for the public.

And if that doesn't work—if both public and private patriarchies are unavailable or have been compromised—they can, and do, become politicized. "Men divested of economic authority," Aslam writes, "tend to adopt political trajectories that facilitate the restoration of (lost) honor."[13]

This, then, is the gendered political psychology of extremism: patriarchal cultures come with sets of obligations for men about proving masculinity, accompanied by a set of entitlements and rewards. Cultures of honor require successful performances of masculinity, in both public and private spheres. A threat to either or both forms of patriarchy leads to feelings of humiliation and shame, as masculinity is a social performance and other men are constantly evaluating that performance. Breakdown requires restoration, retrieval, reclamation. Little wonder that these young men believe dozens of virgins await them in heaven after martyrdom. What could more strongly represent masculinity restored?

Following Aslam, I argue here that "although not the singular cause behind jihadism, gender as a contributing factor in militant-jihadist Islamism and/or Terrorism has to be recognized."[14] I claim something similar about extremist right-wing politics: I add an understanding of that dynamic as specifically embodied in the emasculation and humiliation, and the physicality of masculinity's restoration, in the worlds of young skinheads and neo-Nazis in Sweden, Germany, and the United States.

In this book, I follow the lead of Aslam and Bjørgo, but add a salient dimension to the otherwise fascinating portraits offered by other terrorism scholars. It's not that they're wrong; it's that their analysis is incomplete. They see the social-psychological need for connection, but they don't see it as a gendered quest. They see wanting to fit in, but they don't see why the men stick out in the first place. They see the social rewards these "people" may receive, but they fail to see why it's *so* important, why the stakes are so high; and so they fall back on explanations of a vaguely generic human need for connectedness.

Just for a moment, then, let's pay attention to gender and see where it takes us. I do not suggest that once we understand gender, we will fully understand the lure of violent extremism. Of course not. We still need to take many other factors into account. A host of structural variables provide much of the foundation of extremism, including economic displacement in an increasingly interconnected global economy; the threats to, or collapse of, domestic patriarchy (wives working, children getting an education that circumvents paternal authority); political marginalization. Onto this foundation we add the psychological variables: childhood trauma, bullying, child abuse, sexual abuse. Women's employment and education have also set dramatic changes in motion.

But I argue that we cannot fully understand violent extremist movements without a gender analysis. And, more than that, we cannot adequately meet this challenge without understanding how gender—masculinity—is so deeply and intimately enmeshed in participants' experience. I argue that there is a *gendered political psychology* of extremism: that the men who join do experience the need for camaraderie and community; the threats to a solid, grounded identity; the desire for a life of meaning and purpose; and the inability or obstacles to achieving that life as specifically gendered feelings, urges, and emotions.

Research by some of the major figures in this field, especially Tore Bjørgo and Daniel Koehler, relies on a framework of push and pull factors to explain both entry into and exit from radical extremism. What factors make some young men more susceptible to radicalization than others? What pushes them in, and what pulls them in? One might say, for example, that many young recruits are pushed into extremist politics by the economic dislocation of neoliberal economic restructuring, or by the alienation that young British Muslims feel in a world where they experience racism every day. Or young men are pushed toward radicalization by feeling alienation, a loss of identity, a sense that in this world they don't matter. And young recruits are pulled in by the camaraderie, the community, the sense of historical or even divine "mission"—to save the white race, to establish the Caliphate, to restore Germany to its rightful glory by purging all immigrants. Words like *honor* and *devotion* loom large here. But so, too, do the visceral experiences of embracing your brothers, feeling as though you belong, feeling as though you are seen—seen as a man.

Similarly, push and pull forces operate on getting out. Koehler cites a form of "cognitive opening," some rupture or break with the movement that begins to unravel the tightly wound connections of emotional and political commitment. Push factors are those "negative social incidents and circumstances that make it uncomfortable and unappealing to remain." The active extremist may begin to doubt the ideology; he may become frustrated with the group's hypocrisy; he may decry the violence that the group visits on its own members. Or he may feel pulled to have a normal life, to have a family, children, a steady job. He may feel himself aging out, into that new, more stable and settled life. He may develop new, positive relationships outside the movement. All of these push and pull factors are evident in the chapters that follow. If we are to develop support systems, policy initiatives, and mechanisms that help these men leave the movement, we are going to have to understand the pushes and the pulls, both in and out—and, more than that, how specifically gendered they are.

So this is how it works: These young men feel entitled to a sense of belonging and community, of holding unchallenged moral authority over women and children, and of feeling that they count in the world and that their lives matter. Experiencing threats to the lives they feel they deserve leads these young men to feel ashamed and humiliated. And it is this aggrieved entitlement—entitlement thwarted and frustrated—that leads some men to search for a way to redeem themselves as men, to restore and retrieve that sense of manhood that has been lost. Joining up is a form of masculine compensation, an alternate route to proving manhood. To not see this as gendered is to miss the point.

I am not claiming that gender explains the attraction of violent extremism or that explaining the attraction is impossible without gender. I do say that gender is a vital, necessary, and irreducible element of the experience.

Journalists and researchers usually start by focusing on the content of radical extremist ideology and then work backward to search for the fertile political and economic ground in which such hateful ideologies can take root. Such research strategies can explain long-term political and economic causes, but they can't explain the filter mechanisms by which thousands experience the same political and economic circumstances yet only a handful are smitten by the cause.

It is common to then move immediately from these large-scale macro-level explanations to an individual psychopathology model. There must be something "wrong," with these particular guys, something in their family life or their upbringing. It seems possible—probable—that their fathers beat them, abandoned them, were implacably ruthless with them. Or perhaps the boys were victims of abuse and bullying from male peers.

Psychological reductionism runs rampant as an explanation of violent extremism, but it begs the same question as the overly macro-level structural explanation: in the vast universe of kids who are abused, beat up, abandoned, bullied, and otherwise mistreated by a hostile world, why do only a few of them ever blow themselves up as suicide bombers or begin training to defend the white race from "outsiders"? Why these particular boys and men and not all the others?

In a sense, these two explanations turn understanding on its head. We need to ask why there are so *few* who end up in extremist movements, not why there are so many. After all, there are thousands—no, hundreds of thousands—of boys in America who are bullied and gay-baited every single day. Yet they don't pick up assault weapons and "pull a Columbine" in every middle school and high school in the land. So we need to ask what are the structural features of those schools where they do pick up assault weapons, as well as the psychological characteristics of those particular boys.

What mediates between these overdeterministic structural explanations and the reductionist psychopathological ones is gender. Masculinity. It is the specific ways that specific groups of young men understand and enact masculinity that help us navigate between the macro and micro, between the structural and the psychological. It's within the gendered connection between humiliation and violence where we will find the key to understanding how some young men get into extremist politics and, therefore, how we, as policy makers, civil and community leaders, parents, religious leaders, and citizens, can provide a route they can use to get out. We need to explore the experience of deep emotional connection, belonging, compensation for shame and humiliation, and purpose and mission in life—the sense of finally living a life of glory and strength and power that provides the emotional nutrients that generate a breeding ground for young men eager and energized to prove their manhood.

It's quite astonishing really, after listening to these guys talk (in my research for *Angry White Men* I interviewed forty-five "active" white nationalists in the United States, and for this book I interviewed more than seventy "formers"), that there is virtually no mention of gender, of masculinity, when policy makers get together, when law enforcement officials discuss strategy, or when journalists profile activists. Not even when the experts get together. For example, a groundbreaking conference in Dublin in 2011, the Summit against Violent Extremism, is generally credited with inspiring many organized efforts to understand the experience of extremists groups—neo-Nazi skinhead organizations, jihadists, inner-city gangs, ultraleftist groups, and others—in order to develop strategies to facilitate deradicalization. Sponsored by Google Ideas and organized by Jared Cohen, senior fellow at the Council on Foreign Relations, this conference was the founding moment of Life After Hate, the North American organization that helps ex–right-wing extremists and skinheads get out of the movement. It brought together groups so disparate that they'd never been in the same room together, yet they found much in common to discuss.

The documents the conference produced aggregate the survey findings of these different groups. The researchers identified virtually all of the routes of entry, as well as the most successful strategies of disengagement. But their analysis missed entirely the one crucial variable that provides much of the experiential glue that both attracts young men to these groups and binds them when they join. "A need for a sense of belonging, an identity, and a sense of purpose" they write, "drives individuals down the path toward radicalization."[15] "Individuals." Although that's true of course, these questions of identity, purpose, and belonging are experienced as profoundly gendered experiences. Yet the documents contain not a word about gender.

The same is true of the work of other serious researchers in the field. For example, Daniel Koehler, who once guided me into the world of EXIT Deutschland and who is one of the most astute observers of the scene across many different venues, has now established the German Institute on Radicalization and De-radicalization Studies (GIRDS), one of the most important research centers addressing radical extremism. In his collected work and in two books published simultaneously in 2017, he develops a structural and processual model of radicalization and deradicalization, a useful typology. It is perhaps the most ambitious effort to map the various trajectories into—and out of—extremist movements.[16]

Yet the word *gender* appears only once in the text, and not at all in the index. Where *gender* does appear is in a single paragraph in Koehler's brace of books—a paragraph that discusses women. The role of women—as extremists themselves or as mothers, sisters, partners, wives, or daughters—factors not at all in the analysis. This, despite the fact that his major case study—the National Socialist Underground (NSU) cell in Germany responsible for ten murders, three bomb attacks, and fourteen bank robberies between 1998 and 2011—was a neo-Nazi love triangle among Uwe Mundlos, Uwe Bohnhardt, and Beate Zschape. (Both men committed suicide in 2011; Zschape is currently standing trial.) While Koehler notes that gender has been "only marginally discussed" and acknowledges "the need for gender-specific disengagement," the notion never appears again.[17]

But does it matter that these "individuals" drawn into these movements are virtually always male? Does this craving for a sense of belonging, this need for an identity, this desperate desire for a sense of purpose differ between women and men? It does, and this and the following chapters explore in depth the reasons why.

Gender—masculinity—provides both the psychological inspiration to young men to join these groups and the social glue that keeps them involved. Challenging violent extremism, therefore, means engaging these young men *as men,* not simply as jihadists or neo-Nazis or white supremacists. It means offering them new ways by which they can prove their masculinity, to feel that they are real men, that their lives matter.

But just as my grandmother's preparations for some new, American Holocaust were based on a fantasy of vulnerability and invasion, so too are the machinations of these young men, who ride, as Bruce Springsteen so famously sang, "through mansions of glory in suicide machines." Theirs are gendered fantasies of glory, of brotherhood, of mattering—as men. Women—or, more accurately access to women—are their reward, whether the myriad virgins promised in heaven or their wives, girlfriends, and comrades here on earth. Or both.

Whereas the former neo-Nazis and skinheads in the United States and Europe wanted to usher in the new Reich in their lifetimes, and to be around to celebrate the fall of the "Zionist Occupied Government" (ZOG), their Islamist neighbors harbor no such illusions. They know the establishment of the Caliphate will take centuries of struggle, and they seek their rewards more immediately, if transcendentally. Most dream of going out in a blaze of glory, martyrs to a cause, in order to reap their rewards in heaven in the form of the hot virginal girls they couldn't meet in real life. Suicide bombers are the Muslim version of American school shooters who, since Columbine in 1999, almost always end their school massacres with suicide. Theirs is "suicide by mass murder"; the goal is to die and to take as many with you as you can.[18] These are young men who feel small, who resent being made to feel small, and who are looking to get big by destroying others. They search, sometimes literally, for that magic bullet that will make them a real man.

THIS PROJECT

Healing from Hate is about what brings young *men* into radical extremist organizations, and what we can do to help them get out. Drawing on in-depth interviews with more than seventy "formers"—ex-activists, ex-neo-Nazis, ex-jihadists and -Islamists, and ex–anti-immigrant skinheads—and on organizational profiles of those groups helping to bring about social and personal deradicalization, I strive to fill in the big blank between ideologies of extremism and their organizational manifestation, to connect the dots between word and deed. That connective tissue is social and emotional.

Developing such a gendered political psychology requires that we look underneath the stated reasons to the emotional foundations of both radicalization and deradicalization. It's more important to focus on these experiences than on the ideologies these young men espouse. To focus only on the ideologies in order to deradicalize—to attempt, for example, to provide a rational, market-based explanation of why immigration might be a net positive economic benefit for European and American society—is to doom that effort to failure. The motivation to join is emotional, social, psychological—and, even more, visceral, physical. Those motives must be addressed. After all, the ideologies are so broadly professed, yet while many would be chosen, only a few feel called. At the same time, to treat these young men as if they were simply an aggregation of mentally ill individuals, a collection of zombies following insane leaders into maniacal fantasies, likewise misses the rational foundations of radical extremism.

To know the seductions of extremism—the visceral, emotional, psychological excitement that accompanies recruitment and enlistment—is only half the story. Once in, how do they get out? How can we, a concerned public, help them get out? And how are the organizations that have sprung up to help facilitate their exit helping them?

For my earlier book, *Angry White Men,* I interviewed forty-five American neo-Nazis and white supremacists to understand how they experience masculinity on the extreme right. I heard many stories of what I came to call aggrieved entitlement—a gendered sense of entitlement thwarted by larger economic and political shifts, their ambitions choked, their masculinity lost. Joining these right-wing groups lent a gendered coherence to their sense of emasculation and frustration; their manhood had been taken from them by unseen conspiratorial forces, and their recruitment was seen as a way to reclaim their manhood and to restore that sense of entitlement. To "take our country back," in the words of the Tea Party slogan.

Once inside, these men developed a worldview that constantly shored up their own sense of masculinity through the emasculation of the "others" against whom they were fighting: feminist women, immigrants, Jews, gays—all depicted as not "real men," but unqualified poseurs who've taken over the government and turned it against its authentic native sons. So consuming was this seduction of manhood regained that I began to wonder how it would be possible for them to get out. Once you drift into the world of extreme-right political movements, once you completely buy the Manichean worldview of "us" versus "them," is there any hope? Is there any way to reach you? Is the world of the extreme right like the old ads for the Roach Motel: once you check in, you can't check out?

Or is there a way out for these angry white men? Is there a way to return to their former lives, their families and friends, their workplaces, schools, and churches? Is there, as the North American organization I profile here asks, "life after hate?"

The answer is definitely yes. While I've been researching and interviewing men of the extreme right in the past twelve years, I've spent the past three focusing almost exclusively on the dynamics of "exit"—how to help them get out. Do they drift away, having grown impatient preparing for a war that never comes, or fed up with the hypocrisy of their leaders? Have turns of events led them to question the ideologies to which they were once so committed? Or are they disgusted by the horrific consequences of some of their beliefs?

Those are some of the questions I address in this book. I have not only interviewed ex-extremists in the United States but also gone to Europe, where there are excellent established programs entirely devoted to deradicalization of young extremists. And I've gone to Canada and London to meet with members of an organization that is helping ex-jihadists leave the radical Islamic sects that have been so successful in recruiting them.

I've been fortunate to have been granted access to clients of EXIT, in both Sweden and Germany, organizations that have been helping neo-Nazis, skinheads, and other far-right extremists for more than a decade to "jump" from the movement. Swedish EXIT was the first such organization, founded in 1996 by Kent Lindahl, himself a former skinhead white supremacist. Working through the youth center in Stockholm (Fryshuset), EXIT is today a well-run and well-funded organization that has seen nearly 400 clients—375 male and 25 female—and provided them with job training, group therapy, individualized job counseling, and safe houses and transport if they are threatened by the organizations of which they were members.

In Germany, EXIT has been a somewhat less formal affair, in part because of a greater need for secrecy (due to ongoing threats from neo-Nazi organizations) and in part because the government does not directly fund it. Begun in Berlin not by a former skinhead, but by a former East German police officer, Bernd Wenger, EXIT has relied mostly on word of mouth and contacts with the prison system, especially parole officers, to identify and reach out to potential clients. (In Germany, EXIT recruits most neo-Nazis in prison after their arrest for petty crimes, such as burglary, and so they are in the system on probation or parole when they jump.) EXIT provides counseling and safe houses, but lacks the infrastructure to help formally with job placement.

In Sweden I have interviewed 35 clients (29 male and 6 female), and in Germany I have interviewed 20. I've interviewed the founders and the current heads of the organization, as well as ministerial-level government officials about their understanding of the work that EXIT can do. I am therefore in a position to present a novel, interview-based analysis of the gender of violent extremism.

In Germany I interviewed a young man whose neo-Nazi activities offered an opportunity for an intergenerational reconciliation, and a middle-aged woman who saw Nazism as the only alternative to global socialist domination. In Sweden I interviewed a young woman who came into the movement because her sister had been beaten by her Iraqi boyfriend, and I spoke with several guys who came for the parties and stayed for the fights. And I have conducted three interviews with Jackie Arklöv, "the most hated man in Sweden," who is in a maximum-security prison serving a life sentence for murder, after killing two police officers in a botched bank robbery to raise money for the Nazi organization. (I am, to my knowledge, the only US researcher to have interviewed him.)

And I have been granted access to clients' files (except for therapeutic information) and also examined the organizations' libraries and archives. (I have had helpful translators in both countries.)

In the United States, I've interviewed 8 formers whom I met through my old contacts in the movement, and all but one of the founders of Life After Hate, a relatively new organization whose sole formal presence is on the Internet, but that is working to provide support for guys who are getting ready to jump out. I also rely here on the initial interviews I did earlier with 3 dozen actives in the movement.

Finally, I've interviewed 12 former jihadists in Canada and Great Britain, some through the Quilliam Foundation, a London-based organization that helps Islamic extremists deradicalize. I've interviewed the young Canadian Muslim who infiltrated the Toronto 18, the terrorist cell that was planning the single biggest terrorist attack in Canadian history, a plot to assassinate the prime minister and members of Parliament and take over the Canadian government. I've also interviewed a white Canadian convert to Islamic extremism who came perilously close to blowing himself up in jihad.

Not everyone agrees that this type of organization—nongovernmental and nonideological in the case of EXIT and Life After Hate; nongovernmental and decidedly ideological in the case of Quilliam—offers the best way to help young men get out of the movement. Daniel Koehler, at GIRDS, is skeptical about nongovernmental organizations in general. Quilliam, he concedes, is successful "because their passive contact approach is specialized at a later stage of the disengagement and deradicalization process," and because the guys they work with "display an intrinsic and credible motivation to leave a radical environment."[19]

But EXIT, in both Sweden and Germany, earns his skepticism because of their susceptibility to corruption and recidivism. For example, he cites Kent Lindahl, the founder of EXIT Sweden, who resigned and left the organization after some 60,000 Swedish kronor (about $6,500) went "missing" and he was asked to reimburse the organization. And another EXIT staffer, in the small town of Motola, was one of the leaders of a plot in 2010 to steal and sell the entry gate sign at the Auschwitz concentration camp and memorial site.[20]

It is true that EXIT Germany has had some wobbles in personnel, and some recidivism. But rates of recidivism among the EXIT members who were contacted in prison are no greater than among other prisoners, and many committed crimes again but did not return to neo-Nazism. Those who did may also be part of a longer-term in-and-out-and-back-in trajectory encountered again and again in these stories. This alone hardly seems justification for dismissing the important work that these organizations do.

THE GENDER OF EXTREMISM

This book represents my effort to tell these young men's story. Or rather to tell a story about them—one of many stories that can be told, that need to be told. I'm especially interested in understanding what draws young men to the movement, what keeps them there, and what strategies enable them to leave. I show how proving masculinity plays a central role in recruitment, or entry, into the movement. In Sweden young men enter the movement in their early teens—the average age of EXIT clients is about seventeen (and remember, these are people already *leaving* the movement). They come because they experience downsizing, outsourcing, or economic displacement in specifically gendered ways: they feel themselves to be emasculated. This political-economic emasculation is accompanied by a more personal sense of emasculation: they come because they are isolated or bullied in school, and feel they need the support of something much bigger than they are.

Entry is a gendered effort to ward off the shame that comes with their failures—their failures as men. "The emotion of shame is the primary or ultimate cause of all violence," writes psychiatrist James Gilligan in his stunning book *Violence*. "The purpose of violence is to diminish the intensity of shame and replace it as far as possible with its opposite, pride, thus preventing the individual from being overwhelmed by the feeling of shame."[21]

Recruits stay for the parties and the music. Their activities consist largely of getting rip-roaring drunk, downing a handful of painkillers, and going out as a group looking for someone to fight with. Finding an opponent is easy enough; there are plenty of groups of anarchist anti-Nazis or immigrant teenaged boys who are likewise drunk and juiced on painkillers, equally itching for a fight. They are sympathetic to a generally nationalist message—Sweden for Swedes—and come to identify as white. But it is when they confront the more political aspects of their membership in the organization, and as they grow older and begin searching for jobs and consider starting a family, that they begin to question their participation.

In Germany, these young men are often petty criminals, arrested for street crime (assault, robbery) or more property-related crimes like burglary and breaking and entering. In prison, organized groups of neo-Nazis rule the prisoners and ensure the separation of white prisoners and immigrants, who outnumber the white prisoners by significant margins.

Four very different countries: Germany, Sweden, the United States, Great Britain. Four very different groups of men: adolescent boys in Sweden, former petty criminals in Germany, ex-jihadists in Canada and Britain, and ex–white supremacists in the United States. Four different entry points into their extremist politics. But one thing in common, one trait that binds them all—and that helps to explain both their entry and their exit: they are men.

And it's not just that they are male—anatomically so, chromosomally so—but that they see themselves as men. They enter feeling like failed men, like men who need to prove their masculinity, need to feel like real men, yet are thwarted at every turn. Top of the corporate ladder? Able to provide for a wife and family? Sexual prowess among the ladies? Competitive prowess among the guys? A man among men?

To a man, the ex-Nazis, jihadists, and white supremacists I have interviewed felt like failures as men. But instead of turning that sense of emasculation inward toward depression, interpersonal violence, suicide, or self-medication through drugs or alcohol, these young men were somehow convinced to externalize their sense of emasculation, turn it into righteous political rage, and lash out at those forces that they came to believe responsible for their emasculation. Their failure was not theirs, as individuals; it was something done to them—by an indifferent state, by predatory corporations and rapacious bankers, by a host of "others" who had preyed upon global sympathies to get special bargains. They were not failures; they were victims.

It is this sense of victimhood—that they are the new victims of the politically correct, multicultural society—that lends a degree of righteousness to their political activities. For the extreme right-wingers, theirs is a movement not to take power, but to restore authority to its rightful heirs, white men—"us," not "them." To restore what was, and what should have been. And, in the process, to restore their manhood. And it is through their participation in the movement that they see an opportunity to retrieve that sense of masculinity that has been stolen from them by illegitimate poseurs and their government and its corporate henchmen.

Their paths to entry are deeply gendered. The overwhelming majority of the members of every group I've worked with, and of every group that's been studied, are attracted to the movement because it will give them something they are not getting in more traditional ways: a pathway to manhood.

Many come from deeply dysfunctional families. Divorce isn't the half of it. Many were abused, physically or sexually, by stepfathers or mothers' boyfriends. The fathers of many were absent, simply nonpresences in their sons' lives. Others might as well have been absent, they were so emotionally shut down, opaque, phantom presences in their own homes.

Nearly two-thirds of all the people I interviewed for this book were targeted in school as well. Some found it hard to make friends; others didn't fit in for some reason or another. Overweight or underweight. Too smart (condescending egghead) or not smart enough ("retard"). Acne, bad at sports. Maybe just being the new kid or wearing the wrong sneakers on the first day of school. As we all know, middle school and high school children are amazingly creative in the criteria they develop to make other people feel worthless and like nothing. The drift into extremism helps redefine the situation, transforms shame into power, and transforms one's own fear into others' fear. "Just being part of [the gang was] like, 'You're the man,'" says one former. "So you went from being a nothing, a nobody, to being somebody, and it just happened overnight."[22]

Let me be clear that I am not in any way arguing that entry into these extremist organizations is preordained by adverse family lives or social isolation in school. The number of cases of young people being abused, bullied, abandoned, or humiliated is far greater than the numbers who end up in extremist politics. There are many routes from such sad and terrible beginnings.

Two logical fallacies often blind us to the element of choice as well as the element of randomness, coincidence. First, we often fall prey to the compositional fallacy. Quite simply, we assume that since all members of group A are also members of group B, all members of group B are therefore also members of group A. This is not necessarily the case. To cite a standard example in logic, from the fact that all members of the mafia are Italian it does not follow that all Italians are members of the mafia. That virtually all recruits to extremist organizations come from dysfunctional, abusive, or otherwise broken families does not mean that all survivors of those family conditions are members of extremist politics. That should be obvious.

Second, we often explain the trajectories of actions from back to front, teleologically. We see an outcome and go back looking for possible explanations that determined the outcome. For example, let's say a search of a convicted rapist's home reveals a stash of pornography. Aha! The rapist's obsession with pornography must have "caused" the crime. The problem is, of course, that the home probably also had a Bible, and there are far more rapes in the Bible than in an average porn magazine. But no one ever says "Aha! It was the Bible that caused it." Believing is often seeing.

So now let's look again at these young boys. Alone and isolated, bullied and beaten, emasculated and sad: this describes a few kids in probably every single middle school and high school in the United States and Europe. Yet not even a tiny fraction of such young men find their way to becoming skinheads or jihadists. Some retreat into a fantasy world, playing video games all day, blowing up imaginary galaxies rather than actual buildings. Some self-medicate with alcohol or drugs. Some harm themselves. Suicide is the second leading cause of death for all Americans aged fifteen to twenty-four.[23] For a large number of teenagers, adolescence is a world of pain.

I argue that it's a gendered pain. Boys and girls experience that pain differently. And while there are a large number of girls who, like many boys, turn that anguish on themselves—self-harming, self-medicating, self-annihilating—those who decide to go out in a blaze of glory, opening fire in their high schools before turning the guns on themselves, are far more likely to be boys than girls. It is almost entirely boys who decide to blow up their schools, murder their parents, or join extremist political movements.

Some find their way to the Internet, and some, while there, search out others, and find them. Others just like them, or others whom they want to be like them. They find a virtual community—others who understand, others who have experienced the same torments, the same abandonments, the same humiliations. And sometimes the recruits are sought out on websites, actively recruited on Facebook and Twitter. One of the guys I spoke with described himself as a "keyboard warrior."

(I confess that it is a constant source of wonder to me that this quintessential twenty-first-century medium the Internet is the primary way to recruit religious or political fundamentalists. Whether it's Islamists who yearn for a caliphate that would take us back to the seventh century, or those hardcore right-wing survivalists living in cabins in rural Montana, everyone seems to have a website and is connected to others just like them through the most modern technology. These wired anti-modernists have websites and cell phones and use the Internet constantly. Their idea of the sixth-century Caliphate seems to include cellular technology and modern explosives.)

Others have a relative—a cousin, typically—or some older neighbor who is already in the movement. Movement entry usually demonstrates what sociologist Mark Granovetter called "the strength of weak ties." Whether it's finding a job or meeting the person you will marry, Granovetter argued, the connection is generally not the result of strong ties—immediate family members or your closest friends. It's a "weak tie," one or two removes from your immediate circle. How do you get a job? A friend of a friend. How do you meet your mate? A friend's partner knows someone who is single and available.[24] The same is true for recruitment into the movements I discuss here. A neighbor, a cousin, a new guy in the neighborhood who comes with a crew.

The group's dynamics—the intense bonding, the camaraderie, the parties, the fights—forms much of the glue that keeps the groups together. Ideology comes later, if at all. For some of the Swedes and Germans, the ideology was a negligible part of their movement participation. For others, the ideology becomes just another sticky part of the group dynamic. "In the beginning, it was purely social and had nothing to do with the views that were involved," says one former female American white nationalist. "I pretty much tailored my racism according to whom I was involved with."[25]

What is important about the ideology, though, is not its content, at least not its content alone. The vast Zionist conspiracy, the great American Satan—these are not just ideological constructs based on rational assessments of political events. Such ideas are the substance of paranoid politics, vast webs of seemingly isolated incidents rolled together to form a coherent incoherence, a worldview in which every shred of random detail proves the vastness of the conspiracy and the depth of the corruption and deceit of those in charge. Paranoid politics also serve as a glue, a way to keep people connected. Where else would you get that knowing wink, that bemused shrug, that wise nod from someone who knows an event or occurrence illustrates exactly how "they" are taking over? Ideology is not just content; it is also form. Sharing the ideology—any ideology—provides the glue. If racism is the warp of the paranoid political blanket, then the fact that we share that racist ideology is its weft.

Recruits feel both connected and isolated—connected to one another through their intense bonding, and isolated from the rest of the world. There is a hostile world out there, and only in the combination of maternal care and paternal authority do we re-create a family that is a haven in a heartless world.

ENTRY AND EXIT

Most analyses of radicalization and deradicalization follow the analyses of Norwegian researcher Tore Bjørgo, who is now the director of the Center for Research on Extremism: Right-Wing Extremism, Hate Crime and Political Violence (C-REX), at the University of Oslo. It was Bjørgo who initially conceived of the idea of EXIT, an organization specifically designed to help people get out of the movement by addressing the psychological and social factors that attracted them in the first place. Bjørgo is not insensitive to the role that gender plays in their trajectory.

This book attempts to take Bjørgo's and others' analyses one step further, to specifically "gender" the experiences of entry and exit. In the stories you'll read in the pages that follow, some guys just get tired and age out of the movement. What seemed exciting at age fourteen doesn't seem so exciting at thirty-four. And it's downright unseemly at fifty-four. The raves, the all-night binges, the drinking and fighting, these can get old after a while. And since for many of these guys the commitment to the ideology was never that strong to begin with, it's relatively easily discarded.

Aging out may not be purely a function of age, but also of life circumstance. A few of the men became fathers and had moments of rupture with their extremist groups when they considered what kind of life they wanted for their baby. Or a relationship, most often with a woman, put in stark contrast the life they were living and the lives they wanted to be, or could be, living. Mothers, girlfriends, and wives often forced the guys' hand: the movement or me. The formers I spoke with are the ones who chose the real world, the actual women they loved. The ones who made that other choice are still out there, lost to us, choosing ideology and group membership above all else.

Others get disillusioned with the ideology. Paranoid politics doesn't wear that well after a while. There are too many unexplained random events that cannot quite be hammered into those neat little slots. Or the ideology propels some to do things that others find repugnant or even contrary to the very ideologies they're espousing. Once members break ideologically, it's not uncommon for them to swing wildly to the other side. Quilliam Foundation research found that some of the ex-jihadists careened from Islamism, with "all sorts of crazy ideas about Jihad this, bomb that," to becoming counterterrorist spies for the British government, and from preaching hate to preaching love and empathy.[26] Several of the Swedes I interviewed had gone from National Socialism to supporting the Social Democrats in the most recent elections.

And others become disillusioned by the group's dynamics. Too much hypocrisy. Several of the formers I spoke with found it unsettling that the group's leaders seemed to be playing by other rules. One Swedish leader was sleeping with an Iraqi immigrant. Another told me that the former leader of the Danish National Socialists, Povl Heinrich Riis-Knudsen, who was also the head of WUNS (World Union of National Socialists), was having an affair with a Palestinian woman. One or two of the Swedes complained to me that the leaders were eating meat (Hitler was a vegetarian), drinking and taking drugs, and were not living the pure Nazi life they insisted on from their followers. Several times I heard that men became disillusioned because the group abandoned them in a fight or during an argument. When your membership in a group depends on your comrades having your back, without question, all the time, it's a rude wake-up call when you turn around to find no one there.

All of this means that to help these young men get out of the movement, we have to give them an alternative way to feel successful *as men.* They need to believe that there are alternative paths to manhood besides either capitulating to their subjugation by the forces of political correctness or violently rising up in defiance of those same forces. They need to feel like successful men. Or at least they need to see a path *toward* that successful restoration of masculinity.

Any program that promises deradicalization must address gender. It must substitute new ways to demonstrate masculinity—a visceral, sexual, physical sense of embodied power (fighting, partying, moshing at concerts), coupled with a grounded sense of masculine identity that comes from pride in one's work, civic and political participation, and perhaps even the beginning of one's own family. One cannot ask these men to jump from their extremist views into a genderless void where they don't know any other way to be a man.

Radicalization is a deeply gendered process, one that virtually no one has addressed, because the gender composition has been so normal that it has passed entirely under our analytic and journalistic radar. Becoming an extremist is a way to prove your manhood, to feel like a man. And just as the process of radicalization is deeply gendered, so too must be the process of deradicalization.

Although I pay only a little attention here to the women and girls who are tempted to join, I do pay attention to gender overall, and not just to masculinity. I've interviewed some of the female clients of EXIT in both Sweden and Germany, as well as some of the women involved in Life After Hate. So there are stories to tell. Different women enter through different paths. Some, especially those who join traditional racist organizations like the Ku Klux Klan, are frustrated that they cannot establish families like those of their grandparents' generation; they yearn to stay home and raise their children, but their economic situation prevents it. Some young women ache to be fierce skinhead women, as kick-ass and ferociously racist as their brethren. (Some encounter serious problems of acceptance; in the United States, only the White Aryan Resistance welcomed young women as equals.) Some come for the same reasons as the boys: drinking, partying, and dancing. (But they often leave for very different reasons, as they become frustrated by gender inequality within the movement and resent the guys seeing them only as "mattresses.")

Do I think that once we have addressed gender, we've solved the problem and will successfully deradicalize these young men? Of course not. But I do think that unless we take gender into account, we will not be able to offer these young men anything they consider worthwhile enough to encourage them to jump.

EXIT Sweden addresses these questions by providing group counseling that supports and sustains formers' efforts to find alternate paths to manhood: landing a job, supporting a family, developing civic pride through environmental nationalism and youth efficacy. EXIT Sweden is the model for its German and American counterparts, while the ex-jihadists are still a ways from any sort of formal organizational infrastructure. Working with law enforcement, counterterrorism psychologists, and social workers, we can give these young men a new way to feel like successful men. If we do that, we can offer these men, poised to jump from their extremist pasts, a safe place to land.

There are many differences among the four groups I write about in this book. One of the cases involves ex-Islamic jihadists in London and

Canada, and the other three, to varying degrees, involve anti-Islamic, white supremacist, and anti-immigrant groups. I have tried to remain sensitive to the specific differences. But what if there are commonalities, points of contact among such disparate cases? What if all of these young men have a similar emotional, visceral, and gendered narrative about the attractions of extremism? Similar paths in—and often similar paths out? Then wouldn't it be a wise policy move to also address the aspects they have in common as well as the ideological positions they espouse that keep them apart?

That is the challenge of this book.

Matthias

INTERGENERATIONAL NEO-NAZI

To walk down the streets of Berlin is to feel, at times, as though you are in an open-air historical museum. The past is always there, imprinted in the streets, written on the sides of buildings. But to me it is a museum of the invisible, of what is no longer there. It's a monument to the missing, a constant reminder of what has been taken away.

You can hardly walk down a street in, say, Charlottenburg without stepping on or over the brass plaques permanently anchored into the sidewalks. Part of an art installation titled *Stolpersteine* (literally, "stumbling blocks or stones"), by German artist Gunter Demnig, each plaque memorializes the Jewish families who lived in the house in front of which you are standing. Each stone says, "Here lived," followed by the name of a person who lived at that address.[1] Most also include the date of deportation and the location of the person's murder. It is a living reminder of what happened and of who—concretely, not abstractly—is missing. To be honest, I find it difficult to walk down those streets without tears welling in my eyes, not only in sadness at the atrocities that befell these now-memorialized individuals but also in admiration of a country that is at least willing to try to come to terms with its own past.

Figure 1. The *Stolpersteine* project places small brass commemorative plaques in cobblestone streets or sidewalks throughout Germany with the names and life dates of the Jews (as well as any Roma and Sinti, homosexuals, dissidents, Jehovah's Witnesses, and victims of euthanasia) who lived in the houses and apartments on that street. Products of a project developed by artist Gunter Demnig, the plaques memorialize the destruction of the Jewish community under the Nazi regime and in a sense returns the Jews to their rightful homes.

Even the haunting Jewish Museum speaks with no voice. The rooms that document the history of the Jews of Germany are notable because the various stations where in other historical museums artifacts would stand in synecdoche of the historical moment—a typewriter on a table to show a writer's life, or an old sign from a store—feature only reproductions of paintings that might depict something of the past. The actual artifacts are missing, as are the people to whom they belonged. It wasn't just the people who were exterminated. The plan was really to eliminate the entire idea of the Jews of Europe.

Living in a country, as I do, that inhales the legacy of slavery with every breath, and whose government has never exhaled one word of apology, it's hard not to be even a little envious of the courage it must have taken for that first generation of Germans born after the war—the generation into which I was also born—to confront this past, the immediate past, this past of their parents and aunts and uncles, this past that took place, almost inevitably, in the very house in which they were born. Many of my German contemporaries have agonized over this past, especially the '68ers, the generation that galvanized the radical movements that swept over Europe. While their older siblings who came of age in the 1950s whispered some misgivings, it became a full-fledged shout in the late 1960s, as young people probed and pushed their elder relatives, uncovering some disturbing truths about their own family's wartime activities. They've bravely confronted their past, acknowledging collective responsibility and guilt.

I remember a story my graduate school roommate told me. The grandchild of a Wehrmacht officer, he had as a teenager organized a soccer team in his home town of Bremen to tour throughout Israel and play tournaments all over the country to provide some means of connection with the grandchildren of the Nazis' victims. Younger generations in Germany are as committed to a country free of racism and discrimination as any young generation in the world, perhaps more. And institutionally, Germany has tried to prevent the past from seeping into the present. Swastikas and other Nazi paraphernalia are banned, National Socialist speech is prohibited, and any anti-Semitic utterances are censored.

These thoughts are running through my head today as I leave my hotel and walk down Pfalzburgerstrasse towards the U-Bahn station at Hohenzollernplatz for my first interviews with clients and the director of EXIT Deutschland. It was one thing to meet the Swedish skinheads and former neo-Nazis. Seriously, what do they know of National Socialism? They're Swedes! They were "neutral" during the war. But this is Germany, where National Socialism was born, where it took root in the fertile soil of a comfortable, long-standing tradition of anti-Semitism. These are the grandchildren of the ones who murdered six million people simply for being Jews or otherwise "non-Aryan," the grandchildren of the ones who may not have pulled triggers or flipped switches, but who spat on, shoved, punched, and kicked their neighbors as they were rounded up; who laughed as others did so; or who stood by silently as those same neighbors, whose children played with their children, were herded onto cattle cars. And these were the grandchildren of those Germans who gleefully moved into those abandoned apartments where only a plaque now remains to remind us of whose home this once was.

Contemporary Germans are not simply the grandchildren of those bystanders. My stepfather's older brother was killed only a few days before the end of the war, in the Ardennes Forest during the Battle of the Bulge. These are the descendants of men who had fired machine guns at my people. And by "my people" here I also mean Americans.

And these are also the grandchildren of those who continued to deny what happened and to even justify it. In one recent survey in Germany, about half of all respondents believed that their parents or grandparents viewed Nazism negatively; only 4 percent believed their families viewed it positively; and only 2 percent thought their family's view was "very positive." Could this be true? Weren't they, as Daniel Goldhagen wrote, Hitler's "willing executioners"? Were they actually more like Hitler's unknowing executioners?

I didn't think so. And my research began to confirm it. I read an interview in a recent report about this question in which ninety-one-year-old Elli Krug insists today that she had no idea what a concentration camp was, even though she lived only a few miles from Bergen-Belsen. But she remembers distinctly that, after the war ended, the former inmates of that camp she didn't know about passed through her village, and that she was forced by the British occupying army to open her home to them as they began their journeys to what may have remained of their lives. She was not happy about it; indeed, she felt a terrible burden—as if she had been the victim:

> The Jews were the worst afterwards. They really harassed us. . . . They sat there and made us serve them. . . . We had this big hayloft [where] they slept overnight. . . . The Jews and Russians, I always made sure I didn't get them. They were really disgusting, you know? I always stood down the street, in front of the gate, and when they said "Quarters," I said, "No everything's full!" If the Jews . . . came, I said "It's all full of Russians." . . . And when the Russians came, then I said the same thing, that there were Jews here.[2]

Ingo Hasselbach, the former neo-Nazi "Führer of Berlin" who founded EXIT Deutschland, recalled the little old German ladies who used to bring the movement prisoners food and cigarettes when they were in prison. Many of the Help Organization for National Prisoners (HNG) were the widows of Nazis, and, as Hasselbach recalls, they grew most animated when the conversation turned to Jews. They'd be "venomous," furious; hatred of Jews was "their deepest conviction."[3]

So, I ask myself, do I really want to meet them? For years, I had resisted going to Germany at all, turning down every invitation I'd received to speak at conferences. I worried about how I might react, how conscious of being Jewish I would feel. Would my rage consume me, and would I want to go up to every man my father's age and scream in their faces, "What did you do? What did you know?" Or every seemingly innocuous little old lady and ask what she did, who she turned in, and how she feels about it all today?

At the same time, how would I feel if I sensed that same old anti-Semitism? Yes, I am a social scientist, and the son of a psychoanalyst. I know how to remain inscrutable during an interview, to let the subjects of the interview reveal themselves to me without my disclosing much of my own feelings. But I'm also a sentient person, a historical actor in a place and time, interacting with other historical actors. Can I find their ideas odious and yet like the people who hold them? This had been the case when I had interviewed some of the active white nationalists in the United States. I won't say I liked them especially much, but there were quite a few I felt a connection with, some spark of recognition of a shared humanity, even some points of agreement. And I had actually liked a couple of the ex-neo-Nazis I'd interviewed in Stockholm—one of them enough to remain in contact and today consider a friend.

And what if they immediately "made" me as a Jew? This was an issue among some of the white nationalists in the United States. The second I opened my mouth, they could hear that New York accent, that slightly adenoidal intonation. Unless you believe that all Americans sound like Jerry Seinfeld or Woody Allen, you'd pretty much be able to figure out my street address—or at least the borough where I live—just by my accent. I'm Brooklyn through and through.

And then I quietly nursed perhaps the most disconcerting of all my worries: What if I actually *liked* them? I mean, I'm part German myself. These are "my people." What if I felt comfortable? What sort of betrayal would it be to those six million, a few of whom were distantly related to me, that I was now having a pleasant lunch and laughing with the grand-children of the people who had murdered them?

But then, isn't that the point? Isn't that exactly the dream that Martin Luther King Jr. so passionately articulated, that one day, "sons of former slaves and the sons of former slave owners will be able to sit down at the table of brotherhood." OK, maybe we're not on "the red hills of Georgia," but what about a café next to an auto parts store on some nameless side street in the former East Berlin? That is where I found myself on this cloudless November morning as I turned the corner onto that utterly charmless street.

I met Matthias in the back room of that auto parts store on a nondescript side street in one of those former East German neighborhoods that have not yet been "rehabilitated." Rows of five-story houses, graffitied walls, deserted streets. Nothing that might even remotely suggest that the country's main organization to assist the deradicalization of neo-Nazis would have its offices there. The only signs on the windows of the store were for spark plugs and oil additives.

Which is just how EXIT wants it. The location of their offices is a semisecret, as previous locations have been attacked and occasionally clients have been assaulted as they left the office. Even today, as I arrived and doors were unlocked, someone peered down both lengths of the street to be sure that I'd not been followed and that there were no menacing types on the street. I walked through the main office of the auto parts store to a side room, which led through a small warren of offices and alcoves to a larger conference space in the middle of the main room. Matthias was waiting for me at the conference table, along with a couple of staffers, other clients, and Bernd Wenger, the former East German police officer who founded EXIT after decades of work with East German youth gangs.

Matthias (not his real name) is a short, wiry thirty-four-year-old whose blond hair, parted in the center, and angular nose remind me of a young Tom Petty. Part of the second generation born after the end of World War II, he remains confused and slightly unsettled about where he and his generation fit in. His mother, he tells me, knew exactly where she fit: in a generation that entirely repudiated their parents' Nazi-era past. His mother was a hippie, lived in a commune, and proclaimed herself an anarchist. But while she was busy finding herself through a thorough repudiation of the family, she paid little attention to the impact of her choices on her son. "I'm still not sure who my father is," Matthias tells me, in a tone without affect. "It was, you know, a time of free love. It could be any one of three guys who were at the commune at the time. My mom told me she had no idea. Whatever. I had no father. Christ, I barely had a mother."

He grew up in a small house in Berlin, raised largely by his grandparents. His grandfather, an architect and engineer, was an especially caring parent. Devoted and nurturing, he was also unapologetically pro-Nazi. "It wasn't like he wanted me to be a Nazi or anything," Matthias tells me. "He just told me not to believe everything they tell you in those schoolbooks, you know, the ones that say it was all bad." His grandfather didn't push the ideology, but "we just sang songs from the time, you know, like it was fun and all."

Matthias found it hard to find his place in the school pecking order. By the time he was in seventh grade, he felt he'd better belong to some group, lest he be alone and vulnerable. The punks and anarchists were identifiable by their tattoos and hairstyles and music. But it was the skinheads who captured his imagination. They had great parties, and everyone seemed afraid of them. "They really represented what it meant to be a strong man," he said. By age thirteen, he was one of them, outfitted in flight jackets, high black boots, and a shaved head. His teen years were spent partying and crashing football matches with other right-wing soccer hooligans, looking for—and finding—constant fights.

One day in high school, a Jewish writer came to speak at the school, and Matthias petitioned to present the other side of the case. "I wanted to expose him, like where did he get his watch, where did he get his Porsche, who is paying him for this? Jews can be 'sneaky, tricky,' my grandfather had once said, so I had every cliché in the book ready for him." When his school refused the petition, he protested, and went so far as to threaten the school principal. He was expelled, and the police were notified that Matthias might be a right-winger.

He argued with the teachers every chance he got. "They weren't capable of arguing against me," he says. "I came to school with facts, and they just had bullshit." He especially enjoyed debating about the Holocaust. He denied it.

I look at him quizzically. "Really?" I ask. "Oh no, I didn't deny that there were camps or that there had been deportations," he said. "But I thought the numbers didn't add up. No way six million. A couple of thousand maybe. But that was it. Actually I didn't think they went far enough." He continued: "I thought that the Holocaust story was a sneaky way that the winners, especially the Americans and the Russians, were tying the hands of Germany, sort of like after Versailles. Like a big heavy backpack of debt that we can never pay back. Just weigh us down. Which is what they wanted—to keep Germany from rising again." Now a high school dropout, Matthias found a job as a metalworker, but maintained his contact with his soccer hooligan skinhead pals. He also got serious about studying and thinking about the movement. "I read a lot about the time, you know, and decided I didn't want to be just a sidekick, but a major player."

He gradually drifted into a far more serious political engagement with the movement and began to work as a youth organizer—a damned good one. "We stirred up a lot of trouble because we were really good at mobilizing these kids. They had nothing going for them, the government didn't care at all, so we offered them after-school programs, concerts, movement building. And we staked out the neighborhood as 'our' neighborhood. We finally had a place that was ours." His group of friends were like a "sect," he tells me. Just like a gang. Remember the Little Rascals, and their "He-Man Woman Haters Club"? The clubhouse, the man cave, the locker room—that place of solace and camaraderie. A man needs a posse, and he also needs a saloon.

Matthias's early twenties were a cascade of White Power concerts, demonstrations, and serious political organizing. He'd sworn off drugs and alcohol, and he wasn't really into the fighting anymore. It was all politics. He formed a new organization called Berlin Alternative Southeast Organization, or BASO, not connected to any particular party, but organized simply to do youth outreach in the former East Berlin. For three years, he hung out with kids, played basketball and soccer, and made sure kids had enough to eat. "If they wanted to talk politics, I was into it," he says. "But I didn't push it. It was definitely part of my plan, yeah. But my goal was to give them a feeling of community, brotherhood. The politics weren't nearly as important as that."

Of course, when local politicians moved against the group, it gave him an opportunity to rant against the government. "But it was always because we had to defend out turf, our neighborhood from those criminal politicians." The police were not persuaded by this apolitical posture, and they reported the group to local politicians as a neo-Nazi organization. BASO was outlawed in 2005. To support himself, Matthias took part-time jobs, offering himself as a private security force, as a bouncer at clubs, anything in which "I could look menacing and scare people." His grandfather gave him money, and he even ended up living on the generosity of the hated state. He was on the dole.

In the mid- to late 2000s, violent conflicts became more frequent, as organized groups of anarchists and anti-fascists began to roam the same streets in the former East Berlin that were once the sole province of the right-wing gangs. "Maybe it's like from gentrification, all these yuppies coming into the former East you know, and they bring their leftist pals with them to take over our streets."

After one demonstration, about a dozen neo-Nazis, two of them women, were on the U-Bahn with a French television crew that had come to film them. As they got off the train, they were attacked by about thirty or forty people. "They called for me especially," he said. They were armed with chains and sticks and threw rocks. "It was awful," he recounts. "I got a big gash on my head, twenty-seven stitches. There were a lot of injuries. Those people were animals and they were just lying in wait."

Conflicts and fights became more frequent. Germany had a crisis on its hands, from the gangs of right-wing skinhead neo-Nazis and the anti-fascists, to the leftist anarchists who were equally marauding gangs of young men, to the gangs of immigrants, especially young Turkish German men tired of being singled out and harassed individually. "There were some neighborhoods where you just knew there would be a fight between at least two of these groups pretty much every week," Matthias says. "We actually got to know some of the people who worked at the hospitals."

One evening, he returned to his grandparents' house for dinner. He explained to his grandparents the work he was doing, the anti-immigrant position he had taken, his growing anti-Semitism and anti-Islam views. His grandparents listened intently. After dinner, his grandmother cleared the dishes into the kitchen. "Come upstairs to the attic," his grandfather said. "I have something to show you."

They climbed the three stories to the attic—nearly an entire floor under the eaves. As they arrived at the door, locked with a padlock, and as he fiddled with the keys, his grandfather turned to Matthias and said, tears welling up in his eyes, "I've been waiting my whole life to show you this." They entered what might legitimately be called a museum of Nazism. Matthias let his grandfather's Hitler youth scarf fall between his fingers, and he touched his Youngfolk and Wehrmacht uniforms, in perfectly brushed condition. Books and pamphlets lined the shelves, along with medals, buttons, and several revolvers. "We were right," his grandfather said. "We just didn't finish the job. You, and your generation, you can finish what we couldn't." They embraced there, grandfather and grandson, intergenerational Nazis, separated only by the intervening, outlier generation of liberal baby-boomer hippies.

Over the following few days, Matthias's grandfather poured out his heart to his grandson. It turned out he'd been a stalwart Nazi; he was one of those giving orders, not merely following them. These were not skeletons in his closet; this was a shrine. His grandfather had fought on the Eastern Front, against the Russians, and had even fought in the Battle of the Crimea. He'd saved pamphlets, maps, his own orders, and a hand-drawn diagram of the German army's retreat route.

But even with this deep intergenerational family connection, something was nagging Matthias, something making him uncomfortable. The politics, the ideology, "just didn't feel right" anymore. "I reached some boundaries or something. I can't tell exactly what happened, but I know something definitely began to shift inside. I couldn't logically sustain my position without lying. It wasn't adding up right. I was confused, and started feeling really unhappy, like I was getting trapped."

During a criminal trial in which he was a defendant, Matthias was approached just outside the courtroom by two people who identified themselves as social workers with an NGO that focused on helping youth. "They just asked me, really calmly, if I had listened to myself. 'What are you really saying?' they asked. Like what did I believe, what sort of person was I becoming." He was brought up short. "I have no idea why, but the combination of the way they said it and what they said made me start thinking. I went home that night and I started asking myself what I was doing. I was twenty-seven. I had no wife, no children, no job. What have I accomplished in my life? What was I doing? Would I even live to see thirty if I kept up this life?"

Not long after, he was talking with the mother of one of his recruits. The young man was in jail, having been arrested following an attack on two anti-fascist youth. "She kept making it like we were the victims, you know, like we were just minding our business and these other people were attacking us. It was like this big lie, you know, like we were just minding our business as a country and 'they' came, and they were trying to take over, and poor us, we were the victims. And it just sounded phony and wrong."

Something was shifting. On the TV news, he "saw some footage of some violent assaults, and all the attackers were my friends." He started to feel the one thing he had always refused to feel—as a hooligan, as a neo-Nazi, as a German. He began to feel guilty. "I'd built this whole identity on never feeling guilty for any of it, like *we* were the victims and victims don't feel guilty. They did this to us!"

Like many people when they begin to experience these unsettling emotions, or begin to experience some transition, Matthias started to write. As he and I talked, he laughed: "Did you see *Jerry Maguire*?" he asked me. I had. "Well, I wrote one of those manifestoes, like changing my life by confessing everything. Oh, God," he says, his hands covering his face in mock embarrassment. "Well, there it was." And he took it to those two social workers from the NGO who had confronted him a couple of months earlier in court.

He didn't hear from them for a few days, but then one of them came by. "I have no idea what to say to this," he said to Matthias. "We just need to start talking." And so they did. For six months. They would meet every few days and they would talk, read books together, and then discuss them. "It was the first time I had an honest conversation about any of it, not to get challenged, but a mutual discussion." He contacted EXIT. After a discussion with Bernd Wenger, the organization's formal head, Mathias decided to drop out of the movement.

But leaving was not nearly as easy as he thought. He had an idea: to use a pending court case as a pretext, saying that he needed to leave the public eye and he didn't want to implicate any of his friends and comrades. He began slowly, methodically, just easing himself away. But he sensed his comrades were suspicious that he was betraying them. In December, at a Christmas market, he was surrounded by about a dozen of his neo-Nazi comrades in a planned confrontation. "What is going on with you?" they demanded to know. "Just leave me alone," he said; "I don't want have anything to do with you."

He took a taxi home, and by the time he arrived at his apartment about a half hour later, he had voicemail messages, emails, and texts denouncing him. "These had been my good friends," he says sadly. And there was more. "You'd better not be there when we get there," said one phone message. He left his apartment that night and EXIT arranged a safe house. Staff also arranged for job training and found him a job.

That was three years ago. He's been assaulted and beaten up pretty badly since then, but he's out for good now. He completed his A-level exams, enrolled in the university, and has crossed over and is doing social work with young people, anti-Nazi organizing on the same streets he used to work as a neo-Nazi organizer. Police watch him now, less because they suspect he might commit a crime than because others may find and attack him. He has a live-in girlfriend; they are planning to have a baby. And, as you can imagine, he and his grandfather have not spoken since.

"Jumping is never a one-time thing," he tells me. "You have to decide every day not to go back. It's been painful—and scary. But it was so dishonest that I just couldn't live with myself if I stayed in."

2 Germany: Anti-Semites without Jews

Here's what I know as I make my way to the address I have written on a scrap of paper, for the office where I will meet Matthias and the other clients and staff at EXIT Deutschland: Reunification brought together two Germanys that had diverged culturally and symbolically as well as politically and economically after World War II. In the GDR (German Democratic Republic, or East Germany), resentment against the oppressive regime of the pro-Soviet regime of Erich Honecker was often expressed as nostalgia for Nazi-era anti-Soviet resistance. Hatred of the Soviet Union could be expressed through Nazi references, a shared symbolic universe. Nazism was a language of anti-communist resistance.

The economic juggernaut that characterized postwar industrial development in the former FRG (Federal Republic of Germany, or West Germany), by contrast, brought into the country an enormous number of non-German economic migrants, initially from places such as Italy, and later Turkey and Croatia. Most recently, they've been refugees from war-torn Middle Eastern countries such as Syria and Iraq. Racism in Germany has a new target: Muslims. You don't need Jews, apparently, to be anti-Semitic in Germany these days. As Joachim Kersten writes, a form of "secondary anti-Semitism" has emerged, one that "substituted 'others' as the objects of hate and dehumanization in the absence of a significant Jewish population. *Ausländer* (foreigner) became the functional equivalent of what traditionally used to be the Jew."[1] Jews are an idea, an abstraction. Hated, to be sure. But if you really want to be a passionate defender of the Fatherland, you have to have something concrete to throw out of the country.

Sadly, Jews just can't answer that concrete need for someone specific to hate—there simply aren't enough of them. At reunification in 1990, around the time that a lot of these young skinheads were born, there were only 23,000 Jews in the entire country; even today there are just over 250,000 Jews—which is 0.3 of 1 percent of the country's population.[2] Jews don't figure in the new cosmology of German neo-Nazis. Ingo Hasselbach says that in the East Germany of his youth (the 1980s), there were fewer than 1,000 Jews, total. And, he confesses, he'd never met one.[3]

Their small population does not mean that Jews don't figure in the German consciousness—or in historical memory. Underneath the tolerant and inclusive culture, many of the old anti-Semitic tropes still have a small amount of currency, and even the notion that Jews are "different" probably still informs many people's worldview. A small stream of anti-Jewish sentiment is always flowing underneath German society.

The river, the torrent, the flood of vitriol—that's reserved these days for Muslims. Muslims are the new Jews of Germany and, in that sense, the new Jews of Europe. If the German neo-Nazis are anti-Semites without Jews, Muslims are the Semites they are "anti" to. They're everywhere and they are supervisible. The Muslim population of Germany at reunification was already 2.5 million, or slightly more than 3 percent of the population. By 2010, Muslims accounted for 5.2 percent of the German population, or 4.2 million people.[4] In fact, Berlin is the fourth-largest Turkish city in the world, after only Istanbul, Ankara, and Izmir. "They don't need to wear yellow stars," Josef, one of the clients at EXIT, said. "We can always tell who they are."

Several high-profile murders have revealed how extensive the right-wing extremist network is, and how eager some are to use violence against Muslim immigrants. And, sadly, how inept—or indifferent—the German police have been in tracking down these criminals. For example, in November 2011, police finally cracked the case in which a terrorist cell called the National Socialist Underground (NSU) had, over seven years, murdered one Greek and eight Turkish shopkeepers, and one police-woman, not to mention committing more than fourteen bank robberies and detonating a bomb outside a shop in an immigrant neighborhood in Cologne in 2004, an explosion that wounded twenty-two people. The police never considered a right-wing connection among these crimes, all committed by the so-called Zwickau cell of the NSU, until the lid blew off when two members of the cell killed themselves after a botched bank robbery. The Office of Constitutional Protection, Germany's national security police, thwarted local police efforts because it was afraid the police would expose its informants and agents who had infiltrated the group. The effort to bring down this cell was a mess—equal parts incompetence and deliberate runarounds. The police went so far as to blame the victims, calling the murders the "*doner* killings," a reference to the meats available at the Turkish shops the victims ran. "There is still a lack of public will to go after National Socialist groups in a sufficient manner," said Hajo Funke, an expert at the Free University in Berlin.[5]

These revelations prompted a new wave of national soul-searching, but also some outcroppings of hate that were unexpected and troublesome. The local soccer team's fans chanted "Terror Cell Zwickau" at a recent match, and one of the players actually responded to repeated chants of "*Sieg*" from the crowd with a "*Heil*." He was fined.[6]

While Berlin is the epicenter of most anti-Muslim activities in Germany, the tiny town of Wunsiedel has become a mecca of neo-Nazism, in part because it is the final resting place of Rudolf Hess, the unrepentant Nazi deputy führer, who committed suicide in 1987 in prison at age ninety-three. (His tombstone, since destroyed by the town, said simply "Ich hab's gewagt" [I have dared].) For some years, the anniversary of his death was an unofficial neo-Nazi holiday, and movement members would come from all over Europe to celebrate in this tiny town.

Only slightly less important symbolically to the movement, Dresden has become the touchstone city of the extreme right. An industrial hub in the former GDR, bombed to near oblivion by the Allies in February 1945, Dresden is now the home of many who seethe with anger at the Russians, East Germans, and the West in general. This anger erupted into the open four years ago. Much to the dismay of most local residents, not to mention political officials at the Saxony provincial level, as well as many Germans across the nation, a new group founded in October 2014 holds weekly anti-Islamic demonstrations in the civic center. The group Patriotische Europaer gegen die Islamisierung des Abendlandes (Patriotic Europeans against the Islamization of the West, or PEGIDA) has since demonstrated for tighter immigration restrictions on Muslims. In language terrifyingly similar to anti-Jewish propaganda in the early 1930s, the organization describes cultural and religious differences as cancerous lesions eroding the "democratic" fabric of European society. Anti-democratic sentiment is mobilized in the name of democracy. (No sooner did PEGIDA emerge than it imploded when a photograph of the group's founder, Lutz Bachmann, posing as Adolf Hitler surfaced in January 2015. Many in the group scattered. But they still march in Dresden every Monday.)

PEGIDA is part of a trend of spontaneous expressions of right-wing extremist sentiment in Germany. Right-wing extremism appears to be on the rise all over Europe, and especially in places where Russian occupation was superimposed on former Axis, or Axis-occupied, countries. But it turns out that many of these actions are anything but spontaneous. There is a wide network of neo-Nazis and their sympathizers, along with a pyramid of support and, what may be worse, indifference.

THE NEO-NAZI SCENE

Actually, it's not so easy to be a neo-Nazi these days in Germany. A whole slew of activities, symbols, and behaviors are prohibited, such as singing Nazi songs or even having them on your smart phone, giving the Nazi salute, wearing swastika tattoos, displaying a picture of Hitler, and waving the *Reichskriegsflagge* (the red, white, and black flag with the swastika in the center). It wasn't until 2016 that the ban against publishing any edition of *Mein Kampf* was lifted. (And this after furious debate ended in the deal allowing it to be reprinted in a monstrous, heavily annotated, scholarly tome of nearly two thousand pages; it quickly shot to the top of *Der Spiegel*'s nonfiction best seller list. The more than 100,000 copies probably did not all go to academic researchers.)[7]

And forget free speech. You cannot say any of several Nazi-era mottos: not "Ein Volk, ein Reich, ein Führer" (one nation, one empire, one leader) or "Blut und Ehre" (blood and honor, the slogan of the Hitler Youth). You can't even say "Sieg Heil."[8]

It is indeed difficult to be a neo-Nazi in Germany these days, but it's certainly not impossible. There are hubs of activity, as skinheads hang out with soccer hooligans and committed racists, going to White Power concerts, listening to neo-Nazi rap artists like Fler, or playing neo-Nazi video games, such as "Concentration Camp Manager," in which players sort the incoming hordes into those who will work and those to be exterminated immediately.

Today there are about 22,600 active neo-Nazis and members of other extreme right-wing groups in Germany.[9] Less than half are estimated as ready at any moment to commit acts of violence. But these small numbers are nested atop layers of support found in large swatches of the country. The older far-right political party Nationaldemokratische Partei Deutschlands (German National Democratic Party, or NPD) escaped a judicial ban in 2015 because the courts found it too irrelevant to bother with. But its members have been absorbed into the Alternative für Deutschland (Alternatives for Germany, or AfD), which received 4.7 percent of the national vote in 2013, just shy of the requisite 5 percent to gain a seat in Parliament. Still, AfD has elected candidates to provincial parliaments, and one former leader took a seat in the European Parliament for the first time in 2014. Underneath party politics is significant support among Germans. A 2011 study found that half of all Germans believe too many foreigners live in Germany and that more than half (53 percent) would have a problem moving into a neighborhood where lots of Muslims lived, an increase of 6 percent since 2004.

Who, then, are those 22,000+ actives? My interviews with clients at EXIT in Berlin reveal a pattern of young men, aimless and apolitical, marginalized in the new, EU-based Germany, who take refuge in a nostalgic, romantic Herderian notion of Germanic folk exceptionalism: the traditional village versus the cosmopolitan city. Tending to come from a specific class fraction—downwardly mobile, lower middle class—they look backward longingly at a purer past, with fewer of "them," a world made just for "us," as it was decreed, as it was meant to be. As global capitalism proceeds, it leaves some groups discarded like so much trash at the side of the road. That's how they feel—discarded. Discarded yet entitled. Entitled not to be tossed aside, entitled to have what their fathers and grandfathers had. Entitled to feel like men. And if it isn't going to be given to them, then by God, they're going to take it—take it from those to whom it's been wrongly given.

Grandfathers loom large in these young men's cultural imaginations, if not, as with Matthias in the preceding profile, in their concrete lives. Their fathers, after all, are the 1968 generation of wimpy men who rejected National Socialism and embraced a hippie lifestyle of anarchism, androgyny, and acid. Not to be overly psychoanalytic, but there is some Oedipal drama playing out here: rejection of the father's rejection of the grandfather. In a near-throwaway footnote in his classic study of identity development, *Childhood and Society* (1950), Erik Erikson located the origins of young men's anger in a multigenerational story:

> In psychoanalytic patients the overwhelming importance of the grandfather is often apparent. He may have been a blacksmith of the old world or a railroad builder of the new, an as yet proud Jew or an unreconstructed Southerner. What these grandfathers have in common is the fact that they were the last representatives of a more homogeneous world, masterly and cruel with good conscience, disciplined and pious without loss of self-esteem. Their world invented bigger and better machinery like gigantic playthings which were not expected to challenge the social values of the men who made them. Their mastery persists in their grandsons as a stubborn, an angry sense of superiority. Overtly inhibited, they yet can accept others only on terms of prearranged privilege.[10]

Neo-Nazism is the grandson of National Socialism; it skipped a generation. But it hasn't changed gender.

MASCULINITY AND THE EXTREME RIGHT

Take a step back for a moment and consider the relationship between masculinity and participation in extremist politics. There's a reason most of the extreme right is male: it's that masculinity is centered on something to prove, a quest. Perhaps, you might think, women have to prove something also; perhaps they "prove" their femininity by attracting a man, getting married, and becoming a mother. Maybe, but it doesn't have the same propulsive force as proving one's manhood. Men must prove their masculinity to other men, in the homosocial arena of other men. Their masculinity must be credited, validated, affirmed by their peers. Historically, of course, they've proved their masculinity in the traditional time-honored ways of their ancestors: in the workplace, as breadwinners. They've provided for their families, protected their homes, and defended their homelands. Take those roles away, and they have to find a new arena in which to prove their manhood.

And that's where the extreme right draws its members. To be sure, there are plenty of stable, middle-class family men at the top of neo-Nazi organizations. It's a profession, a job, and just like any other, the top of this bureaucracy is staffed by company men, committed as much to the organization as they are to its ideology. But the bottom, the shock troops, the recruits—who are they? They are young men who feel that something has been unjustly taken from them. Underemployed at best, they compete for jobs with new economic migrants and often resort to petty crimes (burglary, robbery) to make ends meet.

The extreme right in Germany is a loose confederation of these petty criminals, soccer hooligans, serious professional neo-Nazis, unemployed drifters, skinheads, and disaffected young people. Some enter because they share a general anti-immigrant racism, as expressed by the skinhead band Böhse Onkelz (Mean Uncles) in their song "Turken raus!" (Turks out!). They work sporadically in blue-collar occupations during the day, and at night they flock to White Power concerts or head to a friend's house to drink heavily and then go out looking for someone (or some group) to beat up. According to researcher Joachim Kersten, the hooligans and skinheads are the least political; they are, he writes, "action-oriented young males with a masculinist orientation toward risk taking behaviors." They have no political objectives, no strategic goals, and only the most "superficial" ideology of ethnic or racial superiority. Only a small number end up in the *Kameradschaften*, a tight bond of brotherhood among extremists who orient their entire lives to the re-establishment of the Reich (the Fourth Reich, as they put it).[11]

Many theorists use a somewhat economic determinist model to explain the rise of this panorama of extremism, but their theories omit as much as they reveal. For example, Hans-Ulrich Wehler and the Bielefeld School, reacting against a conservative and cultural trend in German historiography, proposed a reliance on political economic explanations, coupled with social history more broadly. Wehler argued that social disintegration leads to a broad anomie into which many of these disaffected youth fall, only to surface again seeking community on the extreme right. Globalization and modernization, the argument goes, lead to a "loosening of social constraints and support structures. Individuals with limited human capital . . . can find themselves lost, unguided and without perspectives."[12] Other scholars use relative deprivation to explain how so many disaffected young people see "others" getting benefits to which they feel entitled, at the same time that they are eager to participate, through media, in the global culture of consumerism.

While intriguing for providing a broad economic background, such theories minimize cultural factors and familial variables that might explain why some young men enter the movement while others, similarly situated, do not. What's more, Wehler ignores gender entirely, though gender is perhaps the variable that best explains the experience of recruitment (aside, of course, from race).

Other contemporary commentators propose a more process-oriented understanding of entry into extremist groups. This process allows for longer-term structural factors, such as economic upheavals, legacies of domination by the former Soviet Union, and economic dislocation, as critical in creating strata of potential recruits, and then includes subsequent processes and variables (such as family structure and experience, educational experiences, employment histories). All of these factors are understood, along with group formation processes around certain cultural experiences (music fandom and concertgoing) and fashion statements (such as skinhead style), to create a comprehensive picture of how some young men are funneled into the movement, while others drop out.

My perspective has space for all of these factors, but stresses gender, particularly masculinity, as an especially significant variable. These young men feel that an oppressive government has taken their masculinity from them, and they are humiliated, shamed, by their inability to succeed in the system. Yet they also feel entitled to the social goods that the state provides, and they see foreigners, immigrants, and other "others" receiving those goods. They experience what I call *aggrieved entitlement*—a sense of victimhood in being unable to get the economic and social benefits that are rightfully theirs. Their politics are therefore reactionary, nostalgic; they seek to "restore" or "retrieve" what they believe they have lost. They look backward to create a vision of the future, back to a past that was purer and more responsive to their needs.

To be sure, these notions of heroic entitled masculinity are experienced by a lot more young men than those who join extremist groups. But this narrative provides a handy rhetoric and a sense of civic and nationalist mission: restoring the country to past glory. Guys join the movement for all sorts of reasons, but they rarely do so because of ideological commitments. Their embrace of neo-Nazi ideology is a consequence of their recruitment and indoctrination process, not its cause. The cause lies far deeper in the personal experiences of the young men themselves.

As with most of the other groups I've examined, entrance into the German extreme right comes through a youth-oriented cultural scene. It's why youth organizers such as Matthias are so crucial to the movement. They know how to hang out on the streets of former East Berlin, Dresden, or other cities in the former GDR where resentment against the Soviets can be channeled back toward a yearning for the glorious German past. So while it's true that many of EXIT Deutschland members are somewhat older than the formers in Sweden and the ex-jihadists, most of whom are still teenagers, it is equally true that many German recruits start as disaffected youth, hanging out, miserable, lonely, on the streets.

And they are eager consumers of youth culture, which provides a visual community of similar dress and affect that helps many feel as though they do belong somewhere. Music is a big part of that community. It's typical among young people to meet someone and want to know if you are similar and will like each other; you ask what sort of music the other likes. It's a shorthand, a shortcut, to a shared (or not) cultural vision, a sense of community, and probably a sartorial style. We all do this, whether we are Deadheads or Metalheads.

Like their Swedish and American counterparts, young German skinheads and potential extremists gravitate toward hatecore—hard-driving punk anthems with overtly racist lyrics spewed out with rage, suitable for sweaty mosh pits in tiny clubs or large outdoor festivals. But they also like hip-hop and rap, as do British jihadists. There are explicitly racist hip-hop acts, such as Makks Damage (birth name Julian Fritsch), who spits out racist and anti-government messages in music videos like "Überall Nazis" and evokes Aryan mythology going back to the Vikings in "Ragnar der Wikinger." In "Winter von Stalingrad," Damage raps over film footage of the German assault on Stalingrad, a historical montage of the catastrophic decision that spelled the end of the Third Reich's army on the Eastern Front. The German soldiers look happy, determined, and unified. Another rapper, Dee EX, is a multilingual polymath who raps in French and German, and she's a woman! She has thousands of Facebook followers and posts photos of herself in sexy military outfits on her blog. She is the not-so-secret crush of thousands of potential skinhead suitors.

Ingo Hasselbach, the former neo-Nazi who founded EXIT Deutschland, explains a typical recruitment pattern:

> I liked to approach fourteen to sixteen year-olds after school. We looked for kids wearing bomber jackets and Dr. Martens. Usually they didn't really have a political position, but for whatever reason they'd decided it was cool to be right wing. The first thing I did when I met one of these boys was to show him that I wanted to be his friend, to hang out with him, which, coming from someone older, especially someone over twenty, was a real compliment. I'd act a lot like an older brother; we'd go into the woods together and do things like Boy Scout exercises, building forts and making trails. I'd always slip in a bit of ideology against foreigners along the way, saying some racist things like how there are such big differences between the white and black races, for example. But only casually at first.[13]

It's quite a leap from building forts and hanging out with a quasi–older brother to desecrating Jewish cemeteries or blowing up kebab houses owned by Turkish immigrants. So, gradually, Hasselbach and others would introduce current issues to the teenagers and mix Turks into the conversation, making it clear that black and brown weren't really very different, that both were "inferior races."

And that's when they would explicitly introduce gender. Masculinity. The big contrast with those inferior races was captured in the difference between the *Untermensch* and the *Übermensch*. All history was a conflict between the great races of men—specifically men, not as in some generic "mankind," but the males of each race and the ideas of masculinity those men supposedly represented. They'd look at the map of Europe in 1937, and Ingo would tell the boys how the Germany of their grandparents was a great nation, and then, after the war, Germany had vast swaths of land—Austria, Poland—"stolen from us." You'd "inflame the recruit's feeling of injustice," Hasselbach writes, and then you'd create a powerful combination: injustice and victimhood on one hand, and a glorious sense of gendered destiny as the *Übermensch* on the other. That is how aggrieved entitlement is born among disaffected youth who had no political sensibilities at all to begin with.

Finally, Hasselbach notes, he'd tie it all together in a neat little anti-Semitic package. It was the Jews, Hasselbach would explain, who had "stabbed Germany in the back" after World War I, and then during World War II "created the lie of the Holocaust." And "you could watch a fourteen year old quickly develop a total feeling of injustice. They were grateful for individual recognition, for praise, and for the communal feeling we could offer them. They got a feeling of power. Many young people don't know what to do after school, for example, and we gave them an answer. No matter how directionless they were, they suddenly had an important lifetime mission."

It was a gestalt: a sense of aggrieved entitlement, a sense of injustice and victimhood, a conviction about who the perpetrators of that injustice were (the Jews and the other enemies), all combined with the experience of acceptance and love within the movement's community of brothers. Guys who felt alone and directionless now had meaning and purpose. And, not to be psychoanalytically reductionist, but they had fathers and brothers for the first time in their lives: authority and community. They felt loved, and they felt seen.

The ones who showed the most independent initiative—who would, for example, go out on their own in the beginning of their recruitment and commit some minor vandalism such as a "spraying action" (say, painting swastikas on storefronts or tombstones)—would be declared heroes and might even be recommended for the Viking Youth, the movement that has, since 1952, been the dominant organizational vehicle for neo-Nazi indoctrination. Part Boy Scouts and part Hitler Youth, the Viking Youth provided direct lines to the NPD and other extreme right-wing parties. And, as Hasselbach notes, once a boy was in the Viking Youth, the die was cast. When one family tried to get their son out, Hasselbach recalled, they received threatening phone calls and their car was blown up.

It's how a narrative cartoon like the one in figure 2 comes to make sense. Here we see a disaffected young man wearing some articles of the Viking Youth uniform: the silky bomber jacket and cargo pants, a gold chain dangling conspicuously from his pants pocket. As he walks along, he sees two swarthy, monstrous Muslim immigrants threatening an innocent German girl with knives. He does what any good German boy would do in such a situation: he beats those immigrants by gouging their eyes. Of course, it is *he* who gets arrested, not those two immigrant thugs (who now seem to be mysteriously joined by a third, a Jew in a yarmulke bearing a Star of David). Brought before a Jewish judge, he is, of course, sentenced to prison. But the story has a happy ending: he carries the beautiful and innocent German girl off into the sunset of a rustic rural setting, with smudged-out insignias around their necks and on the flag behind them. (The swastikas on the side are also partially smudged, because to show them would have been illegal.)

And this is not the only cartoon showing that "they"—Muslim immigrants—are vicious, predatory, rapacious animals who hide behind piety and their Qur'an. In one other cartoon, when a good German man tries to protect his own daughter, it's he who gets arrested. Yeah, the cartoon seems to say, the police always get their man—it just happens to be the wrong one. Such cartoons chronicle masculinity lost and regained, depict violence as a way to recover from the shame and humiliation of foreigners taking over, and tell a story about a corrupt political and judicial administration that at best (the police) fails to understand what is happening and at worst (the judge) conspires in the erosion of German honor.

INGO HASSELBACH

It might just as well be Ingo Hasselbach's story, almost. Hasselbach began his neo-Nazi career in 1987. He was sitting in an East German jail cell, having been incarcerated for shouting, "The wall must fall!" in a public place. Tall (six feet, six), blond, blue-eyed, and handsome, Hasselbach was a prime recruit for the movement. He'd been physically abused by his father, a committed communist. One of those extremely rare West Germans who migrated to the East, his father eventually became the chief

Figure 2. German neo-Nazi comic strip.

of the official state radio in East Germany. The voice of his father was literally the voice of the East German state.

Hasselbach's teen years were spent in the chaotic streets of East Berlin,
a city of "occupied houses, police raids, and gang wars where everyone was
on one political side or another," fighting immigrants, attacking hippies
and punks, dodging the police—all the police forces, namely, the Stasi (the
GDR's notorious secret police), the local police, and the state police—
getting arrested and finding community with others just like him, all from
broken homes, and "always in and out of prison for some offense or other."
By age fourteen, his Stasi file pegged him as "a potential disturber of the
socialist peace." Apprenticed as a bricklayer, he had no interest in doing
anything that even remotely supported the East German state, which he
regarded as oppressive.

A gifted youth organizer and potent street fighter, Hasselbach was
spotted early by Michael Kühnen, the founder of postwar neo-Nazism and
one of the architects of the neo-Nazi movement after reunification.
Kühnen was the father figure Hasselbach so sorely needed (Kühnen was
eventually exposed as gay, and he died of HIV in 1991). "Most of my life I'd
been searching for a father figure," Hasselbach writes, "and in the
Movement Michael Kühnen had been happy to fill the role" (or perhaps
the role of a grandfather). Under his guidance Hasselbach rose to become
deputy führer of the entire movement, the neo-Nazi führer of Berlin.

If Kühnen provided the paternal authority to give life direction, the
Kameradschaften provided community that gave it emotional meaning.
Most of the other members had good jobs as bakers, shoemakers, and
roofers, and some were educated professionals—lawyers and doctors,
economists and engineers, even a smattering of academics. He "saw the
entire universe as a struggle between cosmic racial-cultural forces culminating in a final clash between the forces of Nordic light and Jewish dark-
ness." Here was the band of brothers serving the people, as well the moral
authority of the self-proclaimed new führer. It was a heady mix.

Until it began to unravel. Ironically for Hasselbach, one of those flashes
of insight came while he was playing a game. "Mensch, Ärgere Dich Nicht"
has been one of the most popular board games in Germany for more than
a century. Its name roughly translates as "Man, don't bother yourself," but
in today's slang it probably means something closer to "It's no big deal."

Each player gets four pieces, and the object of the game is to move your pieces around the board toward the center.

Hasselbach and his *Kamaraden* bought a version of the game remastered by a neo-Nazi mail order house in Nebraska and named "Jew, Don't Bother Yourself." In this version each player got four figures: three were Jews and one was an SS officer. Each player moved his Jews around the board with the goal of getting them to the center, which was a gas chamber, depicted by a gray gate bearing the words "Arbeit Macht Frei" ("Work sets you free," the slogan over the entrance to Auschwitz and other concentration camps) and the chemical symbol for Zyklon B, the gas used to murder the Jews. The idea behind the game's title was "Jew, don't get so upset that you're getting sent to the gas."

But playing the game began to confuse Hasselbach, even make him uncomfortable. On the one hand, here was a board game that celebrated the mass extermination of Jews in the concentration camps. On the other hand, Hasselbach had already spent an enormous amount of time arguing that the Holocaust had never happened, that it was all a fabricated story told by dissembling Jews. How could he be celebrating an event that never happened?

After the firebombing of a Turkish family in Mölln in 1992, he decided he wanted to get out. And as he began a new romantic relationship, he realized that doing so was going to take some effort. "You know, Inken," he told his new girlfriend, "this Nazi shit makes me want to puke now, too. I'd like to get out of the scene, but I don't have a clue how to do it." He knew all too well that "the worst violence was reserved for those who tried to quit." The result was EXIT.

GETTING OUT

Hasselbach founded EXIT Deutschland in 2000, modeling it after the Swedish organization. He was met by stony silence from various ministries when he sought funding for a program to help young skinheads get out of the movement (in stark contrast, as chapter 3 shows, to the experience of Kent Lindahl in Sweden, where ministers fairly lined up to fund

EXIT). Hasselbach eventually found an ally in Bernd Wenger, a "retired" former head of the GDR criminal police.

That would be the former *East* Germany, which meant that Wenger, too, was met by some suspicion and reticence by the new unified German government. Was Wenger a Stasi agent? It was true that the neo-Nazis had found fertile soil for organizing in the former GDR. After years of communist rule by Soviet puppets and corrupt apparatchiks, National Socialists had mobilized anti-Soviet sentiment into a return to Nazi-era politics. Germans in the GDR hated the Soviet Union, and, well, whom did the Soviet Union fight against in the war? Germany. In the strange world of "the enemy of my enemy is my friend," East Germans drifted toward the extreme right because it offered an unapologetically national-ist response to what they saw as Soviet occupation. Right-wing groups engaged in what they called "cultural subversion" and attacked foreigners, gay men, and even the few Jews who were still left in Germany. By the end of the 1980s, as the East German regime began to collapse and glasnost signaled the end of Soviet domination, the GDR had a serious problem with unemployed youth drifting further and further to the right.

Bernd Wenger had a front-row seat. Not only had he been the head of the police, but he was also in charge of the youth crime division. At unifi-cation, he went to work at the Institute of Social Work in Frankfurt, part of a federal program to develop strategies for youth problems during reunification. A gang-related crime wave was gripping East German cities as young skinhead neo-Nazis attacked foreigners and gay men, sprayed graffiti on public buildings with slogans like "Jews out of Germany," and patrolled soccer stadiums and rock concerts looking for any opportunity to start gigantic melees. The fall of the Berlin Wall in 1989 only made mat-ters worse. Left-wing gangs would skirmish with right-wing gangs, soccer matches became increasingly unsafe, and new Islamic gangs emerged to counter skinhead violence.

The government's response was heavy-handed, repressive, and largely ineffective. It succeeded in putting a lot of young people in prisons and juvenile facilities, but didn't touch the underlying problems. Wenger had a different idea, using local civic cultural institutions to reach boys and integrate them into this newly unified country. He founded the Center for

Democratic Culture in 1997, a nongovernmental organization that had morphed into EXIT by 2000, when he teamed up with Hasselbach. Their idea was simple: combine political education with youth development work, bring young people into the society as stakeholders, and infuse them with a strong anti-fascist message.

That message had to be tailored to contemporary conditions. Since 2001, EXIT Deutschland has handled nearly five hundred cases of young skinheads and neo-Nazis who wanted to jump. Four out of every five were male, the average age was about twenty-six, and virtually all fell within the twenty-five–to–thirty-five range. These are not the post-adolescent Swedes or the long-committed ideologues in the United States described in chapters 3 and 4.

Typically, the German youth engage while young, through recruitment either from the streets or, more often, in prisons. German prisons are teeming with immigrants, mostly Turks, and so an apolitical white prisoner soon finds "his people" among some of the harder-core Aryans. The young men enter the movement without much in the way of ideology, but they like the scene, connect to the music, and love the community and camaraderie they experience, especially after being loners for so long. From within the prisons, ironically, they feel for the first time that someone has their back. Many are unemployed, and those who have jobs are wage laborers or craft workers. Bernd Wenger gave me a bit of a profile of them.

To begin with, he was quite certain that all of them had a "break" with their families in some way prior to their drifting into the neo-Nazi scene. Their parents were divorced or they grew up in foster care. Some were abused, one or two sexually. Some knew their sisters were being abused and felt powerless to help. "It's not so much the abuse, or the broken home. It's that feeling of injustice being allowed to exist, and that feeling that they are powerless to stop it. They all have felt that powerlessness—and they are absolutely determined never to feel it again."

That observation, of course, matched my observations of every group I examine in this book. The experience of isolation, of emasculation and humiliation at having been abused or ignored or raped—these feelings compromise one's sense of self, thus posing a core existential threat, and also, not coincidentally, compromise one's sense of self as a man, capable of acting with power, autonomy, and purpose. Something essential has been stolen, and some of these guys seek an outlet for it on the streets. Of course, as I've said, it is not the case that all abused, ignored, or bullied young boys become neo-Nazi terrorists. There are many other paths that they can and do take. But the fact that virtually all those who drift into extremist politics come from such a background ought to suggest that we pay attention to these family variables.

Especially when those family variables parallel their political observations of society. Their fathers may have lost jobs, had to close the family store, or had the family farm taken away, and such losses often correspond with their observations that society is sinking into a degenerative state of decline and despair. "Almost every one speaks of the atomization of society, which they fear," Wenger explains. "They want stronger institutions, stronger structures to act as a barrier to this general cultural decline." They want a wall. They may have been happy to see the Berlin Wall come down, but they surely wouldn't mind a new one, between "us" and "them."

In addition, Wenger says, the young prisoners see immigrants as the means by which this decline is occurring, and they see their own misguided corrupt government as the vehicle by which this takeover is being accomplished. Immigrants are "parasites," "ticks," "rats," or other bearers of pestilence in Old Testament terms. The leaders of the country are too soft, too Americanized, to recognize what is happening.

As they see it, the multiculturalism that Europe now embraces is an American import. "Germany is being colonized by the United States," a client named Christian tells me. Germany is being weakened to the point of extinction. This spells the *Volkstod*, the death of the people, he tells me, borrowing a term used during the Third Reich. By contrast, Germany's "primal democracy" is the culturally pure riposte to multiculturalism.

When they point to a civilizational decline that is steep and steady, they mean that literally, by the numbers. Evidence? Well, mostly it's about sex. The declining birthrate is one example (Germany's birthrate is below replacement levels), along with the perceived "scourge" of abortions that tilts the number of births away from pure Germanic people to the immigrants, who do not practice birth control and don't allow abortion. "The wrong people are having babies, and the wrong people are having abortions," says Rike, another client. "We just have to turn it around." And homosexuality is equally anathema to a pure race. "The media creates this image that it's OK to be gay," says Christian. "They actually encourage it, with marriage and all, and anti-discrimination policies. This only further weakens the people. We have to reproduce!"

Finally, Wenger tells me, the young recruits are quite confused about "Semites." The essence of Nazism is anti-Semitism, of course. And they see themselves as anti-Semites. This raises two problems. On the one hand, how can you be an anti-Semite in a country with virtually no Jews? And second, how can you hate Jews when Israel is your major ally in fighting the Muslims, who are, after all, also Semitic? In fact, it's the Turks and other Muslim immigrants who are the targets of the contemporary neo-Nazi rage, the ones to whom they refer when they speak of "parasites," "rats," "vermin," or "cancer."

Most of the EXIT clients I interviewed fit exactly the profile Wenger described, and they followed the same trajectory. Take Christian, for example. Christian is a thirty-two-year-old with a brawny thick build, a jowly face, and arms covered in tattoos, some reminiscent of his neo-Nazi days— an iron cross on one forearm—and others more connected to band names and paganism. Raised on a publicly owned state farm near Leipzig, Christian had a relatively protected childhood, attending a church school until fourth grade. Unification, when he was eleven, proved especially tough, since the farm dissolved and everyone sort of scattered to cities. High school proved difficult too, both socially and academically, and he felt caught between the old East German communist past, which didn't seem so terrible, and the Westernization that unification ushered in. Adrift and apolitical as a teenager, he was found by the recruiters, nurtured, and groomed.

As his father drifted in and out of work, the family had suffered, and consequently moved increasingly to the right in the new unified Germany. "At least communism provided for all of us," Christian tells me, much to the surprise of one of the other EXIT staffers, whose path to the neo-Nazi movement was marked by a profound hatred of the Russians. "Well," Christian insists, "they did. But after unification entire communities went broke, and the government closed kindergartens but opened up shelters for immigrants. 'Fuck that,' my father said. Even after being reunified, he thought it should still be 'Germany for the Germans.'" It was that uncritical nationalism that led Christian toward radical politics. "The government was so corrupt," he says. "All these new Social Democrats, selling drugs, hurting others. I didn't like that. This unification was bad for the East."

It wasn't too far a leap to old-style National Socialism, beginning with a critique of the war debt—the war debt from World War I, mind you. "Having to pay all that, after both world wars, kept us down. Germany was already so poor, and now what's their policy? Bring in more poor people! It's crazy, man." Here, he shifts to Muslim immigrants, substituting "Muslim" or "immigrant" or "Turk" where his grandfather's generation would have used "Jew."

"They're a fucking cancer—they live off us, like they're a parasite and we're the host, you know? They live on welfare, and who do you think pays their taxes that support them? We work hard so that they can relax. And why can they bring their culture here, but our culture, the proud German culture, is suppressed and even illegal! Christian culture is suppressed."

"Who is suppressing it?" I ask.

Christian pauses. "Well, a while ago, it was the Jews, right? But that got taken care of. Now it's the Turks, and the Muslims in general. They've infiltrated the government, and in the name of multiculturalism, they are replacing German values with their values. Same problem, different group." Here, then, was the first conscious link between the contemporary neo-Nazis and their forebears. The Jewish Question was "taken care of." But the problem remains, so now the "immigrant question" has to be taken care of.

"How will you 'take care of' the 'immigrant problem'?" I ask, using the air quotes to refer back to his earlier statement. Christian pauses. "Send 'em back. Plain and simple. Just get rid of them. No murder, no, no. Just send them back. Or, I guess, make them want to go back."

Like most of the young men I met through EXIT in Germany, Christian ended up in prison for petty crimes -- robbery, blackmail, and assault. (He had assaulted his father and sister in a drunken rage during the height of his alienation.) Unlike the many young men who are radicalized after they come to prison, Christian came already radicalized; a couple of comrades were in his cellblock and he expected to feel connected and safe. But they were potheads, whereas Christian had, for movement discipline, sworn off drugs. He couldn't stand the contradiction. "I felt humiliated by them taking drugs," he says, which showed them to be such liars and hypocrites. "I felt like a dope for being a true believer. Fuck that. I was out."

EXIT was waiting for him when he got out of prison. They helped him find work as a medical assistant, and he and his former girlfriend got back together. He has not seen any of his former comrades since he got out, now almost five years ago. His sister has forgiven him for the assault, and he keeps in touch with his mother and his three sisters. "I've built a new life," he says proudly. "I'm not that crazy kid anymore. I don't even miss him." Still, many of the things he says and believes are reminiscent of that earlier "crazy kid." Ideological consistency is not a requirement for working with EXIT. It's still true, he tells me, that Germany is heading down the wrong path. "Immigration is still bleeding us dry," he says, and globalization is not good for everyone. "I still don't understand why Germany is paying so much for everyone else."

ENTRY POINTS

Most of the clients I interviewed in Germany were radicalized in prison. They'd been arrested, as far as they could tell, just for being a good German, a good German man. It is in prison, most often, that these young guys find their brothers. Kersten argues that the crowded juvenile prisons in the former GDR "have turned into right-wing cadre institutions."[14] In German prisons, as elsewhere, groups form around racialized identities: the Muslims hang with other Muslims, the black prisoners with other black prisoners. And white prisoners, disparate and apolitical, find themselves in a cauldron of racialized identity. Fights erupt strictly along racial lines; you'd better be part of your group, lest you become an especially vulnerable target. All of a sudden, they're white, German, and proud. Their inherent Aryanness provides a sense of both victimhood (persecuted by the multicultural state) and superiority, simultaneously. This is a heady and seductive brew, both one-up and one-down. An explanation of the present and a glorious vision of the future.

That was Peter's story. Sentenced to three years for burglary in his midtwenties, he was a drifter, a high school dropout, but hardly a radical. "Inside, it was like crazy," he told me, expressing a casual racism that recalls his earlier virulence. "The Turks, the Arabs, the Iraqis, the immigrants. They were everywhere with their fucking prayer mats and praying all the time. But there were some brothers there, some skinheads who had been arrested for street crimes, assaults on those very same immigrants. And those *Ziegenficker* [goat fuckers] were fucking scary."

Most clients hadn't been especially political beforehand, but inside it was a different world, a world of gangs and groups where "you'd better pick one because you couldn't stand alone." As in the United States, inmates felt that the prison system encouraged the ethnic-based gangs as a form of social control, a way to keep the population divided and therefore conquered, focused on one other and not on the system. "They wanted us to fight," says Peter now. "They encouraged the rivalries. I heard that one guard even slipped one of us [Aryans] a knife once."

On the other hand, several of the clients I met had been racist skinheads when they went into prison, and began a process of deradicalization while they were inside. "I couldn't stand the drugs and the hypocrisy," says Ernst, echoing Christian. "It was all bullshit and I wanted to get out." He contacted EXIT from prison, and they were waiting for him when he was released.

That was also true of Peter. Yes, he'd become radicalized in prison, he tells me, but it was only a survival strategy, "a way to get by inside." He never really agreed with all the political stuff. In fact, he admitted, "I was really pretty apolitical if you want to know the truth. But I needed to be safe."

He needed to be safe when he got out, as well. So as his sentence neared its end, he contacted EXIT and asked to meet with them. EXIT picked Peter up when he was released from prison, provided a place to stay, and helped him find a part-time job. (It's now full-time.) He's become far more committed to helping neo-Nazis jump than he ever was committed to jumping in himself.

What happened with Niels is another typical story, though not so much about EXIT's success as about the difficulty in helping guys leave the movement for good. I heard his story not from Niels himself, but from one of the EXIT staffers, Robert, who had worked with him a bit. Recruited by neo-Nazis in prison, Niels had been sentenced to a three-year term for robbery and assault, charges arising from a string of violent robberies on the streets of Dresden. He was seventeen. When he got out, he wasn't sure he wanted to stick with the neo-Nazi group that had recruited him, and so he reached out to EXIT, hoping to start a different kind of life. "It was

really hard," Robert tells me, "because his girlfriend was still in the movement, and as soon as he got out, they got back together." But he tried. With
the help of EXIT, Neils began working with a social worker. "But she got
sick," Robert says about the social worker, "and had to stop working with
him." And, apparently, she'd done little to help reintegrate him into society
after prison, to rebuild a network of friends and a sense of community.
"Like I had a choice, right, like go back to my people or be completely
alone. That's no choice." Without a home or a job, he returned to Dresden
and quickly got back into the movement.

"We couldn't hold him," said Robert sadly. "It was like he sees the pit,
jumps in, and then wonders how he got there." Now he's twenty-three.
"And we haven't seen him since, though I hear he's unhappy again in the
movement, but still can't see a way out."

In Stefan's case, the anger was familial. As a teenager, he hated his
father, a left-wing intellectual. The father "hated everything on the right,
everything Nazi, everything past," Stefan says. "So I was drawn to it." He
saw his father's leftist politics as yet another expression of his feckless and
indifferent parenting style. "He was a terrible father, just didn't care about
his kids, cared about 'the cause,' whatever that was." Although he was an
indifferent student, he was clever and technically savvy, and wanted a
way to be noticed, to "feel like something besides my father's son, you
know?" At fifteen Stefan started making videos for the movement—
anti-globalization, anti-Zionist, anti-multiculturalism, and anti-pluralism
in outlook. And he found a home, a community.

"But I'm not stupid," he assures me. It became clear to him that while
everyone was benefiting from the PR offered by his videos, he was doing
all the work. "These people weren't dedicated," he sneers. "They were lazy
and stupid. They just wanted to hang out and make fun of everyone else."

At nineteen he decided to leave, and enrolled at a university. There, he
was able to have the sorts of conversation that he'd been hungry for. "But
it made me rethink everything, all that propaganda bullshit I'd been fed,"
he says now. "These people [in the movement] didn't know history, they
didn't know about religion, they didn't know anything. They just mouthed
off bullshit." In one course, he wrote a long paper about the movement's
contradictions, the hypocrisy of its leaders, and the utter vacuity of their
ideas. The professor thought he might want to connect with EXIT, since

Stefan had made it clear that he had been part of the movement. "I used that paper as a first step in my jumping," Stefan told me.

EXIT provided the deeper, more meaningful—and more philosophical— conversations he wanted. Unlike other EXIT recruits, Stefan wasn't searching for community, a band of brothers, a way to feel like a man. He wanted a graduate seminar, a serious engagement with texts. Now twenty-three, he's studying philosophy at the university. The irony of his family situation isn't lost on him. "It's funny," he says, leaning back in his seat so that his long thin frame is nearly parallel to the floor. "I got into the movement because my father was such a serious intellectual, he didn't have time for me, or for anyone else in the family. And what happens? I become a fucking philosopher! I don't think I'm going to become him. But, well, it's strange, right?"

All the men I interviewed had similar visions about gender. It was a simple, binary world they lived in—or at least, that was the world they wanted to live in. We are real men; they are not. We are men; women are women. They wanted that world, the world of their fathers and grandfathers and even further back in time. A world where they had a good steady job, earned a living, and provided for a family. And a world in which their wives could stay home, raise the children, and keep the house. The reason, they believed, they could not have that life wasn't because their wives or girlfriends had actually wanted to work, but because they *had* to work because the old jobs, the ones their fathers had had, were no longer available to them. Because "they" had them.

And "they" are not real men—at least according to the clients at EXIT. "I believed that German men were stronger, healthier, more intelligent," said Marcus. "We were superior by tradition and by birth." Christian agreed. Immigrants are "sad" figures, "pathetic," worthy only of contempt and pity, but not admiration.

"It was humiliating," Christian says, "to have my government take from us to give to them. The current system has it upside down: 'they' should be paying 'us'—rent for the place they now are able to live, taxes to keep the system running. Instead they are sponges, parasites, sick creatures that attach themselves to the healthy organism and suck it dry. They should be grateful, but they're just leeches."

It all seemed so familiar: Aryan men are the real men; Muslim immigrants are failed men, irresponsible, incapable of supporting a family, dependent, parasitical. If I were to substitute the word "Jew" for "Muslim immigrant," these sentiments would have been current in 1939, not in 2016.

And while these young men claimed they enjoyed partying with skinhead women who were righteous right-wingers and enjoyed the drinking, the brawling, and the sex, the truth was they were not at all comfortable with the idea of women's equality—either in the extreme right or in the broader society. They wanted real feminine women for their wives and partners, women who would be good mothers and housekeepers—much unlike the mothers they grew up with.

It was a neo-Nazi version of the dual image of women as "Madonna and whore." They wanted the badass skinhead women to party with and have sex with, but they wanted to marry the virginal Barbie, the homemaking Heidi of National Socialist fantasy.

Yet women are also one of the chief routes out of the movement for many who seek to leave. As with the other groups of young men I discuss in this book, the routes out of the movement in Germany require some process-based experiences, experiences that, in stages, enable, encourage, and even support the unraveling of the intense bonding with comrades.

Disillusionment can come from a general malaise or from a gnawing sense that what one is doing is either pointless or even contrary to one's own values. This can be a serious rupture, a cataclysmic break, in which what a person does and what he believes come into such sharp contrast, such intense cognitive dissonance, that he cannot continue. That sense of cognitive dissonance is the tension that results from the attempt to reconcile contradiction, either between behavior and action or between two sets of beliefs. Humans tend to need to resolve that dissonance; it's very hard to sustain living with or within contradiction.

Some members find the growing sense of malaise comes from their life experiences, from an external driver, such as becoming involved in a serious relationship, having a child, or dealing with the demands of a job. Others attribute a growing discomfort to the hypocrisy that is rife in the movement—a sense coming from a more internal driver, relying on internal dynamics. People at the top, these members observe, hold themselves to different standards than those to which they hold everyone else, and that can begin to wear pretty thin. For example, many guys have experienced being with a group of comrades who abandoned them during a fight or, worse, set them up to be beaten up and didn't come to their rescue or, worse still, beat them up themselves. Just for fun. At those moments, the brotherhood, the comradeship, is exposed as a fraud: nobody actually cares about you in the way they proclaimed.

Such routes out—or at least the beginnings of the exit process—are often not so clear-cut, but rather fuse several strands into a stronger fiber, capable of bearing the increased weight. For example, one German member said:

> For me it was simply that in the moment what was in my head, what I wanted to make into reality, didn't work. It just didn't work. If you then think about such a comradeship and look at it, and look at the people, there's nothing. Somehow no one has . . . no one has this life under control, no one has a goal in any way for something else but they tell you how it should work. But you can think and look at them and you think "*Boah Alki* [German slang for alcoholic], unemployed, who wears women's clothes and hits his children." Then you think to yourself, "What should I do here then?" It doesn't work.[15]

Another man added his relationship with his child to his growing sense that the movement was not the right place for him, even if he continued to agree with the ideology: "[My relationship with] my child was the dot on the *i* because, when you pass through the entire structure and actually observe the ideal that you have in mind and that is communicated to the outside through comradeship, it isn't there. It simply isn't there."[16]

Or a relationship with a woman may be a way out. Combined with getting older and a bit more responsible, many guys grow tired of the skinhead party scene and actually find themselves in a more serious relationship with a woman. Enough of the drinking and partying and sex-just-to-get-off kind of relationship. What if you actually like her? Want to get married or live together? Want to start a family?

Those women, the ones you want to settle down with, aren't the same women whom you've been partying with or having sex with. *Those* women are unlikely to be fellow skinheads, or skinchicks. They're more likely to not be in the movement, and if they know about your life in the movement very much at all, they barely tolerate it. This can bring a moment of reckoning.

"It was, like, when she said I had to choose between my comrades or her," says Ralf, a former. "I never would have imagined it, like because they were my brothers, my comrades, my family. But I chose her. It just seemed like she was the future, you know. Those guys were the past."

Women, children, aging, hypocrisy—these tend to be the most common routes out of the movement. But what about the women who are in the movement? What do they experience? How do they get out?

NEO-NAZI WOMEN

While men are often recruited in prison by older, more experienced neo-Nazis, or through the skinhead punk scene in the cities, women are recruited exclusively by the men in their lives, especially boyfriends. The women's boyfriends are either already in the movement and they find that affiliation exotic or sexy, or they both are hanging out around the margins of the movement, going to parties and concerts, and then enter together. Either way, it almost never lasts.

That was pretty much the story I heard from all six women I spoke with. (As of this writing, about sixty have gone through all stages of the EXIT client experience.) Rilke was fourteen when she entered the movement, through her boyfriend at the time. She married another leader of the movement, and she became an anchor on a neo-Nazi radio show. But when her husband became abusive, she took her two young children and sought refuge in a shelter for battered women. While there, she was approached by someone from the Ministry of the Interior who offered her a chance to work for the government against the neo-Nazis. Now in her mid-thirties, she credits EXIT with offering her the therapy she needed to stay out of the movement, despite the constant threats and the tenderly solicitous efforts to bring her back.

Katharina was fifteen when she, too, had a boyfriend who was on the margins of the movement. He saw Katharina as a way to be cool with the other guys, since she was pretty and sexy. But she was ambivalent, and wrote a letter to EXIT asking for help. With EXIT, she developed a comprehensive coaching plan, including engaging her parents for support. Over the following year, she dropped her boyfriend, pulled away from her former contacts, and eventually moved to another city and got a job and a new life. Now twenty and a nurse, she says that the combination of love and extremism was "so powerful, like a drug, like sex and power. I can understand now the hold it had on me, and how close I came to being dragged under."

Rosa was thirteen when her boyfriend brought her into the movement. Having grown up in a broken home, she felt herself to be a "searcher" and a "hanger-on." Living with her mother and grandparents, she'd heard right-wing propaganda as long as she could remember. Her grandfather had been a solider in the Wehrmacht, and still adhered to Nazi ideas. Germany, he told her, needs a strong leader; democracy was weak and ineffective.

Her boyfriend agreed. By age fifteen, she was hanging out on the movement's edges, furious at how drug dealers and foreigners were wrecking Germany. Her boyfriend had begun working for the Free German Workers Party (Freiheitliche Deutsche Arbeiter Partei), or FAP, as it was known until it was outlawed in 1995. Together, they believed they were creating the Fourth Reich, which would cleanse the nation of impurities—the "flood of foreigners," Jews, and even American influences. They were "saving the white race."

For twenty years, from 1985 to 2005, the movement engaged in street brawls and petty crimes, all ostensibly in the service first of the FAP and later of quasi-religious and spiritualist groups such as Germanic Faith and Viking Youth, which promoted ideas of biological racism and sought scientific proof that the Aryan race was physically superior.

And during those twenty years, Rosa was a mainstay in the movement, almost like a mother to dozens of young Aryan boys searching for a family and community. She'd married one of the movement leaders, Josef, a regional leader of the FAP, and they had four children. From the outside, they looked like an advertisement for wholesome Aryan family life. They condemned all U.S. influences and railed against globalization. "Every hour of every day was devoted to the racial question," she says. "We never ate at McDonalds—it was the fucking Americans."

Rosa had found her ideal German man in Josef, a "political soldier," a man of action, authentic, committed, spiritually and physically strong, and racially conscious. And the movement promoted a sense of pride in their being German. "We were real men," she tells me, undisturbed by the use of the first-person plural. "Those others, especially the globalists and the multiculturalists and the fucking immigrants—they're not real men." Immigrants, she had believed, were stupid, weak, subhuman.

But all was not as it seemed. One of her daughters died as a result of an eating disorder. And every time Rosa spoke up, anywhere—at home, in meetings, at social events—her husband would hit her, sometimes on the spot in public. She tried to "endure the violence," to swallow her pain for the good of the cause: "It was all about the movement anyway, and I had to just take it like a good German wife."

By 2002 she'd had enough. She began to fantasize about breaking from the movement, not because she had any sort of ideological change of heart, but because she was "tired of being a punching bag." Still, it took her three years to get out. In 2005, she took her kids, and what remained of her life, and bolted.

Since jumping, she's faced constant pressure from her former comrades. Young boys whom she'd nurtured as movement pups were now full-grown snarling, rabid pack wolves thirsty for her blood. She has been constantly pursued, harassed, threatened, and her ex-husband has targeted her, seeking to punish her at every turn. "I wonder if I could even call it a life now," she says sadly.

And yet she wants to turn it around. Having worked with EXIT, she calls it "the only place I could go where people would understand me." She still has unbridled disdain for politicians, who are all, as far as she's concerned, corrupt and indifferent. But she's especially concerned with the way society mistreats the disabled, and wants to "stand up" for them because there are so few services for them. "I lost a lot in the movement," she says, looking back. "But mostly, now, I feel that I can say something about the dignity of all persons." She pauses, looks down at her feet. "Good God," she says softly, shaking her head. "I never thought I would say something like that."

Rosa's story is similar to the other women in EXIT, in both Germany and Sweden. Virtually all got into the movement through boyfriends, and virtually all were terribly mistreated by those same boyfriends and then by other guys in the movement. "The guys couldn't decide if they wanted us to be fierce fighters, right alongside them, or sweet little wives in the kitchen," said Dorchen, who had gone through the EXIT program a year earlier when I talked to her. "It was like whatever we were, they wanted the other one. It drove me crazy. Like my boyfriend, he wanted a hot babe who loved sex, but then when I was like that around anyone else, like just at a party or something, he got all crazy jealous that the other guys wanted to fuck me too."

And virtually all the women I spoke with got out because of the way they were treated by the guys. "This is such a man's movement," said Dorchen. "These young skins all trying to puff up and show how masculine they are by beating others up. It's hard to be a girl there. They treat you like shit."

EXIT THROUGH EXIT

Rosa's story, though, was notable for another aspect, something I found truly surprising in interviewing the clients and staff of EXIT Deutschland. She was the only person I interviewed who had anything negative to say about Jews. She wasn't the only one who mentioned Jews; one or two of the other EXIT clients talked about them, but only in relation to supporting Israel because Israelis hate Muslims and they hated Muslims too. Rosa was the only one who spoke of Jews in Germany, even referring obliquely to the National Socialism of her grandparents' generation.

Many of EXIT's clients actually professed alliance with, if not allegiance to, Israel. When the Nazis held power, Ralf explains, the Jews were seen as the problem. "But now it's the Muslim immigrants, and so we look around and see which countries are most opposed to Muslim immigrants." And it's Israel! "I mean, I don't suddenly like Jews or anything, and I still think that Jews are a problem in, like the US, the way they control all the media," he says, I think to reassure me that he hasn't completely lost his Nazi credentials. After all, though traditional Nazi paraphernalia and literature are prohibited in Germany, anyone can still communicate with American neo-Nazis, who remain just as anti-Semitic as Germans of the 1930s. "Let me put it this way," he continues: "We're all probably still anti-Zionist. But we like Israel's policy on the Arabs." As far as they are concerned, Israel is the local bulwark against Muslim contamination of the rest of Europe.

EXIT's vision is clear—it's about providing emotional support and comradeship to replace the camaraderie of the movement; about depoliticizing the radicalism and repoliticizing the clients' sense of being stakeholders in the system. It's about finding meaningful work and a stable long-term partnership as a way to anchor identity outside the movement. And it's evident that EXIT staff have understood the experiences specifically of young *men* in the movement as a way to help to get them out. Their approach is far less about ideology than it is about the experience of being young, isolated, and often feeling alone—whether the youth are among the half who go to prison and are radicalized there, or the half who join up earlier through White Power music and the skinhead life in which they experience community, camaraderie, connection. They ache for that experience as youngsters, and their sense of isolation is easily answered by the ready-made intimacy of the gang. In that sense, they are no different from other gangs in major cities around the world. Gangs are a rational response to miserable economic conditions; they provide jobs, whether selling drugs or organized petty crime, or participating in something more "political" such as demonstrations and handing out leaflets. The neo-Nazi cell is a family for those with no family, a family of equals, a brotherhood without the father. (The father is the more abstract führer in some cases.)

Thus, appeals using rational argument about why the National Socialist vision is either immoral or politically inappropriate are bound to fall on deaf ears. "This isn't a campaign for hearts and minds," says Daniel, a postgraduate researcher working at EXIT. "This is about skin, flesh and bone, the experience of connectedness, of brotherhood, that has been lacking in these guys' lives. If we just try to convince them rationally, we fail. We need to provide for them an alternative experience of brotherhood, a new masculinity, a way to feel like a real man without beating up immigrants, without hating others, but by connecting with them."

To a greater or lesser extent, this appeal to the gendered, the experiential, informs the other programs that help Germans leave the movement. For example, the Federal Office for the Protection of the Constitution, the German federal security service, has organized the Bundesverfassungsschutz (the domestic intelligence agency). The BvF's typical dropout (another word for a former) is between twenty and twenty-five years old and male. The agency recruits mostly from former East German small towns and rural areas, and most of its contacts have serious alcohol or drug problems.

One of its programs specifically targets leaders of extreme-right organizations. With these leaders, the approach is rational. The BvF explains that the groups' political goals are unattainable and offers dropouts a "contract": if you tell us everything you've done and every crime you've committed, and agree to leave the movement, we will not prosecute you for those crimes. The agency's second program is more passive: it waits for fellow travelers and followers to contact its agents through a hotline. For these people the program involves more psychological counseling and support. A dropout who complies with the program then "actually leaves the scene, stops committing criminal offences, adopts another world-view and distances himself wholeheartedly from all extremist values."[17]

One of the requirements is that dropouts "clean house," which means they must remove literally everything connected with the movement from their lives. "In the most serious cases this can result in the person being left with very little clothing, losing his entire music collection and staring at blank walls."[18] If you're going to ask this of a dropout, you'd better be prepared to offer something to take its place. Dumping all your stuff, all at once—the stuff that you've accumulated, that has given you meaning and purpose and enabled you to feel like a man—well, removing all of it could make you feel more isolated and more bereft.

Sadly, some of these programs fall somewhat short when it comes to offering something to replace what has been relinquished. The program may insist that you renounce your past, but it has few well-established programs to help you envision a future. And so some of the men drift back into the movement. One of the EXIT staffers told me that they might initially lose about 20 percent of their clients, but then some return. In fact, says Robert, the fact that guys who try to leave often get "jumped out"— threatened and sometimes assaulted by their former closest friends—is one of the things that confirms their decision to exit. Those in the movement experience a dropout's betrayal as such an existential threat that they must purge it.

Some of the other programs currently being developed pay little attention to gender, and they have met with only limited success. One such program is organized by the Ministry of the Interior in the North Rhine and Westphalia areas. Originally, it was simply a telephone hotline, but no one called except anxious parents and inquisitive journalists. Their new program reaches out directly to the young guys, mostly young skinheads involved with the *Kameradschaften*. Most are addicted to drugs and almost all have a criminal record.

The Hessian Disengagement Program, called IKARus, also tries to split the leaders from the followers. The prevention program targets young (thirteen to sixteen years old) entry-level followers and explains where their lives will inevitably lead if they follow their current path. Somewhat analogous to the "scared straight" programs used with young offenders in some US cities, this is fairly successful, especially if they can point to alternative youth cultures the young guys can get involved in.

A second part of the IKARus program seeks to extract those who have been in for a couple of years. Slightly older (eighteen to twenty on average), these Hessian youth are also often involved with drug or alcohol abuse. IKARus has found that many come from stable middle-class families in the area around Frankfurt-am-Main, where casual xenophobia and anti-Semitism are part of the fabric of family life and community culture. They may take it a bit further, but it entirely surrounds them.[19] The program strives to help these young people "build up a positive identity by experiencing success and creating alternative new values."

Those new values may, in the case of EXIT, have something to do with gender—both in the clients' relationships with women and in their understanding of themselves as men. But they may not. I suspect that this inattention to gender, to helping these young men feel that they are not re-entering an anomic world where their masculinity is uncertain, will limit their effectiveness. "If you are asking me to renounce a subculture that validated my masculinity, that gave me those feelings of brotherhood and purpose," I can hear these guys asking their new handlers, "what are you going to give me in return?

Daniel has been my guide for a couple of days, and he clearly plays to my research interests in understanding how gender, how masculinity, plays out in the recruitment and retention of young men in the neo-Nazi movement. Now that we are in his car as he drives me to the airport, we can unwind a little and talk about my underlying interests in all these interviews. But he's not just parroting the concerns I laid out for him earlier as my motive for getting to speak with EXIT clients. "I don't want to go too far, here, and say that, like, after World War I, Germany was a lost soul searching for a way to feel like a real man or something. That's overly psychoanalytic." But, he says, many of the guys who come to EXIT are lost and feel weak, emasculated, and are struggling and sometimes drowning in a multicultural pool that no one has taught them how to swim in.

EXIT tries to offer an alternative to that—not an alternative ideology, but an alternative *experience*. The opportunity to build a community of brothers (and sisters) committed to one another—and committed to staying out of the movement. Committed to helping these guys find ways to feel more masculine by helping them find steady jobs, thereby developing a sense of economic efficacy. Committed to helping them build a masculine identity anchored in their communities and in healthy relationships.

"Have you ever thought of a dating service?" I ask somewhat sarcastically.

"We have," Daniel laughs. After all, we both acknowledge immediately, there are already neo-Nazi and white supremacist dating sites on the Internet, including whitepeoplemeet.com and the Aryan Dating Page at Stormfront.org, the white nationalist portal based in the United States.

It's not half-crazy as an idea. EXIT has struggled for private and public funding and institutional support. Its lack of success is due in part to a sense among public officials that this is a police matter, not a political one. "The government doesn't want to acknowledge that these political factions are so alive and active and organizing," Wenger told me. Nor does the government exactly trust an organization run by an ex–East German police officer. (I had heard rumors that Wenger had been a Stasi agent. And if I had heard them, they must have circulated widely, because I'm hardly on the inside of these rumor mills.)

Because funding has been an ongoing challenge, and because some of the programs, such as the safe houses and therapy, require significant funds, let alone the constant need for secrecy of the organization itself, EXIT has had to be creative. And it has been. To gain some visibility and credibility with the government, as well as to expand its footprint in the public conversation about the dramatic rise of the neo-Nazis and other far right parties in Germany, EXIT came up with what I think may be the

Figure 3. The "Trojan T-shirt" campaign by EXIT Deutschland—the shirt's front before and after washing. For further information, see EXIT's video of the campaign on YouTube. Photo courtesy of EXIT Deutschland.

most brilliant, if short-lived, marketing strategy ever. The Trojan T-shirt (figure 3).

At Rock für Deutschland in August 2011, a festival of white-power music and organizing run by the NPD, EXIT members dressed up as neo-Nazis and passed out free T-shirts to 250 of the attendees. The T-shirts were really cool: black, of course, with a menacing logo on the front "Hardcore Rebel" was emblazoned under a skull and two flags with no insignia. Underneath that, the slogan read "National and Free." Awesome, right? And free! Skinhead swag! Attendees immediately put it on, and an entire "Hardcore Rebel" corps was suddenly dancing and moshing and drinking and having a great time.

Apparently guys at the festival loved these T-shirts. Until, that is, they got home and washed them, at which point the T-shirt changed. The phosphorescent paint that had proclaimed their slogans, "Hardcore Rebel" and "National and Free," had disappeared, and instead a new slogan emerged: "Was dein T-shirt kann, kannst du auch" (What your T-shirt can do, you can too), along with the message "We'll help you break with right-wing extremism" and contact information for EXIT Deutschland.

Brilliant, right? And also pretty unrepeatable. Imagine how skeptical you'd be going to the next white-power music festival and having someone offer you a free T-shirt. No way you'd take it.

But the campaign did its job. According to the manufacturers of the T-shirt, it resulted in more than 30 million hits on Facebook and was one of the most cited media campaigns of 2011. Most important, the number of people who contacted EXIT for help in getting out has tripled.

Despite the Trojan T-shirt campaign's unrepeatability, EXIT has continued to stage clever PR stunts. In 2014, citizens of the town of Wunsiedel grew tired of the annual neo-Nazi demonstrations in their town, on National Heroes Remembrance Day, at former the grave of Hitler's deputy Rudolph Hess. The townspeople had tried everything—petitions, blockades, and even counterdemonstrations dedicated to peace and tolerance—with little success. Finally, they tried a new approach: under the slogan "Rechts gegen Rechts," (Right against right), they solicited money for a cause. As with any walk-a-thon, corporations and wealthy individuals pledged ten euros for every meter walked by any of the marchers—with the money donated to EXIT! All along the route, the neo-Nazi demonstrators were greeted with banners and placards that announced how much money had been raised. Only at the end of the march did they realize how they'd been pranked into mobilizing contributions of more than 10,000 euros to EXIT.[20]

THE ONGOING PROCESS

As I finished my interviews on the last day I was in the EXIT office, Rudy came into the room. He said he was "desperate." Many of the staff already knew who Rudy was. At twenty-six, he was well known in right-wing circles as a militant Aryan, soccer hooligan, and skinhead. He and his girlfriend, Ann, were legendary; since her father was a prosperous contractor (and also a neo-Nazi), they had been poster children for the neo–National Socialist family.

Rudy had been arrested the year before for violent crimes against immigrants. Released from prison a few months earlier, he and his girlfriend had decided to jump. She'd broken with her family; her father had sworn revenge against his daughter and her "pussy" boyfriend. Rudy now had a job, but the company he was working for didn't know he'd been a neo-Nazi. And, of course, they were under surveillance by their former comrades, who'd made it clear that if Rudy wanted to "jump," they were going to "jump him out," meaning they'd beat him so senseless that he might not even survive.

He came to EXIT knowing he was being watched, followed, threatened. He didn't feel safe anywhere. How could he tell his boss about his past and not get fired? How could he and Ann find a safe place to live? (They'd been couch-surfing at a few friends' homes, but even those friends were getting edgy.)

The EXIT staff leaped into action. One started calling around to find someone with a guest room who could take the couple in temporarily. Wenger and Philipp huddled and strategized how they could go with Rudy to talk to his boss. They suggested Rudy also go to the police—with Wenger, of course—and explain Rudy's situation and hope that the police would also provide surveillance. And Jonas thought he might go have a chat with some of the local skinheads with whom he'd been working.

"Jumping is a process," Jonas said to me, assuming the role of translator he seemed to have taken on. "You can't just jump. You need so much support, and you need to be safe. It's sometimes scarier to be out than it is to be in. We now have to be that community, you know? Every man needs his brothers."

Jackie

Kumla prison is an imposingly secure structure: squat thick windowless concrete bunkers in the middle of a vast flat field two hours north of Stockholm. Kumla is the most secure prison in Sweden, the one to which the three hundred most hardened criminals are sent. As is typical of maximum-security prisons, massive barbed wire fences immediately surround the prison walls, beyond which stretches an open field for perhaps one hundred feet—sort of a dry moat—and beyond that an equally imposing electrified barbed-wire fences forms the outer perimeter. Escape would be difficult.

To visit a prisoner here, one enters the gate in the middle of those thick walls and then walks about fifty yards across a dirt courtyard to the interior prison wall. There, behind another wire gate, there is a door to the prison. You enter a small anteroom with a guard sitting behind a high counter. You present your passport, and in the case of a US visitor, a "certificate of good conduct" issued by the City of New York, which is basically a document that attests that you have not been arrested. (I have been certified a "good boy" by my own city, an accomplishment that ranks right up there with university tenure.) You are then ushered into a small room with secure lockers where you place everything you brought with you.

Everything. I brought a note pad and pen into the next room (metal detectors, guards behind thick Plexiglas), and after passing through the metal detector, the guards took my pen and gave me one of theirs, and inspected my blank pad for coded messages.

They led me down a wide, pleasant, well-lit hallway to a narrow room. Bright and cheery, the room had a window that looked out onto the prison garden, along with curtains, a single bed (with a cotton blanket and pillow, and a rubber sheet covering the mattress), a table, and two chairs. There was a bathroom with a shower. This was one of a row of such visiting rooms, perhaps as many as five, and you could hear the (ahem) conjugal visits taking place in the rooms on either side. An intercom on the wall would ring the guard at the front desk to come and open the door, and a small red panic button next to it behind glass. But these were placed on the wall next to my interviewee's chair, so that he would be sitting between me and those buttons. This made me a bit anxious.

I was here to meet Jackie Arklöv, the "most hated man" in Sweden. Described to me by several journalists and others as the "Charlie Manson" of Sweden, Arklöv was a neo-Nazi, a leader of a small faction called the National Socialist Front. In the late 1990s, to fund the purchase of weapons for the NSF's planned takeover of the Swedish state, Arklöv led a series of daring bank robberies. Cornered by the police after one of these heists, Arklöv shot and killed two police officers. He is serving a life sentence.

During his trial, it was revealed that he was wanted on war crimes charges issued by an international court investigating the excesses—torture, brutality—committed by Croat forces in Bosnia in the mid-1990s. He has pleaded guilty to these crimes as well. That sentence runs concurrently.

I suppose by now you have a pretty good mental picture of Jackie Arklöv, right? Some hulking neo-Nazi skinhead, with a large, shaved head, cold, murderous eyes, and tattoos of swastikas and iron crosses covering his bare chest. Something like a neo-Nazi Lurch from *The Addams Family*. At least that's how I imagined him.

Which made me utterly unprepared for the man who walked into the visiting room to greet me, and who was then locked (from the outside!) into the room with me. Jackie is of medium height, with a powerful bodybuilder's chest and a slim waist, and long delicate fingers. His bright eyes are direct, engaged, and lively, indicating a fierce intelligence. Within thirty seconds of his entrance, he was describing to me the books by Dostoevsky and Coetzee he'd been reading. Of Dostoevsky, he says, he was struck by how the great author had advocated violence, was passionate and political in his youth, but then, in prison, rethought his positions and repented "with real agony." He laughs. "Hey, that sort of sounds like me."

Oh, yeah. Have I mentioned that Jackie Arklöv is black?

Yes, Scandinavia's most feared neo-Nazi murderer is a black man. Well, actually of mixed-race ancestry: his mother was Liberian and his father British. He was born in Monrovia and, at age two, adopted by a Swedish family. And there lies the beginning of his story.

Jackie grew up in Ankarsund, a small town of a hundred inhabitants in northern Sweden (southern Lapland), a village that had never seen a black person before he arrived. Indeed, it's likely that no one in the whole province had ever seen a black person! He was, for certain, the only black person in the entire province. His parents were relatively well-off; his father was a prosperous farmer with thousands of chickens, and his mother was a music teacher. They owned a small country store as well, and lived in the flat above the store. Although remote and inexpressive, they made him feel safe.

Ever the outsider, he was always getting into fights in school. "I was bullied a lot," he says, "but the truth is, I also bullied right back."

He described himself as a "willful learner"—he learned "whatever I wanted" but "not what they told me I had to learn." By high school he had become fascinated with the Nazis. "It wasn't the ideology that interested me," he said. "It was the military machinery, the warfare. I loved war—the fighting, the pageantry, and the glory." The Nazi part was more of a "protest," a way to get attention. "I was always angry, and I needed an outlet for my hate. It just kept growing, the hate."

These three forces—interest in the military, his growing hate, and the painful racism of rural Sweden—led him to overcompensate. "I have to be more white than the other whites," he said. "I knew the Nazis had a racialist ideology that wouldn't include blacks. But I wasn't black. I was Swedish. I was going to show other Swedes that I was even more Swedish than they were. I actively opposed immigrants, complained constantly about refugees. They were parasites, taking *our* jobs."

After high school and an industrial-technical college career, he decided that what he really wanted was a military life. He'd always been interested in the military, devouring books, even as a boy, about battlefield tactics and weaponry. Recruited into the Swedish army, he quickly excelled. He became a Ranger, approved for Special Forces, the Swedish equivalent of the Green Berets.

"The problem for me, though, was that there were no wars. Sweden's such a nice country, they never fight anyone. I didn't want to just be in the military; I wanted to fight in a war."

"I was a warrior looking for a war," he says. And he found one.

Recruited as a mercenary for the Croat army in 1993, he was immediately sent to the war in Bosnia. "It was great," he says. It was among the Croats that he really learned about Nazism, he points out. After all, the Croats had been Nazi sympathizers during the Second World War, unlike the Serbs, who were resisters and were slaughtered by the Reich. Here, committing war crimes against the Muslim Bosnians, alongside the sons of real Nazis whose racialist ideology completely detested blacks, he felt "truly accepted" for the first time in his life. "It was the only time in my life that nobody called me a 'fucking nigger,'" he tells me.

"Sure, when they met me they were a little prejudiced," he says. "But in the army, it's not who you are, it's what you do that counts. And they completely accepted me."

He pauses. "It's like the Norman Mailer novel *The Naked and the Dead*," he muses. "The tensions between the Italians and the Jews in the army." (I confess, every time he cited literature I was a bit nonplussed.)

Though he was active with the special forces in Bosnia, he glosses over his own involvement. "Hell is a place on earth," he says somewhat cryptically. "I saw the absolute worst that people can be to each other." It is the only time in the conversation that he speaks in the third person, about others. He switches to the passive voice. "Terrible things happened. Many, many atrocities were committed." He really doesn't want to talk about what he did in Bosnia.

In 1995 he was taken prisoner by the Bosnian army and spent the next fifteen months in a Bosnian prisoner-of-war camp. Here were Bosnians, Serbs, Croats, all together, and everyone got along "extremely well." It wasn't where you were from, suddenly, but how brave you had been in battle that mattered. Jackie's "heroics" preceded him. He was even, you might say, "popular."

In August 1996 he was freed and repatriated to Sweden in a prisoner exchange. He tried to return to civil society after his experiences in war. It was impossible. He drifted from job to job, place to place.

"I had just been released from prison," he says, fully aware of the irony, "but when I returned to civil society, I felt like I was trapped in a cage, in a box. I couldn't breathe." It was strange. In prison, he felt community, camaraderie, connectedness. Out of prison, he felt isolated, alone, longing for that sense of brotherhood and community. He rented a cheap apartment in Östersund, a small city in the center-north of the country, and fell in with a group of neo-Nazis who were taken with his military experience. "They saw me as a man of action, not words—a man of deeds."

"And I took this northern Swedish idea of being a man to be what a real man is." In the north, he explains, Swedish men are hard, lonely, stoic, inexpressive. They speak with virtually no inflection, in a monotone, mumbling. (I keep thinking of Heath Ledger's portrayal of Ennis del Mar in *Brokeback Mountain*, barely moving his jaw when he speaks.) People in the north seem as cold as the ice that surrounds them, and as dark as the eternal night of winter above the Arctic Circle. "There's no room for happy, fun-loving, expressive, men," Jackie says. "Did you know that they call Stockholm 'Fjollhom' (literally, 'Fag City')?"

In the late 1990s, Jackie became increasingly involved with the Nationalsocialistick Front (National Socialist Front, or NSF; aka the Front), a neo-Nazi faction in northern Sweden that was preparing itself for the glorious and bloody takeover of the Swedish state. "Democracy was all talk," he says. "Sweden was the "bitch society," completely feminized. Everything was corrupt, decadent, weak. Swedish men were cowards: they didn't have the courage to stand up to the police or the immigrants, and were just letting these insects crawl over them. I thought, there must be one man who is willing to stand up to them—and I thought it should be me. I could channel my anger, my hate, and stand up for Sweden." Finally he was a man on a mission. "I believed that we, the Nazis, were the chosen people, the ones who would sacrifice for them. We despised the Swedish people, at the same time as we were willing to lay down our lives for them."

The Front planned its takeover of the Swedish government methodically and carefully, and with its members' paranoia given full reign as it planned a phantasmagorical coup d'état. The militant faction of the IRA was its role model, and members robbed banks for money to buy weapons with which to carry out their terrorist attacks and assassinations (which did not come to pass). On May 28, 1999, Jackie and two comrades entered a bank in Kisa, wearing ski masks and waving pistols. They ordered everyone to the floor and unlocked the safe and took the cash—about 2.6 million kroner (about $330,000 at the time).

The lone police officer in Kisa, Kennet Eklund, gave chase, and eventually got the three to pull over. Arklöv and his comrades, Tony Olsson and Andreas Axelsson, opened fire on Eklund, even throwing hand grenades. A second getaway car had been parked nearby and the three robbers drove away in it. Two Swedish police officers tried to stop them and were murdered. This was not a "shoot-out," as reported in the press, but an execution. The officers were shot in the head with their own service revolvers. Captured a few days later, Axelsson and Olsson claimed Arklöv had actually fired the weapon, to which Arklöv confessed. All three are serving life sentences.

It was in prison that Jackie first began to realize the depraved, insane depths to which he had fallen. The Nazis were "crazy," he says. He means it. Literally. "They were so desperate for members, they would take mentally retarded guys, alcoholics, and especially guys who you would say are paranoid and hysterical," he adds. "Now *they* scare me."

More than that, though, he began to feel a deepening sense of remorse. This was a new feeling, and he wasn't sure where it was coming from. "Where I used to feel hatred, that space inside me became increasingly filled with remorse and regret."

He quotes an old Hebrew saying: When you kill a man, you kill his whole world. "I didn't just kill those policemen; I killed their whole world. Their children, their wives, their relatives, their friends. I feel that every day." (Of course, he says, the fact that he killed two cops in a shoot-out has made him somewhat of a folk hero among other prisoners. He refuses any praise, and tells inmates that he is "not a hero.")

Consumed with guilt, Jackie began thinking and reading and writing. He wrote long, anguished letters of apology to the widows of the two police officers he murdered. (These letters were not answered.)

He says now that he has spent considerable time rethinking his past. Eventually, he reached out to EXIT. He began to work with the organization in 2012, and hopes that when he is released, in another fifteen years or so, he will be able to work with EXIT to help others turn around.

At this point in our first interview, our lunch is served. He has arranged for us to eat in the visiting room, and the guards wheel in a tray of a hot meal, bread, and milk. While not exactly nouvelle cuisine, it is entirely edible. I decide that if I am ever going to be sentenced to a maximum security prison, I'd like it to be in Sweden.

After lunch, Jackie takes out the thick loose-leaf binders he has brought to show me. Inside are printouts from the Internet about Husserl and Wittgenstein. He has been reading Wittgenstein lately, trying to understand the roots of violence and especially of racial and ethnic hatred. He links anti-modernism with economic displacement from globalization, and then links the feelings of invisibility ("being pushed aside") with arrogant invincibility. He asks if I can send him the book *Male Fantasies* by Klaus Theweleit, about the crazed violent fantasies of the Freikorps before and during the Nazi era.

I'm a bit taken aback by suddenly having a conversation about Wittgenstein in the visiting room of a Swedish supermax prison. I can barely get my PhD students to talk with me about Wittgenstein! Jackie is pursuing a joint degree in history from the university at Uppsala and in sociology from the university in Gavle. He reads constantly, and conducts classes by telephone and correspondence, and with visiting instructors. His English is nearly flawless.

Suddenly, the guards walk in, looking at their watches. Visiting time is over. They make sure that Jackie has not given me anything from his large blue binders, and they look through the reams of printouts from Web downloads. He's led out after an awkward and somewhat rushed goodbye, with Jackie reminding me to send him those books.

Which I did when I get back to New York. Not long after, I received a typewritten letter. He was reading *Male Fantasies,* he wrote, but found Theweleit "sometimes too narrow" when describing the experiences of the Freikorps. After all, he told me, "much of their views on women is a general one, a view of mostly all males in that time," so he doesn't find it to be at all special. On the other hand, he was captivated by "their culture of violence and love of fighting."

In the envelope were a couple of photographs of his paintings. While in prison, he's taken up painting, mostly very realistic battle scenes from historical conflicts, mostly from the Middle Ages. Based on precise and detailed historical descriptions of these battles, he typically paints portraits of soldiers preparing for battle and of officers standing on hillsides surveying the field of battle, planning their attacks. The paintings are astonishingly detailed and highly representational; they've even been shown in an exhibition of prison art in Stockholm.

I've since visited Jackie twice more in other prisons to which he'd been transferred. We've continued our conversations, again half about political philosophy and half about his life. The tragedy in Norway in July 2011—when the domestic terrorist Anders Breivik exploded a bomb in downtown Oslo, killing eight people, and then drove to the island of Utøya and executed sixty-nine young people, teenagers mostly, attending a youth camp for a Social Democratic workers' organization—had a profound effect on Jackie. It was as if he had a second identity crisis, the first coming after his arrest. "Why did he [Breivik] do this? Could I have done something like this? If I could have done this, what would that make me? What would I be? Could I have stopped him?"

Despairing and uncertain, Jackie wrote a book manuscript, "*Marrionett-manniskan*" (Marionette Man). It's a brooding work, a philosophical meditation on the questions of individualism versus collectivism. It fits squarely in the European tradition of political theory—half post-Marxist, half German Herderian romanticism—in which the author posits a primitive socialist-collectivist spirit that is replaced by the individualism of modern society. New forms of collectivism—communist, fascist—arise that cultivate that nostalgic longing for connectedness, but these are "artificial."

Arklöv applies these dichotomies first to military organization, and then to theoretical notions of freedom and conscience. Arklöv contrasts the "conscript" model with both collective mobilization and the professionalizing honorific and obligatory elements in military organization. Conscripts must enlist, which means the state assumes that recruits do not want to be there. But the honorific system offers symbolic and cultural rewards, which can be more emotionally compelling. Ranging over the Frankfurt School (Horkheimer and Adorno), then Kantian epistemology, Foucault, and Schopenhauer, he alights gently, like a talented political philosophy graduate student early in his career, on questions and concepts that suggest the limits of free will in modern society, the power of peer pressure, state coercion, and, eventually, the notion of "self-control" as the ultimate triumph of the bourgeois state. Modern notions of freedom are imaginary, as elusive as they are illusory, he concludes, but we are still slightly freer than in earlier eras. Individualism is the biggest trap; the belief in individual freedom is the thing that most imprisons us and keeps us obediently in line.

Along the way, Jackie makes asides about morality and freedom that strike me as only slightly veiled autobiographical musings. In a society in which violence and murder are the norm (for example, the death penalty), it is far more likely that the deviant one, the immoral one, is really the only one capable of acting ethically.

During my third and final visit, having now read the book (or, more accurately, having had the book translated), I ask Jackie about it. He obviously has been doing some serious thinking, and feels that the system that promises freedom and self-expression through consumerism is a far worse prison than the one he's living in. "National Socialism is a fraud," he says, "a complete sham." Its importance lies in its representing "a distorted resistance" to individualism, a "perversion." The community it offers is fraudulent because it is based on hierarchy and exclusion. But, he hastens to add, "that longing for community, for genuine connection—that's real," he says.

Our society promises freedom but delivers "the marionette man." No one is free. No one pulls his or her own strings. I ask Jackie if there is anything else he wants to say. He thinks for a moment, and dangles his arms like a marionette. "When I was free on the outside, I was mentally in prison," he says. "But now it's the other way around."

3 Sweden: Entry and EXIT

People want to be loved; failing that admired; failing that feared; failing that hated and despised. They want to evoke some sort of sentiment. The soul shudders before oblivion and seeks connection at any price.

Hjalmar Söderberg, *Doctor Glas* (1905)

I was so afraid of my pain that I wanted other people to feel that pain.

Christian, age thirty, EXIT client

Jackie Arklöv is an anomaly: an African-Swedish ex-neo-Nazi. He is seriously one of a kind. His adolescent rage, fueled by the casual racism of northern small-village Sweden, led him to fantasies of vengeance that would enable him to prove his manhood. Bloodthirsty and angry, he drifted further to the right, in search of the visceral experience of military glory. He ended up with the Croats, killing Bosnians.

Far more typical of the extreme right in Scandinavia are the stories of Andrew and David. Andrew is a small boy, with short, streaked hair dyed blond and tucked under a black baseball cap. His eyes are bright and blue, and his round, prepubescent face gives an almost androgynous sweetness to his features. He wears a black hooded sweatshirt that says, in English, "Go Fuck Yourself," and a black nylon bomber jacket over that. He sits slouched, his buttocks barely touching the edge of the seat as he strains to lean back as far as the chair will allow. His arms are crossed over his chest in an edgy mix of defiance and resignation as he describes to me what first brought him into the Nazi movement, what he believes, and how he left the movement several months ago. Andrew is thirteen.

David is seventeen; he "jumped" from the Nazi movement two years ago. He's bigger and pudgier, with two studs in his right eyebrow and a labret just below his lower lip. His smile reveals a serious overbite, and his glasses are a bit smudged and crooked. Each of his forearms is tattooed; in one tattoo Bart Simpson smiles demonically, his shorts around his ankles as he moons the viewer. The other is an iron cross.

I met Andrew and David in the Fryshuset, a vibrant youth center in the trendy Södermalm district, in Stockholm. The Fryshuset is a repurposed cold-storage factory (the name means "freeze house"), an ample-sized complex of buildings that represents a collaboration among private philanthropists, the YMCA, the YWCA, and the municipal government. Originally redesigned for sports and music to attract Stockholm's youth, the building's mission has evolved, and it now houses offices for a wide variety of organizations that work with young people. Drama clubs, music classes, and lots of clubs for various interests and hobbies all advertise upcoming meetings on a bulletin board crowded with flyers and announcements. Another section of the board has a list of possible jobs. The cavernous entry area contains a snack bar with tables and chairs around which typical slacker teens lounge purposelessly, waiting for something to happen. There's a large gym with basketball courts and workout equipment, a warren of offices and meeting rooms, and a well-stocked, inexpensive cafeteria. Taken together, the facility feels utterly unlike youth centers in the United States. This one feels more like the authorities and donors asked the young people what they wanted, rather than deciding for them. It definitely has the feel that it is "their" place, and adults, especially one wearing a sports jacket, are definitely the outsiders.

EXIT has its offices here, including several lounges offering comfortable chairs and sofas (one is in near-constant use for group therapy sessions), an open-plan office with file cabinets brimming with neo-Nazi literature, and a modest library with magazines, newspapers, and books about life after the movement. I'm greeted by Robert and Pelle, major figures in EXIT, who have agreed to be my guides. Robert has also agreed to be my translator in case that is needed. It isn't. Even the high school dropouts among the EXIT clients are fluent enough in

English to speak with me. David and Andrew are the first clients I will meet today.

David is from Uppsala, and his father works as a foreman in a warehouse of a pharmaceutical company; his mother is on disability. His stepfather works in a photocopy shop. Chubby, academically disinterested, and feeling marginal, David was a target for bullies in primary school. By sixth grade, though, he and many of his classmates were increasingly drawn into neo-Nazi ideology and affect, and they began to wear the clothing, offer the various salutes, and identify as Nazis. He had a few friends who were into Blood and Honour or the National Youth (NU). "We spent all our time drinking and fighting," he explains, which were the primary draws for him as well.

In seventh grade, his school was so alarmed by the number of kids who were getting interested in Nazism that the administrators called in a member of EXIT to give a presentation. But the life was too much fun. David would go to meetings of more than a hundred and sometimes upward of two hundred kids, with a pretty even gender split. "The meetings would become parties, and then everyone would go out afterwards. The girls used to start the fights, provoking some immigrants or something, but then they'd run away, leaving me to clean it up. But it was OK, and there were plenty of girls."

David felt that the Nazis "had the right idea about unifying the country and unifying the people." He sees Sweden as divided and the politicians as corrupt. He wants them to act, to bring Sweden together again. He would target immigrants "because we hate them. They have no reason to be here. They keep saying they don't like Sweden. So what are they doing here?"

Arrested three times but never convicted, David has had his share of injuries, though none serious. Gradually, he began to feel that movement participation was losing its fun. "I began to think that the people I was hanging out with were not living up to the ideals of the movement, weren't living up to what they were saying. They were drinking and smoking and one of the leaders was actually dating a Thai woman! And it started to get boring, always going to the same parties with the same people." Although he also continued to drink and smoke, David began to drift away. He came to EXIT one year ago, and for a while lived in a safe house. "They said they were going to kill me," he said of his former comrades. He had dropped out of high school and has returned now, has a regular girlfriend, and is about to take his first holiday with her. "I just want to have a good life," he says.

ANDREW'S STORY

Andrew is from Värmdö, a working-class Stockholm suburb. His father is in construction and his mother, a homemaker, formerly worked as a kindergarten teacher. Andrew also felt marginalized—in third grade. By fourth grade he had discovered white power music like Skrewdriver, and that was his point of entry into the White Power movement. He spent his time going to parties, putting up posters, drinking, and driving around in a car with several other kids, yelling obscenities at immigrants. Unlike all the others, Andrew says he was not the target of bullies. "Not at all," he states calmly and flatly. "I was the bully."

Still living at home, Andrew had lots of conflicts with his parents about his beliefs. One of his mother's friends is Jewish and was in a concentration camp. "She's OK, I guess," he says. "My mom likes her. It's OK." But it isn't so "OK" with his mother, who has taken down the Nazi flag he hung in his room and burned it, along with his storm trooper uniform—even in its rather small size.

Ironically, although Andrew had been the bully in his school, as a visible, and visibly small, Nazi, he has now become the target for others. He is constantly harassed and beaten up by violent anti-Nazi groups, "which is really just other kids my age who hate just like I do." The ritual purity of the Nazi movement held no appeal. "I drink all the time," he says casually. Addicted to the video game *Counterstrike,* Andrew now says he likes gaming more than fighting. This past summer, he "jumped." The group's leader, twenty years old, was furious and threatened him. "But my mother's boyfriend knows some Hell's Angels, and I just told him [the leader of the group] that if he messes with me, I'll tell my mom's boyfriend. Now he's incredibly nice to me, and said 'Cool, whatever.' He even offers to drive me home from school." Andrew hopes to become a fireman.

THE NEO-NAZI SCENE IN SCANDINAVIA

While significantly fewer in number than their American counterparts, white supremacists in the Nordic countries have made a significant impact on those normally tolerant social democracies. Norwegian groups such as Bootboys, NS 88, the Norsk Arisk Ungdomsfron (NAUF), Varg, and the Vikings; the Green Jacket Movement (Gronjakkerne), the Danish National Socialist Movement (DNSB), and the Danish Front in Denmark; and the Vitt Ariskt Mostånd (VAM, or White Aryan Resistance), Kreatrivistens Kyrka (Church of the Creator, COTC), and Riksfronten (National Front) in Sweden have had an influence disproportionate to their modest numbers. While some of these groups have disappeared (VAM disbanded in 1994), the most readily identifiable group today is Blood and Honour, a spin-off of the notorious British skinhead group that is an amalgam of right-wing zealots and drunken soccer hooligans spoiling for a fight. The Nationell Ungdom (National Youth Movement) and National Socialist Party are also important groups in Sweden.

These groups are small in number: Norwegian actives number in the hundreds; estimates in Sweden run between 1,500 and 3,000 actives at last count, and the annual Salem march in the southern suburbs of Stockholm on December 11 draws between 1,000 and 1,200 in the largest annual demonstration of the movement in the country.[1] Nevertheless, the idea of neo-Nazi skinheads looms large in a country that prides itself on inclusiveness and providing a safety net for everyone.

Best-selling author Henning Mankell made their glowering subterranean presence the subject of one of his police crime novels, *The Return of the Dancing Master* (2003). In that story, a former police officer is brutally murdered, and it turns out his murderer is the son of a Jew he had himself murdered as a volunteer in Hitler's army. As Kurt Wallander, the police officer's colleague, searches for the killer, he stumbles into a world of unrepentant ex-Nazis and their young followers. "Nothing has changed," says one. "Now Sweden is being undermined by indiscriminate immigration.

Figure 4. Nordfront is a far-right extremist organization extending across various Nordic countries. Members dress in white shirts with black trousers and black ties; their hair is short, but they avoid shaving their heads in order to appear respectable. Photo in the public domain.

The very thought of mosques being built on Swedish soil makes me feel sick. Sweden is a society that is rotting away. And nobody is doing anything about it."[2]

And, of course, Stieg Larsson's global best seller, *The Girl with the Dragon Tattoo*, ultimately centers on a group of depraved and unrepentant ex-Nazis from an aristocratic family that profiteered on Sweden's neutrality during the war. Typical of the muckraking journalist author, Larsson's subsequent novels in the Millennium trilogy see this venomous legacy as running all the way through the government, infecting every level of Swedish officialdom. It takes a kick-ass tattooed punk and a disheveled leftist magazine reporter to tear the smiley-faced social safety net veneer off the swamp of hatred and xenophobia.

Fact may be stranger than fiction. Allan Pred, a geographer at Berkeley, noted this incongruity earlier than most in his well-titled 2000 book, *Even in Sweden*. Here was the model country, built on a social safety net, guided by notions of social equality and justice, yet seething with anti-immigrant sentiment.[3] And it's only gotten worse. In 2014, the Swedish Democrats, a populist party with a virulently anti-immigrant agenda, brought down the minority coalition that was in power.

The Danish National Socialist Party may be the largest, and is certainly the most mainstream, political organization on the extreme right in Scandinavia. A "respectable" amalgam of traditional Nazism with occasional nods to street hooliganism and skinhead neo-Nazis, it runs candidates in local elections, publishes a national e-newspaper, *The Fatherland,* and runs a local radio station called Radio Oasis (www.radiooasen.dk /english.htm).

In the past several years, these disparate Nordic groups have begun to create a pan-Scandinavian movement, the Nordic Front. They've begun to campaign for local and even national political offices, and their political parties are now considered part of the mainstream. Just like David Duke, the former grand dragon of the Louisiana Ku Klux Klan, members have shucked their former identifiable attire. Duke traded his bedsheet and conical white hat for a suit and tie; the Nordic Front wears white shirts and dark trousers or skirts. No more skinhead bomber jackets and Doc Martens, no more black leather and shaved heads. They want to make neo-Nazism respectable.

Most of the groups meet irregularly, with few formal monthly or weekly meetings, but many hold meetings on specific ritual dates, such as Hitler's birthday. But since these groups serve social needs at least as much as they address political questions, they meet informally almost every night, to drink, listen to music, and go out looking for fights. They prowl neighborhoods, frightening passersby and occasionally targeting immigrants with anger and violence. They're especially eager to pick fights with groups of immigrants, and information about an immigrant gang's whereabouts is highly prized.

Most members of the Scandinavian far-right groups share a similar profile: most come from lower-middle class families; their fathers are painters, carpenters, tilers, bricklayers, and road maintenance workers. Some come from small family farms. Several fathers own one-man businesses, are small-scale capitalists, are part of the historic petite bourgeoisie, or work as self-employed tradesmen. In her life-history analysis of her young Norwegian participants, Katrine Fangen found that only one claimed a working-class identity, and his father owned his own business; another's father owned a small printing company, another was a carpenter, and the fourth came from a family of independent fishermen.[4]

Many of the Swedish guys have already checked out by the time they finish middle school. The current generation of Swedish youth is the least-educated in a century. The country has the highest unemployment rate among young people in its history, 23 percent. Most of the young people on welfare have bounced from school to school through middle school, getting suspended, expelled, and finally just being done with it. "No one goes to school," says Elin, a former skinhead, matter-of-factly.

Almost all of the EXIT clients whom I interviewed come from lower-middle-class backgrounds—skilled trades, farming, military, police, and construction trades. One or two have more working-class origins, but in highly skilled trades. And one's father is a successful local politician and was solidly middle class. Their mothers are either homemakers or working professionals—nurses and teachers. A few work in the public sector. Several work with their ex-husbands in their small-scale businesses.

All the former members I met are themselves downwardly mobile; they work sporadically and have little or no control over their own labor or workplace, and none owns his own business. Youth unemployment has spiked, especially in Sweden, just as the numbers of asylum seekers has spiked, along with the number of attacks on centers for asylum seekers. And all but one or two of the Scandinavian participants I interviewed are from divorced families.

The clients at EXIT Sweden range from thirteen to twenty-three; the average age is between sixteen and seventeen. Since its founding in 1998, it has served close to eight hundred clients, all but fifty of whom were male. About twenty-five new young guys are actively participating at any one time, and one new one comes to EXIT every week. They largely fit the profile described above: their parents are divorced; their fathers are lower middle class; they describe themselves as searchers who did not fit in with any of the available cliques in middle school. Having often been targeted by bullies, they describe their first flirtation with Nazism as a way to both express their growing sense of anger and also to entertain fantasies of revenge. "Being a Nazi in a country like Sweden is probably the worst thing you could be," said Lasse, an eighteen-year-old former skinhead. "And since I wanted to be bad—really bad—I decided to be a Nazi."

The staff at EXIT is also composed of former neo-Nazis. In fact, that is one of its major institutional innovations.

Actually, the EXIT model originated in Oslo. Tore Bjørgo, who was then teaching at the Norwegian Police University, teamed up with police, parents of skinheads, and a few young guys who had jumped. Bjørgo's major idea, which is the organization's centerpiece, is that the young recruit's commitment is not to Nazi ideology, but is more experiential, visceral, and emotional. He is less a "Nazi" than he is a comrade, a brother, a part of a living, breathing community. Members are more concerned with validating their masculinity than with scoring ideological points. Bjørgo argued not that young people join extremist groups because they hold these radical ideological beliefs, but rather that they develop these radical ideological beliefs because they join extremist groups. Arguing about theory will never help extract them.

This idea is perhaps the central insight that makes these efforts to reach these young neo-Nazis comprehensible to them. Bjørgo understood before anyone else that ideological commitment matters far less than experiential connectedness. The needs the group fulfills are less theoretical than psychological.

The Norwegian EXIT group launched in 1997 at a Police Academy conference. Sitting in that conference room in Oslo, with police, policy makers, politicians, parents, ex-skinheads and -neo-Nazis, and a few actives, was Kent Lindahl, a Swedish neo-Nazi skinhead who had contacted Bjørgo only a month earlier. He wanted out, and was more or less extracting himself.

Inspired by what he had learned from Bjørgo, Lindahl returned home to Stockholm and immediately set to work founding EXIT Sweden, which is now the model for the rest of the world. His chief innovation was to make sure that mentors are also formers. (They call themselves formers, and I also use the term *ex-neo-Nazi* to refer to them, but only when they subscribed specifically to Nazism.) Having come from the same world, the same movement, the mentors have instant credibility with the clients. They know exactly what the clients are going through, and exactly how to engage with them.

ENTRY TO EXIT

Robert Orell, the current coordinator of EXIT, was thirty-five when we met a decade ago in EXIT's Stockholm office. His father owns a hobby shop and his mother is an assistant in a home for the elderly. Trim, fit, and handsome, Robert looks hip and stylish and blends in easily with other young Swedish men. Pelle, an assistant at EXIT, is two years older and from Norrtälje, a summer resort city; his father is a local politician and his mother teaches nursing. A tall, muscular, hulking presence, he wears what appears to be classical skinhead garb—baggy black cargo pants with a few graffiti-like names written on them, tucked into black combat boots, shaved head with unshaved sideburns, and a red T-shirt with gothic letters surrounding a bloody skull. He laughs about his appearance, explaining that the names on his pants are rave bands, the boots are canvas, not leather, and the T-shirt is actually from a paintball competition. Having been out of the movement for ten years, he feels he can finally return to the comfort of the clothing, acknowledging certain ironic twists and knowing full well that unsuspecting sociologists from New York might get the wrong idea at the beginning of an interview.

It was in conversation with Robert and Pelle, both formers, that I first heard the passage that now forms this chapter's epigraph. The quote from *Doctor Glas* is a touchstone quote for their work. (Söderberg was actually writing, in a 1905 proto-feminist epistolary novel, about a young woman who comes to confide in Dr. Glas. Margaret Atwood wrote an introduction to the English translation.) "I was desperate to be seen," says Pelle. "The more invisible I felt, the more dramatic I got." Robert remembers only that "I needed to feel like I was special, like I mattered in the world."

Both Pelle and Robert describe themselves as having been small, skinny, and easily targeted. Robert now says he was a "searcher," that is, "a young kid looking for an identity, a place to fit in. I felt like a nobody." He was picked on by gangs of immigrants in his school and neighborhood. First, he hung out with some soccer thugs; later he got into death metal music. "Then, the 'Viking wave' sort of hit Scandinavia in the early nineties, and I became really interested in Vikings, and I had a necklace of Thor's hammer. The Vikings were such strong men."

This gradual search was also Isaac's story. Isaac is another former, now a client at EXIT. Skinny and pale, Isaac is from Mora, a small town of fewer than twenty-five hundred inhabitants, a working-class enclave with virtually no class mobility. His father works in a factory and his mother is a nurse. They're divorced, and he lives with his father. Unpopular in school, he was lonely and often picked on. "I felt the anger building up in me," he tells me. "In my town, there were only two groups, really"—left-wing hash users and right-wing racists. That was pretty much it. "I started hanging around with the right-wing guys because they listened to great music." They also drank a lot, and by the time he was fifteen, he had a serious drinking problem.

I heard about the same animating emotions consistently. Insecure and lonely at twelve years old, Edward started hanging out with skinheads because he "moved to a new town, knew nobody, and needed friends." Equally lonely and utterly alienated from his distant father, Pelle, too, met an older skinhead who took him under his wing and became a sort of mentor. Pelle was a "street hooligan" hanging out in gangs, brawling and drinking with other gangs. "My group actually looked down on the Neo-Nazis," he says, because "they weren't real fighters." "All the guys had an insecure role as a man," adds Robert. "They were all asking, 'Who am I?'"

These sentiments were also echoed by Markus, eighteen, another EXIT staffer:

> As a child I had friends, sometimes, but I was completely left out at times. I got beat up a lot, both at home and at school. And I was always told I was stupid. When I was 11 I started looking up to my stepbrother, he was 18 and he was a skinhead. He took care of me, he cared. Once when I got beat up by five blokes (three Swedes and two immigrants), he started going on about "those bloody foreigners." Being only 11, I had no racist opinions but I was affected by what he said. And when I walked around with him, I suddenly got my revenge for everything that had happened to me. Everyone I was afraid of was suddenly afraid of me. It felt great. My stepbrother started giving me white supremacy records, a T-shirt with some nationalist slogan on it, and eventually a bomber jacket. I went straight from listening to boy bands to listening to white supremacy music.[5]

The boys and men I interviewed at EXIT also described themselves as "searchers" or "seekers," kids who felt marginalized, were often targeted, and were looking for a group with which to identify, where they would feel they belonged. "When you enter puberty, it's like you have to choose a branch," says one ex-Nazi. "You have to choose between being a Nazi, anti-Nazi, punk, or hip-hopper—in today's society, you just can't choose to be neutral."[6]

Magnus has a similar story. His parents are divorced, and his stepfather was alcoholic. He started hanging out with neo-Nazis when he was twelve. He sought them out. "We'd moved to a new town and I didn't know anybody and I needed friends fast." Johan had a similar entry point. Raised in suburban Stockholm, he had friends who all seemed to become either druggies or skinheads. "I couldn't get my head around school, so fighting seemed attractive to me," he told a journalist. "That's what got me into the movement."[7]

Tomas's parents are not divorced, he wants to be clear. His mother died when he was twenty, and his father was a chef in a restaurant. He was a good student, but was constantly bullied by older kids. He started fighting back. "I learned to get rid of people who were in my way." He fell in with a group of soccer hooligans because he liked the fights. These weren't necessarily politically motivated. "You could start a fight because someone was wearing the wrong sweatshirt," he says. He drifted into the movement. Immigrants were taking our jobs" and "taking our girls." And the government was just "crap." "Why should I care about society if they don't care about me?" he asked.

Casper also grew up in what he called "a field of violence." He was in a lot of fights, especially with a group of Muslim boys. Constantly enraged, he started listening to what he called "hate music" and dressing like a skinhead. "I'd listen to the music as soon as I woke up in the morning," he says, "so I would come to school already angry." Isolated and friendless, he found new friends through Internet forums, and with them started fighting with other groups after school. Pretty soon, he dropped out and couldn't find a job.

A colleague of mine once interviewed Jens, the most fearsome neo-Nazi in Denmark, who has a similar story. A big guy at six foot, five and about 260 pounds, his entry was also a story of feeling small and humiliated. For his eleventh birthday, he says, he got a pair of Nike sneakers. Walking home from school, he was attacked by a group of Turkish immigrant boys. (Nearly all the clients at EXIT reported being threatened or targeted—or at least being aware of—gangs of Turkish and Pakistani youth who are equally itching for unfair odds when they want to fight.) The attackers were fierce, and Jens was kicked in the head a couple of times. And they stole his shoes. "I could take their beatings," he said; "I always have had that ability, but to take my shoes . . . man, that's just nasty." He remembered when he encountered them again, two years later. This time he fought back, "but there were too many of them. I got in some good punches. Then their leader stabbed me with a knife." That was when he joined up with the neo-Nazis.

Whenever he was out on the streets with his comrades, he would always be on the lookout for that first gang. "We had looked for them many times, but always in vain," he said.

> Then one day we saw them in one of our rounds and we had baseball bats with us. To our luck we were five in this round, so when they started to scare us off, we knew we could beat them. Suddenly one of them draws a knife and started to run over to us. Then we took the baseball bats from the car and started pounding them—and they got a lot! Two of them ran away in the end, while the rest were down bleeding.

Nobody got arrested. "The police knew us and, I think, wanted us to do it."[8]

The contemporary Swedish neo-Nazi movement is not populated only by loners who were bullied in school. In fact, Christian was neither the bully nor the bullied. He was raised in Helsingborg, on the Danish border. (It's across the Oresund from Helsingor in Denmark, the setting for Shakespeare's *Hamlet.*) His father, a butcher, and his mother, a home-maker, were divorced. A huge guy, at least six foot, six, he has straight blond hair and striking blue eyes. In school he really enjoyed being the top guy. "I only kicked ass on the bad boys, and never did anything to the weak students," he said. In a sense, as Christian saw it, he was defending the weaker kids who were being bullied.

When his mother died of cancer, he felt as though he was going to explode with anger. A lack of an emotional vocabulary and an absence of any sort of emotional support are, of course, hallmarks of traditional notions of masculinity. With nowhere to put those feelings, and no social support, he hung out with football hooligans and spent his weekends fighting. "I took drugs before the fight so I could take more pain without fainting," he recalls. "Everybody did." Suicidally depressed (he tried to kill himself several times), he was found by right-wing recruiters who nurtured him because of his fighting ability. One beating left a left-wing activist paralyzed and in a wheelchair. "I feel really bad about that, actually," he says.

Of course, not all boys who have been bullied in school, or who have divorced parents or distant and perhaps abusive fathers, become neo-Nazis. Some drift into other identities; some may even become violent anti-racists, and many of the violent anti-racists' profiles seem strikingly similar to those drawn to violent racist extremism. But that similarity, in a way, underscores my argument that it is dynamics other than the lure of the ideology that brings these guys into the movement. As with the German young men, points of entry for the Swedish young men I interviewed included social activities such as parties and drinking with other kids. Also as in Germany, many in Sweden described relationships with older guys already in the movement who served as mentors and guides. An older cousin, brother or friend is often the gateway to choosing Nazism over other forms of rebellion. Says one: "I joined my cousin to go meet his skin-head friends, drink beer and listen to white supremacy music. And it just went on from there. The music got harder and harder. You'd sit there, not knowing you were a racist. You'd get your boots, your flight jacket and peel off your hair."[9] For others, the push came from a sense of alienation from family, and especially the desire to rebel against their fathers. "Grownups often forget an important component of Swedish racism, the emotional conviction," says journalist Jonas Hallen. "If you have been beaten, threatened, and stolen from, you won't listen to facts and numbers."[10]

Many of the Swedish guys I interviewed told me similar stories of drifting into the movement. They'd been primed for it by early childhood problems—being bullied in school, neglected at home, or even physically abused by their fathers. Loners by temperament or isolated and lonely, they'd drift to the margins and start hanging out with other disaffected youth. Neo-Nazi recruiters would often find them and bring them to parties where there would be loud music, lots of beer, and girls.

Three of them, in fact, told me they had sex for the first time at one of these parties. Imagine you're fourteen, a loner, marginalized and bullied, and you start to feel like a complete loser. And then, these guys accept you, like you, hang with you. And the girls, well, they like you even more. One could see how this might not just appeal but also meet very real and basic social and psychological needs.

That was Isaac's story. A tall, lanky twenty-four-year-old with stringy shoulder-length hair pulled back into a small ponytail, Isaac slouches into the chair to talk with me. When he finally takes off the dark-blue hoodie and worn baseball cap he's been almost hiding under, I notice he's inked up, with a spiderweb that stretches from wrist to elbow and other, Nazi tattoos. With long fingers, acne-pocked cheeks, and the faintest hint of a moustache, he looks barely pubescent, at least ten years younger than his age.

In ninth grade, he tells me, he was hanging out with both the stoners and the skinheads, and he gradually drifted to the right. He dropped out of school and began a life of selling individual cigarettes to other kids and doing petty crimes. When he got into debt, that's when the serious recruiting into the ideology took off. "They told me, 'Just get into the car, and if you come with us and you do this thing we need you to do, it will pay off your debt.' So I went." What the gang had in mind was that he plant a bomb in an immigrant-owned restaurant in the north of Sweden. So that's what he did. The restaurant was destroyed, and Isaac got away. (His comrade was not so lucky and got a long jail sentence.)

Stefan's background was similar to Isaac's, and his story tracks that of other clients I interviewed. A defiant-looking twenty-five-year-old in a road worker uniform, he sits next to his wife, Amelie, twenty, who is visibly pregnant. He's wearing a black baseball hat, and his arms are crossed over his chest. (Like several of the clients I interviewed, Stefan was initially reluctant to talk to me, and his body language let me know that. Through the interview he warmed up a bit, prodded by his wife to be more forthcoming.) Stefan is from a small working-class town of 35,000 about 150 kilometers from Stockholm, where his father is a crew chief at a manufacturing plant and his mother, who had once worked for Ericsson, now stays at home. He drifted into the movement gradually: he initially came for the music, loved the violence, and then got political. By age eleven, he was fighting with the Turkish and Iraqis kids in his school. They tried to hit him, "but I hit them first." Wherever he moved, he'd fight with the immigrant kids. By thirteen, he was a member of Vitt Ariskt Mostånd

(VAM), or the White Aryan Resistance. "I still didn't know what any of it meant," he says. "But I knew it meant fighting." He stopped drinking at fifteen because he knew "the black guys didn't drink" and he "wanted to be able to fight with a clear head."

Finally, at eighteen, he joined the Combat 18 skinheads and really got into the politics. He worked for the National Democrats, a small racist political party, and finally went all-in and became a recruiter for the National Socialist Front. During four or five weeks of immersive indoctrination, he received information that "I had never really thought about." He was in. "I wasn't a Nazi when I was born," he reminisces now. "I became a Nazi."

One must not underestimate the power of White Power music on these young prepubescent boys' decision to "go Nazi" instead choosing another of the variety of rebellious identities on offer. It's a glue, a lubricant, facilitating their acting out. Such bands as Skrewdriver, Arvingarna, and especially Ultima Thule offer angry, hardcore, punk-inspired, metal-inflected driving rock music—almost deliberately amateurish, loud and raucous, with a pounding simple beat and nearly indecipherable lyrics screamed out over the thundering rhythm section. Every song seems a contrived anthem. In short, this is just the sort of music that an enormous number of young suburban boys find irresistible. "The music reinforces the feelings that I am righteous and outside of society," says one.[11]

Ultima Thule is probably the best-known white power band in Scandinavia, the Swedish Skrewdriver. Acoustic neofolkie odes to the *Faderneslandet* (fatherland) and driving anthems like "Jag Älskar Mitt Sverige" (I love my Sweden) double as patriotic anthems and xenophobically nationalist hate music. Love your country; hate those who don't love it by coming here uninvited. Ultima Thule plays a version of Viking rock, fusing those traditional sounds with a thrashing, driving punk. (Though they formally declare their music to be apolitical, no one believes them. Their first album was financed by the National Front.)

Johnny got his start in the movement at age eleven, "painting swastikas, drinking, and listening to Ultima Thule and other White Power bands." As the purveyor of the largest White Power music website on the Internet proclaims, "Music that is hard, music that awakens the warrior spirit in these white people, within these white youth, which stirs up barbarian rages in them—is healthy."[12] Their concerts also provide a sort of instant community—a place to meet friends, get drunk, slam dance, and take out all of one's frustrations and rage.

That's how Stefan got his start also. "Yeah, I may have had some problems with immigrants when I was little, but it was the music," he tells me. "I first heard Ultima Thule on Swedish radio" at age ten, he says. "On the radio! Regular radio. They had, like, several hit songs." He found one of his mother's credit cards and bought some of the clothes online. He was hooked.

It is in modes of dress and affective styles at these concerts that one can best see the dynamics of gender as they play out for these young guys. Alienated young boys searching for a masculine identity, targeted by school bullies, whose family ties are attenuated at best and diffident and abusive at worst—this combination is easily a recipe for adolescent rebellion. Indeed, many of the ex-Nazis in EXIT see their behavior exactly in these terms, more as efforts to secure a masculine identity and experience community than as commitment to ideology. They engaged in a wide variety of affective styles and behaviors—posture, clothing, drinking, fighting—with consciously masculinizing effects.

The concert is the window, the beginning of the evening, not its crescendo. "After about an hour or so at the concert," Markus explains to me, there is usually a "spontaneous" decision to go "do some mischief." They go desecrate a graveyard, attack a mosque or synagogue, and throw some rocks at other guys, preferably minorities, to start a fight.

"Spontaneous?" I ask.

Markus laughs. "Well, let me put it this way," he says. "Toward the end of the concert, I always took my earrings off, just in case there was a fight."

"Ha," I say. "Just in case."

"Yeah, sort of like bringing condoms on a date. Just in case." He breaks up laughing.

Edward, who joined VAM when he was twelve, was called a babyskin because he was prepubescent and had not begun shaving yet. "I felt like such a little boy," he said. "Before I joined," says Robert, "I felt like a nobody, I felt like a loser, I felt, like, worthless. Their world offered me a world where I was better—just because I was white." Another client interviewed in an EXIT self-study remembered his time with VAM as commanding respect and even awe: "It was like joining the Baader Meinhof gang or something like that. Powerful as hell. And it was powerful just standing there with robber's mask and a banner [at a demonstration]. People were shouting at me but I was just standing there, like a statue. I felt invincible, like there was nothing that could break me down."[13]

In an interview with Tore Bjørgo, another former skinhead recounted his experience of masculine transformation as he joined up:

> When I was 14, I had been bullied a lot by classmates and others. By coincidence, I got to know an older guy who was a skinhead. He was really cool, so I decided to become a skinhead myself, cutting off my hair, and donning a black Bomber jacket and Doc Martens boots. The next morning, I turned up at school in my new outfit. In the gate, I met one of my worst tormentors. When he saw me, he was stunned, pressing his back against the wall, with fear shining out of his eyes. I was stunned as well—by the powerful effect my new image had on him and others. Being that intimidating—boy, that was a great feeling![14]

For Pelle, it was a "pure power trip." "I really wanted to fight," he told me, "and the best way to start a fight is to say 'Sieg Heil.' I wanted to fight, to release all that anger and hatred. I think it was a good way for me to rebel against my father; he is a legitimate politician, and the worst thing a legitimate politician's son could be is a Nazi." In the end, Pelle said, "I held the opinions to get the more personal feelings I wanted."

The cultural practices of White Power culture were also masculinizing. White Power music was both "visceral and emotional," says Robert. Drinking also made participants feel like real men. Each of the guys I interviewed described drinking between twenty and thirty beers in an evening, listening to White Power music, or watching certain videos (*Romper Stomper* or *A Clockwork Orange*) to get themselves ready to go out and look for fights. "By the time we'd downed twenty beers and watched the movies, we'd be banging into each other, butting our heads together, and screaming," recalls Pelle. Magnus recounts what a typical evening would be like: "Mostly we hanged at our leaders' apartment. Then drink, and drink some more, and we'd go out on the town and did whatever we felt like that evening. . . . The first years it never was about any politics. Mostly acting like we were dangerous, smashing windows on pizza parlors, nice cars, or shops owned by immigrants." But gradually, older members eased them into increasingly political activities: "When we became part of the Riksfronten," Magnus continues, referring to the National Front, "it became more political, and we were able to go to concerts and happenings and meetings with other NS activists from all over the country. At the same time, we became more and more criminal and finally we got busted and some of us were sentenced as minors."

After everyone was good and drunk, they'd all take painkillers so they wouldn't feel the injuries they'd sustain, and then they'd go out in a large group to look for a fight. These fights were almost invariably one of two types: either they'd come upon one or two immigrants or anarchist punk types and set upon them, beating them senseless, or they'd encounter an entire group of anarchist punks or immigrants who were equally drunk and juiced on painkillers and itching for a fight. Then the melee would begin.

"I don't think we'd consider it a successful fight unless someone— hopefully some of their side—ended up in the hospital," Magnus told me. I asked if he'd ever been injured. "Of course," he said looking at me with a bit of an eye roll, as if to say, What could you possibly be thinking? "Yeah, of course. Nothing serious, though. Mostly bruises and small cuts. Once, though, I was stabbed, and another time I was beaten up so bad that my skull cracked." Another guy, he recalls, "got rammed by a car, and another was stabbed and had to spend like a month in hospital."

Sometimes the crew thought it would be funny to leave a guy hanging on his own. Several of the formers at EXIT told stories of being with a gang of guys, out looking for a fight, and then suddenly being abandoned and left to fend for himself. "Like, we'd be walking down the street as a group, you know," Arno tells me, "and we'd see some immigrants standing there, so we'd all hide behind a wall of a building and urge one guy to go and provoke and fight, so we could all jump in. 'We'll wait for you around the corner and you lure them back here, and then we'll all jump them.' Then we'd disappear and laugh when he got beat up."

Christian told me about one night, in particular, when he was hanging around in his own house with about a dozen other guys. Four immigrants burst in, beat him up, and stabbed him. His friends "just stood around and watched and laughed . . . They were such fucking hypocrites. They weren't there for you at all. I was completely betrayed. Fuck them. They proclaim camaraderie, but in the end they just protect themselves."

On the other hand, many of the rituals the young men shared were deeply intimate and caring. Pelle describes how the skinheads in his group would shave one another's heads as they bonded for "war," and how their physical affection during and after fights amounted to the most physical intimacy he had ever had to that point. "I was hugged very seldom as a kid," he remembers. "I guess now looking back, some of the things we did would look pretty gay."

Becoming a soccer supporter was also a dominant theme in the interviews. In Scandinavia, as in Britain, being a soccer fan is different from American adherence to a sports team, no matter how passionate. For some British and Scandinavians, fandom is the occasion for indulging in massive quantities of alcohol and engaging in serious brawling. In one survey, half of all Swedish Nazis were soccer hooligans.[15] All of the guys I interviewed were avid soccer fans, and were making the transition from soccer hooliganism to simple fandom. Tomas drifted from being bullied to joining the soccer hooligans because they offered protection. Over time, he met some neo-Nazis. They didn't talk much about ideology; "it was mostly just hanging out, drinking, camping, parties, and music."

A cartoon series published in a neo-Nazi skinhead magazine perfectly illustrates this trajectory—and the gendered experience of entry. In the first of the cartoon's eight panels, we see the threat to the bucolic peaceful Swedish countryside: a Jewish puppeteer manipulating the strings of thousands of dark faceless hordes invading. That sets up the narrative of a young boy. In panel 2, he is being harassed and bullied in the school hallways. He is surrounded by a group, including two black boys and an anarchist punk, that is threatening and roughing him up. Meanwhile his only friend is trying to get the attention of the school principal, a balding nerdy Jew, who is whistling and looking the other way. Our "hero" is in trouble.

In panel 3, the pair are on the streets of Stockholm by the T-bahn station, where the friend meets a neo-Nazi skinhead and his female companion, proud and strong, who hand them a leaflet. (The man's T-shirt says, "Death to ZOG.") The two friends take up the invitation in panel 4, and are seen at a skinhead party. Our "hero" is in the center, having his head shaved by a woman in very tight-fitting jeans, while his friend is trying on a cap and wearing the skinhead uniform. Around them, guys with amazingly strong bodies are doing the Nazi salute.

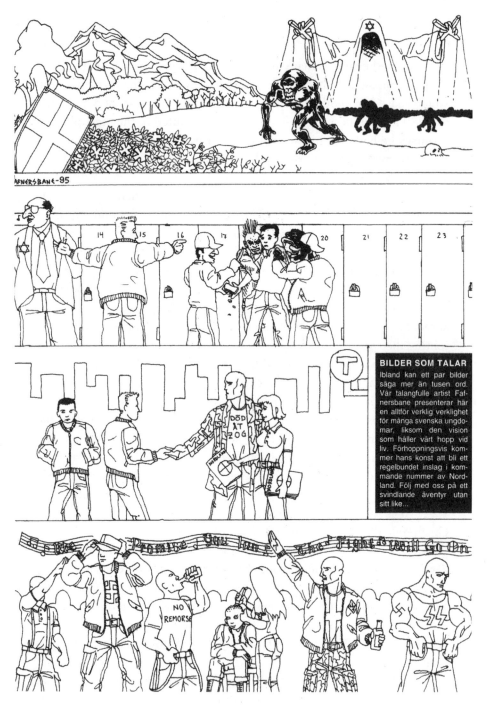

Figures 5 and 6. This two-page comic-strip story of masculinity lost and regained appeared in volume 6 (June 1996) of the Swedish neo-Nazi magazine *Nordland*.

The story continues on the following page. In the first panel, the two experience the transcendent power of a White Power music spectacle. In the second panel, they return to the school, this time with some hypermasculine comrades, and confront the crew that bullied them before. You can see our hero in the back, both fists raised in triumph. He's shown those pretenders! The final panels move back outward to the more political struggle. The skinhead neo-Nazis march past the slain double-winged dragon, the one a with dollar sign and a hammer and sickle on either wing—the true National Socialist path is neither capitalist nor communist. Finally, we see the heroic Aryan Nordic man and woman, commandingly overlooking the bucolic Swedish countryside over which order has finally been restored.

The cartoon illustrates perfectly how reclaiming manhood and reclaiming one's country are intertwined in the skinhead neo-Nazi scene in Sweden. Both masculinity and nation are restored simultaneously, and through each other, in this allegory. And one can easily see how attractive such a narrative might be to young guys in high school, or even middle school, who identify with the young skinny guy getting bullied. Take that, you assholes! And take that, you foreign invaders! We're taking our country—and our manhood—back!

THE ROLE OF IDEOLOGY

Joining the movement has far less to do with ideology than it does with the experiences of adolescent boys. Thus far I have described the points of entry into Nazism as embedded within a developmental psychological trajectory of response to marginalization and the effort to establish and sustain a hypermasculine identity as a hedge against feelings of psychological emasculation. I have said very little about the ideology—anti-Semitism, racism, nativism, and xenophobia. This de-emphasis has been deliberate.

Among the ex-neo-Nazis of EXIT, white supremacist ideology played a relatively minor role, both while they were in the movement and today. Being a boy, growing up to be a man—these were important stages in their developmental process, and occasionally the ideology would serve as a sort of theoretical prop for their masculinity. On the other hand, racist ideology served to underscore the taken-for-granted aspect of their entitlement. "We believed we were superior," says Robert, and "that we had the right to beat up other people because we were white."

EXIT's promotional material underscores the minimal role of political ideology, and instead emphasizes the developmental trajectory for young boys: "Political opinions have little to do with it [guys' reasons for joining], but many of them have been abused early on in their lives. They have felt unwanted or pushed aside, sometimes by 'friends' and teachers, sometimes by ethnic youngsters and occasionally by their own parents. They are used to being picked upon, and find themselves at the bottom of their social hierarchy."[16]

Only one of the fifteen neo-Nazis interviewed by Karl-Olav Arnstberg and Jonas Hallen denied the Holocaust or used any other catchphrases from National Socialism; in my interviews, none of the young men did. In fact, those who expressed any political opinions at all might just as well have been categorized as liberal or progressive, supporting the environment and a strong regulatory state that restrains greedy corporations and promotes environmental stewardship.

If the young men and women who come to EXIT are motivated less by ideology than by other reasons, it makes sense, then, for EXIT to credit their experiences and not wage a full-on assault on Nazi ideology. A critic of this approach, Liz Fekete of the Institute of Race Relations in London, argues that the nonjudgmental, nonideological approach allows these people the opportunity to "skirt around past actions without having to take full responsibility for them." She argues, "The ethos is not to look at the neo-Nazi's ideology; it tends to look at their grievances. They come saying they're frightened to leave the scene; there are all these problems that they've had in their social background. So there is a sense that they are the victims and in that context there's not a focus on what they have done."

Such criticisms miss two essential elements of the EXIT strategy. First, EXIT is dealing with children, or, at most, young adults, who started their entry at twelve or thirteen. Second, an ideology-focused strategy effaces the clients' own sense of their experience. EXIT works front to back, not back to front. By that I mean the organization looks first at how the client entered the movement, what he was searching for, what he feels he found. It doesn't take the client where he "is," at first. That is to say, EXIT pretty much ignores the ideological spewing of National Socialist dogma, knowing that this was not the young men's initial motivation to get in, and thus it cannot be the lever by which they can get out.

I made the same mistake as Fekete when I started doing this research at EXIT. In my first interview with a client, I had a broad schedule derived from my interviews with the active white nationalists I had been interviewing in the United States. I thought we'd discuss their commitments to National Socialist ideas, the inconsistencies in their positions, their abstract anti-Semitism, and the global ZOG menace they saw as threatening Western civilization. I asked Andrew (whose story is related above) what it meant to him to be a Nazi, part of the movement. "I liked the fighting and the attention," he said.

"Yes, but what does it mean to you, you know, to be Swedish nationalist?" I asked.

He looked at me quizzically. His brows furrowed. He clearly didn't understand what I was asking. I tried a simpler question. "Well, what does it mean to you to be Swedish?"

"Dunno. I'm white."

That seemed to be the extent of his ideological commitment. But then, he followed up, not by explaining what it means to be white, but by describing what it feels like to be part of the movement. Being a Nazi "means I'm part of something, part of a group. It gives me a chance to express my hate. I don't care about the words."

Perhaps the only central component of ideology that seems consistent among members has to do with gender, masculinity. They hold "an idealized view of the male as a strong defender of the family and nation," as EXIT documents put it. They maintain a fairly traditional understanding of male-female relations, especially in the absence of positive male role models in their development. To be a man, Magnus tells me, is "to have the strength to be what you want to be. To stand up for what is Swedish and to be true to your race." He pauses. "At least that's what it meant to me then. Now I think it means 'to be a good father and a good supportive friend, a caring and loving husband and a person who tries not to be judgmental.'"

They believe that wild young immigrant boys have been foisted on their schools by a seemingly beneficent, but ultimately blighted government, and they look on with dismay as "free" Swedish girls are attracted to immigrant boys who, in turn, see them as "easy" or "tramps."[17] Swedish boys are cowardly "wimps" who must unite to protect Swedish "girlhood" and reclaim the mantle of masculinity. "Swedish men are such wimps," says Robert. "That's what we believed. They're soft, so easily pushed around. We looked up to the police, the military. We looked up to strength."

And the immigrants were certainly not "really" Swedish and not "real men." "How can they be 'real men'?" says Tomas. "They take money from the state in welfare, they are not independent, they treat their women like shit, and they don't act, I don't know, proud of themselves, head up, you know, proud." And Swedish? As Magnus says, "I used to think that the immigrants couldn't be Swedish, because they didn't look Swedish and they refused to integrate. But by that I meant assimilate. For an immigrant to be OK to me back then, he had to speak perfect Swedish and celebrate all the Swedish holidays and to think their former culture was inferior."

Nazism as a masculinizing project is also easily observed in the movement's symbology. In addition to Nazi paraphernalia, the single most common symbolic tropes among Scandinavian Nazis are references to the Vikings. Vikings are admired because they lived in a closed community, were fierce warriors, and were feared and hated by those they conquered. Vikings also represent an untrammeled masculinity, an "armed brotherhood" of heroes and martyrs. "The Vikings were real men, all right," explains Lars, now eighteen. "They were so strong and powerful, and they never gave up. They also knew who was boss in the family." "Vikings destroyed all those other cultures, conquering them and subjecting them," notes Tomas. "That's what we need to be: Vikings."

Another interesting symbol that unites many Scandinavian Nazis is the Confederate battle flag from the US Civil War, the Stars and Bars. Outside the American South, where it is often celebrated as the hallmark of tradition and loyalty to the "lost cause," the Confederate flag is understood to be the universal symbol for racism. (Of course, some American southerners fully understand it to be a racist symbol, but few outside the South rise to its defense as a nonracial emblem of a fallen nobility.) Scandinavian Nazis sport T-shirts, tattoos, and hats with Confederate insignias, and hang the Stars and Bars in their rooms or from their apartment windows.

Figure 7. Soldiers of Odin are a street patrol group that harasses immigrants. Founded in Sweden, the organization has "chapters" in Canada, the United States, and across Scandinavia. Photo in the public domain.

THE WOMEN OF EXIT

While the overwhelming majority of white nationalists and neo-Nazis are male, there are often girls and women around. Some events are almost entirely homosocial, including the drinking and listening to music before going out to party and fight. "We'd drink a lot and start screaming along with the music," says Edward, "and start hitting each other and slam-dancing into each other. Then we'd go out, and a few girls would join us, and we'd go looking for fights."

While women may have participated in some movement activities, they were not seen as integral to its central projects, all of which revolved around enabling these guys to feel like real men. To be sure, the neo-Nazi ideology to which many clients had subscribed may have been explicitly racist, but it was often just as implicitly sexist, assuming a natural hierarchy of men over women. In fact, many of the guys believed that their proclamation of neo-Nazi ideology entitled them to deference and respect from girls.

My informants described the girls' motives as similar to theirs: they enjoyed the drinking, partying, and fighting. And sometimes they were welcomed, especially at the parties, but other times they were simply, as David says, "nuisances." Recall that he described how the girls might initiate fights, but then would run away.

Of the fifty or so young women who have gone through the EXIT program, I was able to interview six. They had profiles similar to the men's: lower-middle-class family backgrounds, unhappy childhoods in broken homes, and experiences as social outcasts in school. Elma's experience is typical. She's twenty-one and is from a tiny village outside Linköping where "everybody knows everybody." She's short and chubby and wears glasses, and her stringy hair hangs limp and appears unbrushed. Her fingernails are chewed down to bleeding. Always overweight, she says she was never popular because of her size, and she always felt like an outsider. After her parents divorced when she was ten, she became something of a "wild girl" as a way to cope. She felt that it was the only way to be noticed while not being hated. She had few, if any, friends, and was picked on because of her weight. At age fourteen she ran away to Linköping to live with her older sister.

Linköping was a scary place, "filled" with minorities and immigrants. (The city of 104,000 had about 9,000 immigrants in 2016, mostly from Iraq and Somalia.) Her first boyfriend was from Iraq, and during their year together he started to hit her, without warning or even, as she saw it, provocation. Mostly, "he just wanted to show off in front of his friends." After returning to her home village, she ended up hanging out at a bar next to a gas station, and it was there that she started to meet some right-wing extremists. Her new boyfriend was one of them, and she gradually entered that world through her connection to him.

Elma said the group engaged in petty crimes, vandalism, and the occasional brawl. Sometimes they defaced city property, breaking windows and setting a fire at a school. This got her arrested, and while the guys were given one- to two-year sentences, she was held for a few days, released, and sentenced to pay a huge fine. In jail for those few days, though, she began to have misgivings, and when she was alone, while her boyfriend was in jail, she contacted EXIT. She's resisted their efforts to find her a job, and has also demurred on returning to school. When her boyfriend was finally released, he was furious that she was an EXIT client and beat her. She is still in the program, and they are still together.

This sort of hanger-on status for women among Scandinavian skinhead groups may differ from the more central and active role played by some women in American extreme-right groups. The rank and file of many Scandinavian organizations is certainly more gender-integrated than the leadership. There are virtually no women at the top, even though many may be participating at the grassroots. And it also appears that more young women are attracted to these groups than earlier research predicted. However, I saw no evidence that girls and women play a major role in the activities of these neo-Nazi groups. They are girlfriends, partiers, and drinkers and are fun to have around. But their numbers are small, and their presence is relatively immaterial.

"It's tough to be a woman in the movement," Elma tells me. "They [the guys] all say they care about you, but they don't really give a fuck about you at all." There are, she explains, only two roles for women: you can be the perfect girlfriend, sort of like their mother, very traditional; or you can be a skinhead fighter, with boots. "But you'd have to do ten times more than the guys in order to prove yourself." She tried to "do the homey thing." It didn't work out. You need, in a sense, to straddle the line, to be both. "You have to be a Madonna and a whore at the same time," she says, capturing the contradiction that so many women experience, no matter their political position. She had several neo-Nazi boyfriends, and all were violent and abusive. "They feel they have the right to do it because they are superior to you."

The difference between women's experiences in Sweden and the United States may be attributed to several factors. The age difference between the U.S. and Scandinavian groups may indicate a lesser role for the latter girls, as prepubescent girls may be more circumscribed in their evening activities. As I argue below, a younger age also indicates a lower level of commitment to Nazi ideology, which might discourage serious right-wing women from participating. But the lower average age of the Scandinavian neo-Nazi skinheads indicates that their "project" has more to do with proving adolescent masculinity than with spreading Nazi ideology. Their objective, implied or explicit, is the restoration of masculinity, the retrieval of masculine entitlement. And while one might discern support among some women for such a restoration of traditional masculinity, compensatory masculinity projects are almost always the province of intense homosocial bonding as the basis for masculine validation. The presence of women would, as Edward put it, "pollute things."

Eva says that through EXIT she's gotten a work placement that ended up becoming a permanent job. But more than that, "EXIT has given me back my self-esteem. EXIT has taught me to like myself, which I didn't do before, and to see the potential that I can do things, that I'm not worthless, that I do have something to offer."[18] Elma is not so sanguine. She's currently in a job-training program that pays her 150 Swedish krona (about $16.25) a day just for showing up—"which is exactly the same amount if I was on welfare." If she doesn't show up, though, she loses the welfare. She doesn't see much of a future. Without friends, she has an alcoholic mother and a needy sister. "Maybe I'll go back to school," she shrugs.

EXIT STRATEGIES

How and why do Swedish neo-Nazis leave the movement? What do their decisions tell us about masculinity validation as a motivation for participation in the first place? Ironically, it may be the tolerance that Scandinavian societies are so famous for that enabled the neo-Nazi activities. All participants in a two thousand–subject self-study said they wished they had been stopped earlier, but the society of "nice-ism" facilitates their Nazism.[19]

Others described the hypocrisy of the movement. "There is a very strong double standard," one said: "You should look after your body, not drink, and live soundly, but then you live like a pig anyway. I think this was a major reason why I distanced myself from it. When I stopped all the drunken parties, I then distanced myself from the whole thing."[20] For Daniel, it was the hypocrisy that "got to me" after a while. "I read that the Nazis were pure, so I tried to live a pure life. Did you know Hitler was a vegetarian? So I was. Vegetarian, no steroids, no smoking, no drinking, no drugs, no crimes." He laughs. "Well, sex was OK." Some of his friends found the discipline "boring" and they left, but for Daniel it was more about the leaders not following the standards they were demanding from the others:

"People I was hanging out with were not living up to what they were say-ing," he recalled. When one of the group's leaders became romantically involved with a Thai woman, an immigrant, he'd had enough. "Are you kid-ding? By day you are shouting about how the immigrants all have to get out, and at night you are with one? What kind of Nazi are you?"

For Johan, the racism just got too strange. Some of the adults were generating pseudo-scientific theories to support their racism, he said, while he just wanted immigrants out of Sweden. "They started measuring skulls and I felt it was too much," he told a journalist. "They measure the heads of people to decide who was Aryan and who wasn't."[21]

For Magnus, the ideology just started not fitting with his experiences: "I mean, yeah, it was great to have an ideology about being the 'master race' and all, and the idea that everything that was wrong with my life, the society, could be blamed on someone. We had a clear bad guy to blame: ZOG, the Jews, immigrants, gay people, and so on . . ."

"So, what happened?" I asked.

"Well, it was on a personal level. Like there were some immigrants in my school that were cool, they were OK, and I didn't think they were part of the problem," he says. "But I never talked about it."

Consistently, I heard stories of how actually knowing, meeting, hanging out with, and even dating these immigrant "others" often eroded any rac-ist beliefs they had, or at times even prevented those racist beliefs from taking up residence inside the guys' heads. This confirmation of what Harvard social psychologist Thomas Pettigrew called the "contact hypothesis"—that the way to reduce racism or any other discriminatory ideology is to provide opportunities for the groups to work together on a common problem—was evident throughout my interviews in Sweden and, as chapter 4 shows, is central element to the way other extremist groups work as well. According to the contact hypothesis, the process of working with others breaks down ideas about group characteristics and replaces them with an understanding of the many ways in which individ-ual members of a group vary as much from one another as they do from members of one's own group. The hypothesis demonstrates that within-group variation is far greater than between-group variation, and that the real story is not the small differences you might find between, say, women and men, white people and people of color, or Jews and non-Jews, but the enormous variations among women, among men, and within different racial or religious groups.[22]

One EXIT client commented that what he really wanted was "to be part of a disciplined movement. Then you see it's not going to happen, because there are so many idiots and nutters."[23] For others, it was the gradual feelings of guilt about what they had done. One said he "started to feel bad about myself and realized that none of us lived the life we talked about." Several others exit in a rather respectable way: they get married and begin families. "They got a lot of positive regard for that," said Robert, "because they were perpetuating the white race. It was simply the easiest way out." "No one bothers you if you've got a wife and a Volvo," added Pelle.

For several it was a wife, girlfriend, their mother, or another woman who drew them away from the movement. It's often through personal relationships with women that the guys get enough strength to tear themselves away. It's hard. It was the intensity of the male bonds that got them in. That intensity has to be matched—or even exceeded—by the relationships with women.

Take Christian, for example. Once, he got beaten up so badly that he was in the hospital for several months. "No one from my immediate group came to the hospital to see me; no one called or asked about my health." Out of the more than thirty he considered his brothers, his comrades, only two people came to visit him. And one was his girlfriend. "She told me she was afraid she'd lose me," he says. They left the hospital together and checked into a hotel under a false name for three weeks. "I wouldn't leave the room, I was so afraid they'd find me," he says. His girlfriend contacted the police, and he talked for days with a police inspector. It was actually the police who contacted EXIT for him. "Actually, I was afraid that EXIT would reject me," he tells me. They didn't.

When Isaac and another comrade blew up that restaurant in northern Sweden, the comrade was arrested. He's still in jail. Isaac got away, but this episode spun him into a serious depression. Isolated and barricaded in his home, he surfed the Web until he found a chat group of ex-Nazis. They steered him to EXIT. From there, he started talking with one of the female staffers at EXIT, and she really helped him. "We just started talking. It gave me a window out," he says. After a year in EXIT, Isaac has a girlfriend and a job placement in Eastern Europe. The two will go together.

Others drift away into other sorts of activities. Referring to those he knows who moved into more serious criminality, Pelle notes they "had to grow their hair and fit in so they wouldn't be noticed, or they would have been ineffective in the criminal underworld." A few become bikers or other marginal hypermasculine outlaws. Not an insignificant number actually switch sides and become violent anti-racists. "All these groups offer the same sort of brotherhood and community," Robert says, "so they drift into other arenas. It's almost never about making a lifelong commitment to Nazi opinions."

The most common reason for leaving is, as formers described it, getting "burned out." The life is demanding—drinking and fighting, constant arrests, constant violence—and requires such a steady supply of rage that eventually it begins to dissipate. "Am I going to be doing this when I'm forty?" Robert asked himself one day. Casper said it all became "too much." He had found a girlfriend and she wasn't in the scene. When a photograph of him appeared in a local paper as a "key member" of the neo-Nazi group, his girlfriend called EXIT. Pelle described a sort of economy of emotions. "I used anger to express every emotion. If you're disappointed, get angry. If you're sad, get angry. If you're frustrated, get angry. Eventually, I got tired of only expressing anger. I didn't run out of anger, exactly. I just got interested in other feelings . . . It's a lot easier to shout at someone than it is to cry," he concluded.

EXIT THROUGH EXIT

The success of EXIT in Sweden has been based, in large part, on its treatment of Nazism as an adolescent search for manhood rather than as a commitment to a specific National Socialist ideology. "Most young neo-Nazis eventually get bored with the ideology," states the organization's brochure. "The most common motive for leaving neo-Nazi groups is personal development and maturity."[24] In fact, EXIT has been so successful that it has branched out and formed a new organization, Passus, a group without political affiliation that is aimed strictly at gang members.

EXIT founder Kent Lindahl stated as his axiom: "Love the neo-Nazi, not his opinions." While this may sound more like the Catholic Church's notion of loving the sinner but not the sin, it speaks instead to the relative weights the group gives to ideology and the quest for identity. Indeed, ideology is not discussed with the potential client until well into the exiting process, after he has already jumped. Only outside the movement can the young man "reflect" on his ideology and see that it can be easily detached from the demonstration and proof of masculinity.

That personal development and maturity is often accompanied by a good deal of guilt. Several spoke of feeling "ashamed" or "guilty" about what they had done, or what others had done when they were around. "You could say I had too much of it," says one. "I couldn't bear it; I felt bad about all the stuff I did. I wanted something else—this chaos was not what I wanted." Another said he "started to feel bad about myself and realized that none of us lived the life we talked about." Markus Olsson says that he now works for EXIT "to pay off my debt to society. But I just can't forgive myself."

EXIT provides group meetings and individual therapy for these boys and young men seeking to leave the movement. It offers practical advice on rearranging social lives and returning to school and help searching for a job. And it also offers a way to negotiate exit from groups that do not take kindly to those who seek to leave their ranks. Recall, for example, the stories of David and Andrew: Andrew's mother's friend's association with the Hell's Angels enabled him to avoid being threatened by his group's leader; indeed, now that leader offers him rides home from school.

Others report constant threats. The one who quits is considered a traitor who deserves to be assaulted or killed. In one survey, all subjects had been threatened; some actually assumed new identities in different towns or cities. "They were everywhere," recalls one guy. "Once when I looked out the window in my mom's kitchen, I saw this car packed with skinheads staring straight at me." Another reports: "It got so bad, I had to hide for five months. I couldn't even go out in the open. There was a price on my head. Everybody was chasing me and everybody was going to kill me. I hid in Stockholm for two weeks too. The more I hid, the more they wanted to get me, for they knew I was afraid of them."

EXIT can, in extreme cases, suggest potential safe houses and, in many cases, advise the young man about how to avoid any retaliation. After Casper left through his girlfriend's intercession, he got into a protection program, and today they live out of town. When he is occasionally recognized by some older guys, they still threaten him. Casper says now that he wants to live in the country and raise hens. "And I swear I will never hit anyone ever again."

Christian says he never feels lonely anymore. "I'm never alone, and everyone knows about my past," he says. "In ten years, I want to have a house and a big car with a lot of seats because I want to have a big family—like about eight kids." He's started a Big Brother group at the local YMCA, and works with teenage boys to help them find a positive path. "You know, once I wanted to make people feel scared of me. Now I want to protect people from people like I used to be, to make them feel safe—even around me." As long as "I feel good, and I don't make anyone else feel bad," he concludes, "I'm OK."

Stefan got married and got a job. EXIT helped him find the job and still provides counseling support. "I don't have a lot of friends now, but I have EXIT, my wife, and my job and my workmates." And Amelie, his wife, is expecting their first child. Isaac's life has completely turned around. He gets along better with his father now and goes to adult school. "It's still hard, I still struggle." His goal is to become a chimney sweeper. He lives with his girlfriend, and they have a baby. He likes playing *World of Warcraft*, "but that's the only violence" in his current life. "I've made a lot of big steps to change. I used to be angry with everyone, but I was really just angry with myself."

According to those who have left the movement, participation in neo-Nazi groups was a rite of passage for alienated and insecure adolescent males. Their commitments were to a masculinizing project, not a National Socialist ideology. Ex-Nazis in Scandinavia appear to be far less interested in ideology than in action.

Yet, while Scandinavian skinheads are less committed to the ideological project of Nazism than their American counterparts, it is also likely, of course, that this difference is partly due to my having interviewed two different groups of men. While the American white supremacists I interviewed were still in the movement, the Scandinavian men were all *former* Nazis, and they would, undoubtedly, engage in a sort of revisionist re-creation of their participation—one that would underplay the role of ideological commitments and perhaps even overestimate the developmental tasks of becoming adults. Their descriptions of their activities rarely, if ever, referred to ideology. Indeed, it was very difficult to extract the sorts of racist comments from them that came so casually and effortless out of the mouths of the American Aryans. There is no doubt I would hear a greater commitment to the ideology if I interviewed Scandinavian Nazis who have remained in the movement.

I believe, though, that the difference in their ages was at least of equal importance in understanding their relative emphasis on ideology. The American Aryans entered later, in their late teens and early twenties, while every one of the Scandinavian Nazis were out of the movement by age twenty—some for more than five years. Their years of participation were, on average, from ages thirteen to sixteen, with some beginning as early as ten, but none remaining beyond age twenty. So the Scandinavian Nazis were leaving just as the Americans were entering.

As we end our interview, Isaac puts on his blue hoodie and pulls the hood over his head. "I'm going to go home and cook dinner for my girl-friend now," he confides. He cooks, cleans the house, and he even walks the dog. "I like it actually," he says. "I've turned into *den nya svenska mannen*—a new Swedish man." He laughs at the irony.

Frankie

"BORN TO BE WILD"

In the late 1960s and early 1970s, there was a huge billboard off the highway as you approached Philadelphia. "Philadelphia isn't as bad as Philadelphians say it is." Seriously.

This was the Rizzo era, named after the notoriously bombastic and corrupt mayor Frank Rizzo. (He'd earlier been police commissioner, and his younger brother was fire commissioner.) It was the city that saw Rocky Balboa grow up on those gritty streets in North Philadelphia. And across town, in Southwest Philadelphia, it was the city into which Frankie Meeink was born.

Back in the 1970s Philadelphia was a city of ethnic zones, as it still is today. And they tend not to get along with each other particularly well. Philly is more the city of internecine warfare than the City of Brotherly Love. Kensington: Italian. North Philly: Black. Northeast: Irish. Southwest: Black. South Philly: Italian. Don't go walking where you don't belong.

It wouldn't be fair to say that Frankie had an unhappy childhood. It would be more accurate to say he didn't have any childhood at all. Combine a nineteen-year-old Italian American father with a penchant for drinking and brawling, and a seventeen-year-old Irish American mother with an

Figure 8. Sign along the highway leading to Philadelphia, 1968. Photo courtesy of Temple University Library.

insatiable hunger for drugs, and you get Frankie. An ethnic mutt, he was one of those kids who, if he were a puppy, would be cast off as a stray.

The cards were stacked against a guy like Frankie from the start. And Frankie knew it. "I had been raised to hate. I was a Catholic mulatto, a half-mick–half-dago who'd never felt more than half-accepted anywhere, especially not in my own home," he writes.[1] His father was distant, aggressive, and a hard drinker; he owned a bar on the Southside of Philadelphia, the kind of place where you'd expect to meet Rocky Balboa. Or real guys with names like Crazy Cha-Cha Chacinzi or Fat Mike DeRenzio. A tough bar in a tough neighborhood frequented by tough men. And his stepfather was far worse. Violently abusive, John would habitually drink just enough to get motivated to kick the shit out of Frankie every chance he got.

Frankie didn't have a chance, partly because no one gave him one. But it's different now. Now he's making up his own story as he goes, cobbling together a life of purpose from the shards of his past.

You may even think you know his story—some of it will at least sound familiar. Ed Norton plays Derek in the film *American History X*, which is,

Frankie tells me, loosely based on Frankie's life. (For his performance, by the way, Norton was nominated for an Oscar.)

Let's start where Frankie starts, on those mean streets of Philadelphia. Frank Bertone Sr., Frankie's father, was a low-level street thug who owned the aforementioned bar in a Southwest Philly neighborhood in transition. Remember *The Fresh Prince of Bel Air*? Southwest Philly is where Will Smith (as well as the character he played) came from, and the place from which he had to escape to southern California. Frankie (Frank Jr.) never knew where he fit in. He didn't have a rich uncle in a ritzy LA enclave to fly off to, so no TV sit-com for him. His life was the real-life docudrama "Who the Fuck Am I?" Was he his Italian father's son or his Irish mother's son?

In his *Autobiography of a Recovering Skinhead*, Frankie tells one story that illustrates this conundrum. Living with his mother, one day Frankie was wearing a new football jersey she had bought for him—one that had his own name on the back. He was so excited. When his father arrived to visit, he took one look and "his eyes flashed with rage."

"I don't ever wanna see youse wearing that piece of shit again," said his father. Frankie was crushed. Tears in his eyes, he looked searchingly at his father, silently asking why.

"She gave youse a shirt with somebody else's name on it," Frank snarled. Of course, the name on the back was Meeink, her name, not Bertone, his name. While Frank Sr. saw it as a big "fuck you" from his ex, Margaret had said it was only for Frankie's own protection from the furious anti-Italian prejudice in the old-school Irish neighborhood they lived in. "A name like Bertone was like a bull's eye in that part of South Philly back then."[2]

Frankie lived in a world like that in the sitcom *Cheers*, only turned upside-down. Nobody knew your name. Not even you.

Living with his drug-addicted mother and her enraged alcoholic husband, his step-father, was a constant torment. "I wished every day of my life to get hit by a car," he tells me.

"Seriously?" I ask, somewhat incredulous.

"No, no, not to get *killed* by a car," he says, somewhat reassuringly. "Just to go to the hospital. I'd rather go to the hospital than go home."

Actually, he'd rather have gone pretty much anywhere instead of home. One night, beaten savagely by his mom's boyfriend and then thrown out of the house, he showed up at his father's bar across town. That was it. His father wouldn't take him in forever, just for a little while. He was on his own. He was never going back to that house again. He was a middle-school dropout by age twelve. He spent his time on the streets looking for trouble, and finding it relatively easily.

You can see why. Today he speaks in a breathless staccato, juiced on adrenaline, pumped and ready for action. If you're of a certain age, Frankie will remind you of "Action," that tightly wound bundle of jittery energy played by Tony Mordente in the movie of *West Side Story*, the Jet who was always ready to go, to bust out, to explode. Similarly, Frankie is a bundle of energy, difficult to miss.

Frankie wasn't big, but he was fast and scrappy and tough. "I got the crap kicked out of me all the time," he says. But then some skinheads began to hang out in the neighborhood, new guys, not from around there. They were compelling. "They had cars, beer, girls. They were powerful." He tagged along, and they began to talk to him. After a few months, they'd convinced Frankie that a multiracial society "would never work." Just look around. Everybody hates everybody else. You have to choose your people and stand with them. So Frankie made his choice, made his stand. He shaved his head, added red laces to his Doc Martens. "I was fourteen and I was a neo-Nazi skinhead. For the first time in my life, I felt like I mattered."[3]

Part of that mattering was religion. Frankie had always had a spiritual side. Sure, earlier he'd gone to church with his family, especially his grandparents. In fact, he says now, it was in a Bible study class that he first understood the divine mandate of racial division and white supremacy. "I learned how to hate by studying the Bible," he says, laughing at the irony. "Here's what I learned: God chose me. I am a chosen person of God. I'm chosen to defend the white race. It is my sacred mission."

For more than a dozen years, Frankie was a street organizer and proud member of various skin groups. He ricocheted between serious organizing, drinking, getting inked, and street brawling, on the one hand, and, on the other, getting high on serious drugs with his stoner friends who hung out on a nearby street corner. Everything was zoned, right? There was Skinhead Alley, where he'd hang with the other skins, having an occasional tryst with some skinchick against a wall almost out of sight, or smoking, bragging, and Sieg Heiling. And there was the corner of Porter and Second, where the stoners hung out. Frankie became a mid-level dealer.

Finally, it all caught up with him. In a particularly brutal fight, Frankie nearly killed a guy from a rival skinhead gang. He kidnapped him and, worse, he was armed with a gun. Worse still, there was a videotape of the whole thing. At age seventeen, angry and alienated, already the father of a baby girl, he was going to prison for fifteen years.

Frankie was tried and convicted. And he started the Great American Prison Shuffle, getting moved from one facility to another. From Graham and the Sangamon County Jail to Big Muddy, a maximum-security prison where the rules were lax and the drugs were plentiful. He cozied up to the other white nationalists, bikers, and older members of the Aryan Brotherhood. One of them recognized Frankie from the racist cable TV show that Frankie had been running. "There's our boy!" he shouted, and from then on, Frankie was part of the crew.

At Menard State Penitentiary, he had his first experience with the "other." He'd sit in his cell and read the Bible for hours, "praying that I'd get out of prison before my baby was an adult." Suddenly, one day, a shadow appeared at the door of his cell, blocking the light.

"Yo skinhead!" said a deep voice. It was Abel, a six foot, six inch former drug kingpin in East St. Louis. You didn't mess with Abel. And Abel was unmistakably black. "I see you reading the Bible in here by yourself all the time," Abel said. The silent pause was pregnant with possibilities, and, this particular pregnancy being unplanned and unwanted, no one seemed especially happy.

"You know, skinhead," Abel said softly, "we have Bible study in my cell every night at eight. You ought to come down." Frankie didn't quite feel ready for this. While facing "fatherhood and fifteen years in prison had reopened my heart to God," he writes, it hadn't yet reopened his mind. "I would play Spades with minorities, I would take prison survival tips from minorities, but I wasn't going to study the sacred word of the God of Identity with 'mud.'"

And yet there he was, a few minutes after eight that same evening, in Abel's cell, surrounded by six black inmates standing in a circle, holding hands, and reciting the Lord's Prayer. "The two men closest to the door silently opened the circle to me. They took my hands gently in theirs. I finished the Lord's Prayer with them."

"What's your name, skinhead?" Abel asked.

"Frankie."

"Lord, thank you for bringing Frankie to us on this night," he prayed.[4]

Wait. Frankie heard that voice inside: Who are you, you stone racist, neo-Nazi, proud white man, holding hands with a bunch of . . . Who was he indeed? Whoever he was, Frankie was starting to unbecome him.

Transferred again, this time to Shawnee State Penitentiary, he suddenly felt a bit stranded. Aryan Brothers there were few, and bikers were pretty much on permanent lockdown. But sports were everything in that prison yard. Everything. "Sports at Shawnee was bigger than at Penn State," Frankie says. Since the white prisoners seemed relatively uninterested, Frankie asked their permission, as one must in prison, to join one of the other teams. They shrugged their indifferent approval. "Hey, Frankie show 'em that we white guys can play. It's good for us."

And there, on a field filled with black and Latino gangbangers, he was suddenly a player on the Vice Lords football team. Well, almost. Mostly, he sat around waiting for his chance. In the game against the Gangster Disciples team, his teammates finally let him run back a kickoff. "I was a Nazi skinhead playing tackle football in a prison yard with a bunch of black gangsters. This wasn't Pop Warner League." When he took the kick-off, his teammates somehow failed to block for him, missing tackles or just plain falling down. He got stampeded by the Disciples. But then he did something impressive—something that revealed how he felt about his new teammates. He got back up, ready for the next play. Again and again. He ran a kickoff back for a touchdown. By the end of the game, they high-fived him.

Frankie Meeink knew how the game was played. Both the game of football and the game of proving manhood.

Two of his new teammates, Jello and Little G, started hanging out in the yard with Frankie, mostly because this was also their first time in prison and they were trying to adjust to life without their girlfriends and wives and their outside life. They'd talk, Frankie and Jello and Little G, and they pretty much "had only one thing on their minds to talk about." Girls.

"You'd get a letter from your girlfriend and try to figure out all the possible hidden meanings. You'd show it to the other guys, and they'd show you the letters they got. I mean it was intense, like if you wrote 'I love you' a little crooked, we would try to figure out what it meant."

Paroled after three years, Frankie was back in South Philly. He was unemployed, penniless, and still adrift. He needed a job badly. He knew the desperation that could so easily drag him back into that former life. A friend knew an antiques dealer named Keith across the river in New Jersey who needed some help moving and trucking antique furniture. Two days' work, a hundred dollars a day. Frankie jumped at the chance.

"I hadn't had two hundred dollars to my name in like forever," he remembered.

"There's just one thing," his friend said. "The guy's a Jew."

"I don't fucking care, so long as I don't have to talk to him," Frankie said.

"That's exactly what he said about you," said Frankie's friend.

After all, what sorts of credentials did Frankie have for getting a real job? "Education? Ninth grade dropout. Employment history? A job on a concrete crew. . . . Criminal record? On parole for aggravated kidnapping and assault with a deadly weapon." Not exactly a stellar résumé.

So, as Frankie puts it, "an upper crust Jewish antiques dealer hired an ex-convict with a swastika tattoo on his neck to deliver armoires to his suburban clients."[5]

It was strange enough to work for the guy, and Frankie says he kept expecting to be "Jewed" out of the money he was owed. He was braced for it. After all, isn't that what Jews do? Isn't that why they use the word *Jew* as a verb?

Actually, Keith paid him *more* than he had originally promised, and asked Frankie if he wanted to come work for him full-time. According to Frankie's ideological beliefs, this was not going according to plan. And then it took a turn that was far "worse" than Frankie could ever have imagined. It turned out that Keith was a hockey *fanatic*. Like Frankie, he lived for the Flyers. "And if there's anything in this world that can cross a gap as wide as the gap between a Jew and a Nazi, it's loyalty to the legacy of the Broad Street Bullies," Frankie writes. Just getting to know an actual Jew pushed Frankie up against every stereotype he'd ever held. If this very significant stereotype didn't hold true, what could be said about all the others?[6]

As his employment situation started to improve, his relationship with his former comrades began to deteriorate. As he drifted back to his old life, hanging out on Skinhead Alley with Jimmy and Louie and all the old skins, it just didn't feel right anymore. He was drifting away from his former comrades. He was working for a Jew—who was a good guy! Who liked hockey! He'd hung out with black guys. He knew them. And they knew him. He just wasn't into the hate anymore.

And besides, these newbies were all mouth and no action. Frankie remembers sitting at a party one evening and listening to these other new recruits talking trash as a way to pump themselves up.

Those baby Nazis felt as if they had cast-iron balls every time they spat out "nigger" or "spic." They felt like geniuses when they spouted off about how the ZOG-Jew landlords were handing North Philly over to the Puerto Ricans. They felt like gods when they bragged about what they had done, as a pack, to a lone Puerto Rican kid in a dark alley the night before.

He was by turns contemptuous and wistfully nostalgic. "I know for a fact that's how they felt, because it's exactly how I'd once felt."[7]

His former comrades from Strike Force, as they'd called themselves, noticed it and arranged for Frankie to be jumped out of the movement. At what was supposed to be a party for a fallen comrade, members of the Nazi Alliance and Axis Skinheads beat the crap out of him and threw him down a flight of stairs. Strike Force, his sworn comrades, his brothers, just watched. Beaten to a pulp, broken, barely conscious, Frankie lay in the street. "You're fucking dead to us, you fucking traitor!" someone screamed at him. Then they turned and walked back into the apartment and slammed the door. It was over. Frankie was free.[8]

Well, not quite. He may have been jumped out of the movement, but there was still a monkey on his back. It was even harder to resist the lure of drugs. Drugs were a form of self-medication, a way to get numb, just as hate and fighting had sort of made him numb, just as drinking had made him numb. And, to some degree, just as the movement had made him numb. He'd be hyped up on adrenaline, beer, and painkillers, yeah, and looking for a fight, but like a lot of guys, he fought in order to feel something—anything at all. Better to feel pain than to feel nothing. Better still to inflict pain on someone else. You go into that zone; you stand outside yourself, watching yourself get hit and hit back.

You might say he'd hit bottom when he starting shooting up. He'd pretty much left his neo-Nazi past behind by this point and was trying to make a go of it with his wife and baby in tow. It wasn't going well. One night stands out as especially vivid for him. He was hanging out in what was called Badlands, a crack house on the Southside. Just junkies and their suppliers. Frankie was sitting with a homeless guy who was his "helper." I'll let Frankie tell it:

> While he talked, I snuck glances at the other lost souls of the Badlands. Not ten feet away from us, a man who looked like a corpse unzipped his pants and plunged a needle into his penis. The horror registered on my face. My homeless helper followed my eyes to the man, now slumped against the wall, a blissful look on his face, the needle hanging limply from his dick. "Only veins he's got left," the beggar said. He flicked his index finger hard against the pulsing vein in my right arm. "You got nothing to worry about. You got great veins."
>
> I was still staring at the corpse man, thinking, "At least I ain't that bad," when I felt the needle prick my skin. Three seconds later, I gladly would've shoved a three-foot needle up my dick, through both balls, and all the way north until it came out my eye if that's what it took to stay feeling the way I felt when that heroin rocketed through my body. Mainlined directly into a vein, heroin is fucking nirvana. It's a feeling you can't possibly imagine until you're inside it. Unfortunately, it's a feeling you can't ever forget once you've been there.[9]

Jessica left him, and took their daughter with her. Distraught, he checked into rehab, and when he finally stopped stealing other people's meds to get high, he started to stop. He started to get clean.

It was sports again that helped him turn his life around, turn it back toward his family and toward a self he now barely recognized. He saw his experiences in prison as a kind of template around which he could work with young people of different races. If sports could break down some of the hatred that *he* was carrying around under those tattoos, maybe it could work for other kids.

The big break came by accident. In 1996 he was invited to speak at an Anti-Defamation League (ADL) luncheon event. By chance—or celestial design—he was seated next to Jay Snider, whose father, Ed, just happened to own the Flyers. They talked hockey most of the afternoon, ignoring everyone else at the party. Frankie offered an idea of using hockey as a way to build relationships among different groups of kids. "Like taking kids from different backgrounds and coaching them in hockey, but also coaching them in life," he says. Frankie had stumbled on one of the most venerable axioms of social psychology: the contact hypothesis. Want to break down stereotypes? Put different people together and give them a common task.

The problem was that hockey is expensive. Really expensive. This isn't soccer in some Brazilian favela where all you need is a ball and a place to kick it. There are skates and pads and uniforms and sticks and helmets and ice time. It's more expensive than skiing. And it's just about the whitest sport there is.

Joined by the ADL regional director, Snider approached the Flyers' front office. Within a week, Frankie enlisted a local lawyer to help write a mission statement, and they presented it to the management: a community-based youth hockey organization in Philadelphia to teach hockey and sportsmanship to a wide range of kids from different neighborhoods, on the principle that if they played together, they'd get to know one another other and thereby maybe, just maybe, refrain from killing one another on the streets. Uniforms, sticks, skates, ice time, you name it—the Flyers provided it. Harmony Through Hockey was born.

These days, Frankie lives modestly in Des Moines, Iowa, is clean and sober, and is on the road lecturing and speaking for Life After Hate, the organization of formers that he cofounded. And he has a job with the Iowa Chops, an American Hockey League team (sort of the minor leagues of the NHL), running the program he started in Philadelphia with the Flyers. Harmony Through Hockey enrolls young urban kids, ages six to twelve, from diverse backgrounds, for whom hockey is a rich person's sport. Frankie got the team and local businesses to contribute the equipment and care of the skates, and he teaches hockey and life skills, with a large dose of spirituality. Frankie sees Harmony Through Hockey as an alternative to recruitment by extremist groups of all kinds. The kids have discussions about social issues before they lace up, then they skate on the Chops' ice. The rules of hockey they're taught—no hitting or checking, always supporting one's teammates, showing respect—are intended to carry them off the ice and into their lives.[10]

He knows two things. That it's through contact with the "other" that you realize your own capacity for empathy. And that these kids need mentors—just as Frankie did. Because in the absence of parents and mentors, he found his own parents and mentors in the movement.

On a sunny spring afternoon, I watch Frankie talk to the assembled seventh- and eighth-grade students at an Orthodox Jewish Yeshiva in Boro Park, Brooklyn. The boys and girls are separated in the auditorium by a wide aisle. They are a jumble of energy, chattering and joshing each other. But when Frankie speaks, they're silent.

He's clearly dressed for the occasion. T-shirt, shorts, sneakers, and mismatched socks—Frankie is nothing if not informal. I think he cultivates that look because, given where he's come from and where he's been, fashion has never been much of an issue. Photographs on his Facebook page show him in a T-shirt and shorts addressing a roomful of police officers in full uniform.

After Frankie tells his story—a story he has now told thousands of times at events, conferences, synagogues, homeland security briefings, and community forums—he tells a story about elephants in Africa. It's a fable, perhaps apocryphal. Who knows, perhaps it's true.

It seems that a community group, determined to thwart the terrors of elephant poaching, decided to remove a number of baby elephants and place them in an elephant preserve. These are babies from different herds, all about the same age. Protected and safe, they grow to elephant adolescence. And that's when all hell breaks loose. The males are constantly fighting, and they are marauding through the veldt, enraged and bullish.

Their rescuers are beside themselves. What can they do to stop this version of elephant thuggery? The very babies they rescued are now threatening the other elephants. Their former rescuers think they might have to put the rogue elephants down. But one of the rescuers has an idea, and they soon bring a few adult elephants into the safe confines of the reserve. Within a few days, Frankie explains to the now-mesmerized kids, the young elephants calm down and start to imitate the adults.

"No one had ever taught the baby elephants how to be adults," Frankie says, warming to his moral. "They were trying to make it up, and they thought fighting was a way to show they were adults."

"That was me," he says, "and the guys just like me. We had no role models, no mentors. No one ever taught me what it looked like to be an adult, what to do when you're a grown-up, what it looks like to be a man. So we made it up. And we screwed it up." Now he's determined to be for others what he never had for himself. A mentor. A coach. And yes, a father figure to some of these kids. "Be the older elephant," he tells the kids. "You have a younger brother, younger sister? Be the older elephant. With your friends? Be the older elephant."

Getting out of the movement and the drug life hasn't exactly made Frankie mellow. He's still wound up, still on the go. There's nothing meditative about him, but now his energy is channeled, directed, and has a purpose.

He's still quite spiritual; he believes in a higher power—God, you might want to call it. Just as in the old days when he believed that God had chosen him to redeem the white race by attacking others, he believes now that God has given him a second chance to turn his life around, to redeem himself, by helping turn others' lives around. "If today I did none of those things that I used to do yesterday, if I didn't hurt anyone, if I didn't discriminate against anyone," he says, "then I know I don't have to spend my day atoning for those things, and I know I can be of maximal service to God today." Same God, maybe, but this time he's moving Frankie in a different, more Christian direction.

POSTSCRIPT, SUMMER 2017

Well, maybe not only in that more Christian direction. In one of those ironies that life often throws those who seek purity, it turns out that Frankie is Jewish. Part-Jewish, anyway—and certainly enough to have sent him to those very gas chambers he once denied having existed.

4 United States: Life after Hate with "Life After Hate"

It was a bright, sunny Irish afternoon in Dublin in late June 2011 when six formers stood in a circle in their hotel garden, all put their hands in the center, and vowed their allegiance to one another. There were tears and smiles and hugs all around—real hugs, big bear hugs, the kind of hugs you give when you finally exhale and let go of everything you've been carrying around with you for so goddamn long. The five of them—Angela King, Tony McAleer, Sammy Rangel, Frankie Meeink, and Christian Picciolini—were attending a conference, the first ever, the "Summit Against Violent Extremism," sponsored by Google Ideas. Some of them had never met, and they'd never met the attendees from EXIT or other organizations around the world, all working toward the same goal. That day, these five vowed to support one another and, more than that, to create a safe and nonjudgmental space where others in the movement can come and find support. There, in the lush garden of their hotel, Life After Hate (LAH) was born.

After the conference, the five joined two others, Arno Michaels from Milwaukee and T.J. Leyden from Southern California. Both had also been major figures in the White Power movement, and all seven had recently left the movement. They'd done it with different levels of difficulty and

Figure 9. The founding of Life After Hate at the Summit
Against Violent Extremism, Dublin, Ireland, 2011. *From
bottom, clockwise:* Tony McAleer, Frankie Meeink,
Christian Picciolini, Sammy Rangel, and Angela King.
Photo courtesy of Life After Hate.

pain, emotional and physical. Christian felt he was leaving behind friends,
but just couldn't reconcile their rage with the people he was meeting in his
music store on the outskirts of Chicago. Sammy had founded "Formers
Anonymous," a Twelve Step program for gang members who were, he
believed, "addicted" to the lifestyle in the same way that an alcoholic or
drug addict becomes dependent on their form of self-medication. Tony
had been drifting away gradually ever since he'd become a parent. Frankie
had been jumped out, as the previous profile reveals, when he was beaten
senseless by some fellow skinheads as he stepped away from the political
ideology and drifted into a drug scene. Different routes in, different paths
out. But each had done it alone.

They didn't just walk away; they felt their leaving needed to be public
and permanent, a way to set themselves apart in active opposition to the
hate groups they'd been in. And besides, one doesn't just go gently into
that good night when you've been a visible racist skinhead. You're known
to the police and other anti-racist gangs. Heck, you're known to everybody
if you have a swastika tattooed on your forehead. And besides, your former
comrades don't like people to leave. In fact, they may now be swearing to
kill you.

If you don't want to go into a self-made witness protection program, leaving the state and maybe even the country, then you'd better go big so you can go home. Go public. Be splashy. And every founder had been doing just that, going public with his or her story. T.J., for example, had left, visibly and purposefully, by showing up at the Simon Wiesenthal Center in Los Angeles with boxes of materials—pamphlets, newspapers, everything he had, really—and making a public apology. He was, he says, "the first neo-Nazi to voluntarily and publically give up the movement."

The founders' plan was simple: create an organization in the United States similar to those springing up in Europe that would support those who were growing disaffected with the life. They were as geographically scattered as you can be in North America. Tony lived in Vancouver; Angela in a diagonal across the continent, in Florida. Christian and Frankie were in the Midwest, Chicago and Des Moines, respectively. Sammy and TJ were in Los Angeles and Arno was in Milwaukee. No one particularly wanted to move, so the organization had to be decentralized and rely on the newly emergent social media platforms.

By August 2011 they'd registered as a nonprofit organization. Their timing was perfect. Social media were just taking off, and they provided the perfect platform for the new organization. There's no headquarters, no charmless office in some suburban strip mall. Instead, Life Against Hate established a closed-group Facebook page so that people who were considering getting out could connect. Thus far, more than forty people, mostly young men, have reached out and found their way to the page, then been carefully vetted before being allowed to join. (The group administrators have to be careful, as some current actives have tried to infiltrate the group to find out who is thinking about leaving.) An online journal was considered, launched, and later scrapped because, as Angela tells me, it just wasn't the right time for such a platform.

In addition to providing support to those considering leaving, the five current organizers—Christian, Sammy, Frankie, Tony, and Angela—also do a significant amount of speaking and writing. They work to bridge the "trust gap" between academics, anti-racist activists like the Southern Poverty Law Center (SPLC), and law enforcement, which often has an agenda oriented more to punishing past offenses than supporting people who are getting out of the movement. They know that leaving the movement involves a serious "identity shift," as former enemies are now your allies, and former comrades are now sworn enemies. "It's not only your former brothers," says Greg, who left the movement four years ago. "It's people like SPLC. They were like the worst enemy, because they were exposing your comrades left and right. You fantasized about blowing them up! Now, it's like they're your best friends, and you want to sit around with them and help them draw their maps of hate groups."

Since that fateful day in 2011, Arno and T.J. have drifted away from the original group, though neither has lapsed back into movement life. The remaining cofounders now form the group's core. All five have written memoirs of their time in the movement, detailing how they got in, confessing to the terrible things they did, and examining their own process of getting out. Equal parts cautionary tales, personal expiation for their past deeds, and therapeutic confessional, the memoirs illustrate the narrative arc of entry, experience, and exit.

I interviewed all but one of the organization's founders, as well as seven other formers I met through networks of friends and contacts. Since they are a "virtual" community first, I met them all virtually at first. After emails, I conducted telephone interviews with each of them. To be honest, given the enormous surge of interest in what has been renamed the alt-right, I found the staff of LAH to have well-rehearsed answers to my questions, which were, I admit, basic and naïve. Their stories of entry and exit, their backgrounds, what happened to them in the movement, and how they were able to leave, all had an air of familiarity, as if they'd given these interviews many times. And, indeed, they had. Besides writing their memoirs, they've been on various talk shows and been interviewed by magazines and for TV documentaries. Occasionally, I have to say, I found the answers to be so well rehearsed that I wondered if the recitation wasn't formulaic to avoid having to go back "there," back to viscerally confronting their past behaviors. But the second time we spoke (I interviewed most of them at least twice), there was a sort of casual familiarity, and I sensed we were starting to open up to each other more informally and spontaneously and the conversations became exactly that—conversations. Subsequently, I've met with a few of them personally, tagging along as Frankie gave a very personal talk at a Yeshiva in Brooklyn, and meeting Tony a few times, once for a joint interview on film in which we interviewed each other.

EMASCULATION AND MOBILIZATION

Take yourself back to September 12, 2001. The Day After. Here was Rocky Suhayda, Nazi Party chairman from Eastpointe, Michigan. "It's a disgrace that in a population of at least 150 million White/Aryan Americans, we provide so few that are willing to do the same [as the terrorists]," he said. "A bunch of towel head/sand niggers put our great White Movement to shame." And Billy Roper, deputy membership coordinator of the National Alliance added that while "we may not want them marrying our daughters," anyone "willing to drive a plane into a building to kill Jews is alright [*sic*] by me. I wish our members had half as much testicular fortitude."[1]

The terrorists had bigger balls than we did! How many cartoons and images of missiles up bin Laden's ass, or missiles and guns interchangeable with penises, is it going to take to understand that there is a gender component to these reactions? Our national American manhood had been challenged.

It's that sense of shame, that specifically gendered sense of humiliation, of *emasculation*, that I heard again and again among the white nationalists I initially interviewed for my earlier book, *Angry White Men*. No matter where they fell in the organizational matrix on the extreme right—from older organizations such as the John Birch Society, the Ku Klux Klan, and the American Nazi Party, to neo-Nazi and racist skinheads, White Power groups like Posse Comitatus and the White Aryan Resistance, and radical militias—it was the constant refrain: our manhood is being challenged by "them," so we have to show them that *we* are the real men and they are not.

And who are "we"? The Department of Homeland Security, in an assessment of "rightwing extremism" released in April 2009, concluded that "rightwing extremists may be gaining new recruits." Indeed, the SPLC has documented 932 active hate groups in the United States alone—a 50 percent increase since 2000. These groups range from the neo-Nazis and the Ku Klux Klan to militias, Aryan survivalists, white supremacist youth groups, and violent religious cults.

They consist mostly of younger, lower-middle class men in their late twenties, educated at least through high school and often beyond. They are the sons of skilled workers in industries such as textiles and tobacco, and of the owners of small farms, shops, and grocery stores. Buffeted by global political and economic forces, the sons have inherited little of their fathers' legacies. The family farms have been lost to foreclosure; the small shops squeezed out by big-box stores and Amazon. These young men face a spiral of downward mobility and economic uncertainty. They feel squeezed between the omnivorous jaws of global capital concentration and a federal bureaucracy that is at best indifferent to their plight and, at worst, complicit in their demise.

And it's often their younger brothers who are called as well: teenage boys, adrift and alone at school, often friendless, bullied, finding it hard to find their way. Nearly one-third of all users on the white nationalist site Stormfront.org are between the ages of fourteen and seventeen.[2]

The followers all agree that "they" are taking what is "ours," and that *our* mission is to take it back. One fellow traveler once put it succinctly to a friend of mine who was interviewing him for a book she was writing: "Is this a white country, or what?" The answer, they believe, is "what." America is no longer a white country, no longer the country of their forebears. As one issue of *The Truth at Last*, a white supremacist magazine, put it: "Immigrants are flooding into our nation willing to work for the minimum wage (or less). Super-rich corporate executives are flying all over the world in search of cheaper and cheaper labor so that they can 'lay off' their American employees. . . . Many young White families have no future! They are not going to receive any appreciable wage increases due to job competition from immigrants."[3] Their anger often fixates on the "others"—minorities, immigrants—in part because these are the people with whom they compete for entry-level, minimum-wage jobs, or it fixates on those, such as women and gays and lesbians, to whom they feel the government kowtows. Above them all, enjoying the view, hovers the international Jewish conspiracy.

"I don't get it at all," says Alex, a current white nationalist I met in Michigan, when I asked him in 2011 about this notion that white men are the ones who have power in America. (I interviewed him for *Angry White Men*.) Alex trained for a while with a militia unit in Michigan, and he still lives in Grand Rapids. His father and grandfather worked for Ford Motor Company in Dearborn, but Alex never could latch on there. And now there's little to latch on to. To scrape together an income, he drives his 1988 Chevy pickup truck for various contractors around town, doing errands. That's right: a Ford family, driving a Chevy C/K 1500. "We have nothing," he told me.

> Nothing. It's all going to *them*. I mean seriously, they get all the breaks, the fucking welfare, the health care, the jobs. I mean, a white guy has no chance for the job these days—the government says you *have to* give it to them! It's like completely upside-down now. My grandfather and my father both fought to keep this country free, and for what? So their kid could get laid off and some [he looks around the diner, sheepishly] well, you know, the N-word, can get the damned job? This isn't right, man. It isn't right. We got nothing.

It doesn't exactly sound like a man in power. He feels powerless, yes, but he still thinks he's entitled to power—as a white American man—by a combination of historical legacy, religious fiat, biological destiny, and moral legitimacy. Once they had it, perhaps once they even "had it all," but it's now been surrendered or stolen from them by a federal government controlled and staffed by legions of the newly enfranchised minorities, women, and immigrants, all in service to the omnipotent Jews who control international economic and political life.

So who are these hundred thousand or so active white supremacists? In *Angry White Men*, I concluded that they are far more recognizable than I originally thought. They're every white guy who believes that this land is his land, was made for you and me. They're every down-on-his-luck guy who just wanted to live a decent life but got stepped on; every character in a Bruce Springsteen or Merle Haggard song; every white cop, soldier, auto mechanic, steelworker, or construction worker in America's small towns who can't make ends meet and wonders why everyone else is getting a break except him. But instead of becoming Tom Joad, a left-leaning populist, they take a hard right turn, ultimately supporting the very people who have dispossessed them.

They're America's Everymen, whose pain in downward mobility and whose anger at what they see as an indifferent government have become twisted by a hate that tells them they are better than others; who are disfigured by a resentment so deep that there are no more bridges to be built, no more ladders of upward mobility to be climbed. Their howl of pain has been mangled into the scream of a warrior. It's a rage as sad as it is frightening, and distinctly male.

What holds this "paranoid politics" together—anti-government, anti-global capitalism and pro-small capitalist, racist, sexist, anti-Semitic, homophobic—is a rhetoric of masculinity. These men feel emasculated by big money and big government—they call the government the Nanny State—and they claim that "others" have been handed the birthright of native-born white men.

As he traveled through the rural West in the mid-1990s, journalist Joel Dyer constantly heard these refrains: "Environmentalists wouldn't let me run my cows cause some damn little sparrow they said was endangered lived on my place." "They took my farm." "The IRS took everything I owned." "These people," Dyer observes, "believe the government is responsible for where they are, because they are finding themselves ignored, basically, by the economic system. People are losing their homes, their farms, their jobs, their sources of income. Corporations have been allowed to move wherever they want, and to take away jobs by the truckload. People are becoming economically dispossessed."[4] In this view, NAFTA took away American jobs; what the jobless and underemployed see as the "Burger King economy" leaves no room at the top, so "many youngsters see themselves as being forced to compete with nonwhites for the available minimum wage, service economy jobs that have replaced their parents' unionized industry opportunities."[5]

In the eyes of such downwardly mobile white men, most white American men collude in their emasculation. They've grown soft, feminized, weak. White supremacist websites abound with complaints about the "whimpering collapse of the blond male"; the "legions of sissies and weaklings, of flabby, limp-wristed, nonaggressive, nonphysical, indecisive, slack-jawed, fearful males who, while still heterosexual in theory and practice, have not even a vestige of the old macho spirit."[6] According to *The Turner Diaries*, the highly popular white supremacist novel that provided the blueprint for Timothy McVeigh, American men have lost the right to be free; slavery "is the just and proper state for a people who have gown soft."[7] It is here that the movement simultaneously offers white men an analysis of their present situation and a political strategy for retrieving their manhood. As Aryan Nations puts the challenge: "What has become of your men? Are these powder puffs in their sky-blue, three-piece suits the descendants of George Washington, Thomas Jefferson, and Andrew

Jackson? What would your fathers say if they watched you give your country away?"[8]

This thinking is easily visible on groups' websites and online publications. In one cartoon, the poor hapless emasculated white man is surrounded by the signifiers of a multiculturalism gone amok: African American commercialism, Chicanos selling oranges on the streets of LA, LGBT centers, Holocaust remembrance museums. The triumph of the "other" over the white man, who is entitled to it. He has to take it back.

Nowhere will you find a more powerful illustration of white male emasculation than one from the revamped Aryan Nations (figures 10 and 11): a man who stands accused by his beautiful blond daughter of not even standing up to "those dark men" who "took Mommy away." His emasculation is complete: even his daughter sees him as a failed male.

The second gendered strategy I observed when researching *Angry White Men* was the problematization of the masculinity of the "other." White men had been emasculated by the Nanny State, true, but those "others" were but pretenders to masculinity. "We" are the real men, they seem to say, the ones whose manhood has been taken. "They" are not real men.

Racism, sexism, heterosexism, anti-Semitism—these have been cast in gendered terms. "They" are either "too masculine" or "not masculine enough," that is, *hypermasculine* or *hypomasculine*. It was what I've called the Goldilocks dilemma: Like the porridge that was either too hot or too cold, the chair that was either too big or too little, the masculinity of the other is either too much or too little. Never just right. *Our* masculinity is just right, of course; theirs is too hot or too cold. They're either wild, out-of-control animals, violent and rapacious (too masculine, uncivilized), or they are weak, dependent, irresponsible (not masculine enough).

Thus, for example, black men have been imagined as violent rapacious thugs (since long before the stereotype was portrayed in D. W. Griffith's *Birth of a Nation*), but also as irresponsible, welfare-dependent, and slothfully lazy. Hypermasculine and also hypomasculine. So too are Jews weak, effeminate, and nerdy, but also so clever and conniving that they control the economy of the entire world. Hypo/hyper. Women, of course, are supposed to be hypomasculine—it's what femininity means. But feminist women are men in women's clothing, gender inverts who have embraced masculinity so much that they want to have sex only with women!

Figure 10. White Nationalist cartoon (originally found on Stormfront.org) depicting the emasculation of white American manhood.

Or take the portrayal of gay men. To contemporary white supremacists, gay men are effete fops who have men do to them what real men should do only to women. On the other hand, they are so sexually voracious and promiscuously carnal that straight men can only stand back in awe. As Jeff, a twenty-seven-year-old auto mechanic in Buffalo, New York, said:

What Did You Do During The Revolution ?

What did you do in the war daddy? I'm hungry daddy. Why do we have to stand in line for food daddy? Why did those bad men make us move to this strange place daddy? Where have all the White people gone daddy? Why did those dark men take mommy away? When's mommy coming home daddy? Why didn't you stop them daddy? Why didn't you do SOMETHING?

ARYAN NATIONS
Box 719 Lexington, SC 29073
803-233-6601
http://Aryan-Nations.org

Figure 11. This advertisement for Aryan Nations explicitly points to white men's emasculation through their inability to protect their wives and daughters. Poster originally found tacked to a telephone pole in Nashville, Tennessee, in 2009; website no longer exists.

"I read this article that said that, like, faggots have like a thousand different sex partners a year. Fuck! Unbelievable. It's like all they do is have sex. Christ, I can't even imagine. I'm lucky if I can get laid by like two or three girls in a whole year! Damn, I wish girls were more like gay men. Ah [he sighs] that would be a miracle." Websites are flooded with lurid descriptions of "gay public orgies" in San Francisco, including claims that these orgies are public and sponsored by the city's municipal government. Effete femininity of the failed man, savage hypersexuality of the carnal Superman: hypermasculine/hypomasculine.

And, of course, immigrants. Contemporary white nationalists have nothing but contempt for those weaklings, those "huddled masses," those beggars. They're animals; they beat their wives because, obviously, they can't control them; they are desperate for handouts because they swarm like locusts but have no individual souls. The suicide bombers, like kamikaze pilots, are both hypermasculine (wow, look at those guys, willing to blow themselves up for the cause, willing to die like martyrs) and hypomasculine, with no individual self, just another one of the sheeple.

EXTREMISM AND THE RESTORATION OF MASCULINITY

So, if you've been emasculated, and your rightful entitlement has been handed over by feckless governmental bureaucrats to those "others" who surely don't deserve it, then there is only one way to get your masculinity back: join the movement.

White supremacist organizations thus offer themselves as the antidote to America's current social problems by promising to empower men who feel they no longer have any power. The movement seemingly offers white men the chance to prove their masculinity. The fate of the white race hinges upon the need for real white men to act. The movement repeatedly attacks white men for becoming feminized (thus unsettling the natural order) encourages them to become real men by standing up and protecting white women, reasserting their place in the natural hierarchy, and taking over the world. Movement websites are saturated with images of warrior-like men donning weaponry, shields, and armor.

Reclaiming the country, though, is a bit abstract; white men also seek to reclaim their manhood. This challenge provides an enormously successful recruiting strategy: Join us, and we will see to it that your manhood is restored. And you'll probably get a girl. The political really is personal. Even deeper, you will not only become a real man, but you will be embarking on a sacred mission: to redeem the entire white race. Your valor, your courage gets you community and camaraderie with your brothers, access to women who will adore you, and a sacred mission of sacrifice and glory. You've morphed from Loser into Rambo.

No white nationalist leader understood this better than Tom Metzger, founder of White Aryan Resistance (WAR). Born in 1938 and raised in Indiana, which had become a bastion of established "White Wing" groups like the Klan and the John Birch Society, Metzger became an active Bircher and grand wizard of the California Klan after he moved his organization to Fallbrook, California, a small exurban town between San Diego and Los Angeles. (It was Metzger's son, John, who was a guest on the infamous 1988 episode of *Geraldo* during which a brawl broke out on stage and Geraldo's nose was broken.[9]) Metzger and his organization were brilliant at recruiting young alienated white guys at skater parks and dismal exurban streets (Tony McAleer was at one time WAR's main youth organizer). And he did it precisely by playing to their sense of masculinity lost and masculinity regained.

In one of their most imaginative native flyers, WAR repurposed an timeless older story of masculine restoration. In a mid-1960s cartoon familiar to most American men over fifty the ninety-seven-pound weakling transforms himself into the most manly man to ever walk among us: Charles Atlas (figure 12). The ad has nothing whatever to do with white nationalism. It's for the Charles Atlas bodybuilding system, touted as capable of a transformation from emasculation ("Oh don't let it bother you, little boy!") to masculinity restored ("You *are* a real man after all!"). And all by using the Charles Atlas system.

(While virtually every man over fifty to whom I have shown this ad has recognized it immediately, few knew that it was Charles Atlas's actual story. A young, scrawny Italian immigrant, Angelo Siciliano, came to Ellis Island and failed at his attempts to meet girls on the beach at Coney Island. The cartoon illustrates Atlas's life.)

Now have a look at what Metzger and WAR did with the ad (figure 13). Metzger racializes the bully on the beach, so that our young hero's emasculation ("Oh don't let it bother you, white boy!) and subsequent reclamation of manhood ("You are a skinhead after all!") are restorations to a specifically white masculinity. Metzger's head is superimposed on the body of a bodybuilder; his tattoos, laced boots, and suspenders are drawn on. Here is an appropriation that perfectly illustrates the quest

Figure 12. The original Charles Atlas "ninety-seven-pound weakling" advertisement, telling the story of emasculation and the restoration of manhood through bodybuilding.

Figure 13. White Aryan Resistance's unauthorized appropriation and racialization of the Charles Atlas cartoon, in which masculinity is regained by becoming a white nationalist.

of the young guys drawn to the movement: masculinity lost and masculinity regained.

American white nationalism offers American men the restoration of their masculinity, a manhood whereby individual white men control the fruits of their own labor and are not subject to the emasculation of Jewish-owned finance capital or of a black- and feminist-controlled welfare state. Theirs is the militarized manhood of the heroic John Rambo, a manhood that celebrates their God-sanctioned right to band together in armed militias if anyone, or any governmental agency, tries to take that manhood away from them. If the state and capital emasculate them, and if the masculinity of the "others" is problematic, then only "real" white men can rescue this American Eden from a feminized, multicultural, androgynous melting pot.

There are, to be sure, tensions among the different groups on the extreme right; they're hardly a unified bunch. There is an uneasiness, a mutual wariness between what might be called the "mainstream" of the extreme right—the old John Birch Society, the KKK, the American Nazi Party—whose adherents love their solemn ritual gatherings and like writing pamphlets, and the newer groups of young skinheads who like partying, drinking, and fighting and are primed for action. The older organizations may attract a certain nerd-loner who wants to plan, plan, and plan, but most young guys are viscerally attracted to the corporeal hypermasculinity on display among the skinheads. After his first meeting with a group of New York skinheads, Arno Michaels remembers feeling excited. "I wasn't really attracted to the political really, but I liked that these New York guys were huge and covered in ink and really mean and scary looking. I wanted to recreate that in a style of my own."[10]

LAH was created by people decidedly in the latter, nonmainstream camp. To them, groups like the American Nazi Party were simply "a bunch of kooky old white guys who just sit around and complain about how bad things are," writes Christian Picciolini in his memoir, *Romantic Violence: Memoirs of an American Skinhead*. And the Klan? Those small-town rubes "with their ridiculous dunce caps and tablecloth clown costumes," they were hardly role models for this urban street fighter.[11] Arno, in his memoir, *My Life after Hate*, describes a neo-Nazi officer in full-uniform regalia as giving off "a kind of gay S&M effect," with his close-cropped beard and ponytail. These SS-inspired guys spent their time watching an endless loop of

Triumph of the Will, Leni Riefenstahl's film of "Hitlerama," while being "spun out of their gourds on robust biker acid," writes Arno. Listening to the leader of the group, Arno "saw a man who had nothing to offer the world."[12]

Today's neo-Nazi skinheads have a different profile—and it's not just age. They tend not to be from southern small towns, or to be steeped in pre-1964 segregation nostalgia, or to evoke Nazism or apartheid as achievable goals. They're suburban, and some are even urban. Many come from those vast swaths of endless suburbs that link Los Angeles to San Diego, or from desperate cities like Philadelphia or Detroit, where urban desolation meets urban dissolution, and where long-lived traditional ethnic communities are being crowded out by equally poor newcomers whose origins are less European and more South Asian or South American. They may start their careers as one of those burned-out thirteen-year-olds you're likely to see at a skate park in SoCal, or standing alone on a decaying urban basketball court from which the net disappeared decades ago, not much air in the ball, shooting hoops on a court without lights—acne-scarred face, stringy long hair, flannel shirt, aimless, bored out of his skull in a country he feels gives him everything and nothing at the same time. He's on his way to Fight Club or to a dead-end job in a life where his only solace is getting stoned with his bros and driving around looking for trouble. They're disaffected youth, living in a "teenage wasteland" as The Who sang in 1971. They're everywhere in the suburbs, and the skinhead recruiters give their lives meaning, affirm them as somebody important, somebody who has a mission to save the white race from extinction. Having felt their lives were over at twelve, suddenly they feel reborn at fourteen, with a purpose. More important, they feel like men, real men, in a band of brothers. They *matter.*

T.J., for example, grew up in Southern California's Inland Empire, a vast stretch of rural suburbs extending southeast of the LA basin toward San Diego, including Lake Elsinore and Fallbrook (once the home of Metzger and WAR), and east toward Riverside and San Bernardino. This is a fertile recruiting ground for the extreme right: vast, characterless, sprawling suburbs dotted with skater parks, strip malls, and utterly alienated white youth. White nationalist groups proliferate here, and, to be truthful, they spend most of their time fighting with one another. American Firm versus American Front. WAR versus T.J.'s own BBB (Boot Boy Brotherhood).

Christian, Frankie, and Arno, in contrast, were city boys, from Chicago, Philadelphia, and Milwaukee, respectively. All felt like cities that had seen better days: crumbling infrastructure, high unemployment, widespread drug use, and a large number of immigrants who, many white families felt, were stealing their jobs, taking over their neighborhood, and threatening their way of life.

ENTRY

How do the young men get in to the movement? What is the path from exurban blight or inner-city decay to life on the extreme right? How do they get recruited? What leads some to join while others move on to something else? Based on my interviews with about a dozen formers, and the forty-five actives I interviewed in the early 2010s for *Angry White Men,* we can discern several pathways to extremism. (LAH has surveyed about fifty formers, and while I was unable to read these transcripts, patterns were described to me that also buttress my findings.)

These boys and young men rarely, if ever, join because they are racist, anti-Semitic, or even anti-immigrant. Rather, they join and then *become* racist. Christian Picciolini told David Greene on National Public Radio in April 2017: "One day I was standing in an alley at 14 years old and I was smoking a joint. And a guy drove up the alley and stopped six inches from me. And when he got out of the car, he walked towards me. He grabbed the joint from my mouth, looked me in the eyes and said don't you know that that's what the Communists and the Jews want you to do to keep you docile?"[13] In his memoir, Arno writes:

> At the time I could [not] really give a shit about black or white or whatever. I was just overjoyed when I realized the impact that running around with swastikas had. I loved how it really pissed people off. I had no consideration for the Holocaust and the real horrors of Nazi Germany. I had no understanding of it and it never really crossed my mind. All I knew was that now it was me and my friends against the world and that's how I liked it.[14]

Young men like the ones Christian and Arno once were join extremist groups because they're lonely, scared, and miserable. And this isn't just your garden-variety teenage angst. They are seriously miserable—and with good reason.

According to Angela, more than three-fourths of the formers in LAH's survey said they had experienced some sort of trauma, ranging from routine bullying in school to sexual or physical abuse from a family member. Nearly all came from families that could generously be labeled dysfunctional: violent or abusive fathers, violent or abusive mothers, alcoholics and addicts. Some talked about single mothers who had a string of boyfriends, each of whom was more abusive to her sons than the one before.

The single most important factor in predicting who joined the extremist groups was childhood trauma and abuse. "So many had stories of being sexually or physically abused," Angela told me. For those socialized to be strong, powerful, and stoic, these experiences cut deep, to their core, as existential threats to their very sense of themselves. For many, "joining a hate group was a way to get back their own power."

"It's not causal," Tony tells me; "it's not like every abused kid from a dysfunctional family becomes a skinhead. But it is consequential for those who do; it's the place where their pain starts and their efforts to transform that pain into rage."

Take the case of Duke Schneider, a Brooklyn boy born and raised (his nickname harking back to the 1950s Brooklyn Dodgers star Edwin Donald "Duke" Snider). "I grew up warped," he told a journalist. His father was long gone, and his mother "hated me for reminding her of him," while an older relative beat him mercilessly. With a dog leash. He retreated to a world of documentaries about World War II, watching the Nazis marching so proud and strong at rallies. "Why can't I be as tough as they were?" he asked himself.[15] Duke became a weight lifter and joined the professional wrestling circuit. For two decades, he was a corrections officer at Riker's Island before he retired in 1999. And along the way, he became a neo-Nazi.

I heard stories like Duke's over and over as I interviewed the American formers. Guys felt small, weak, ashamed. Many had been brutalized and abused by parents, but mostly they told stories of abuse by stepfathers. These were sometimes accompanied by stories of the boys witnessing their mothers being abused by the stepfathers and being unable to protect them, frightened of intervening—a dynamic that only deepened their shame. One cannot live with such shame and humiliation for very long without serious injury to one's sense of self. Many of the men I interviewed considered suicide; several attempted it, some more than once. The trauma of family abuse and the wounds of shame and humiliation haunted many of these men and led them to seek a way to retrieve, recover, or reclaim their sense of themselves as men. Becoming a neo-Nazi is but one strategy to restore a damaged sense of manhood. The ideology comes much later, a remedy for pain, a tactic to externalize the shame and humiliation of weakness into a fiction of collective strength in defending the race.[16]

Gendered shame and humiliation were part of Tony's story too. A sensitive and intelligent boy from a middle-class family, he was constantly shamed and humiliated by his father—who was a psychiatrist! "You'd have thought he'd know better, right? But he wanted to toughen me up." Tony says now that this "emotional trauma" left him lonely, isolated, and confused. He was set up as a target, and his teachers as well as the students were his tormenters. "Trauma," he says now, leaves you with a belief that you "aren't lovable, smart enough, that we're powerless and weak." He calls it "toxic shame," and the effort to make that shame disappear, or at least dissipate, brought him to his first confrontation as a teenager. He got into his first fight at age sixteen. "It was electrifying," he told a journalist. "The adrenaline rush was intoxicating. . . . People were afraid of us. A false sense of power comes with that."[17]

T.J. opens his memoirs with a question about his abusive, hard-drinking truck-driving father: "How many times had he called me a sissy?" It was a relatively easy jump from his father's admonitions, to never ever backing down from a fight, and giving even better than you got, to being the one to initiate the fights, and making sure you never lost.

Frankie, too, describes being beaten savagely by his stepfather, his mother's denial of that abuse, and his biological father's indifference to it—all of which, of course, left him feeling alone and scared. "Less-than," he says. "I felt less than. And unworthy. I deserved what I had. I was nothing. But I was desperate to feel loved. I wanted accolades."

The consequence of the abuse and the dysfunction is shame, the "toxic shame" Tony talks about. In fact, every single former I spoke with had a story of feeling ashamed, humiliated. Perhaps they were too small or too helpless, or trapped in an abusive family, or they were abused and beaten or raped by family members. One had been abused by a priest. To whom was he going to turn? The single thread that runs through all the stories of entry is humiliation. The movement puts that humiliation to good use, providing a way to feel strong and proud, to feel like somebody, as if you matter in the world. And then the humiliation is slowly manipulated, as shame tends to be an easily malleable emotion, one that can be turned into a rage that can then be directed outward onto others, or onto the entire society, instead of turning it on those who actually hurt you.

And instead of turning it on yourself. Many of the formers I spoke with had contemplated suicide prior to joining the movement, having felt as though they were invisible, as though their trauma and struggles and pain were ignored by indifferent institutions, by callous and often conspiratorial parents. While some of the women cut themselves, the boys projected their pain outward as rage. The path to extreme politics is paved with personal grief. Grief that is politicized can then explode.

Politics gives that anger meaning, coherence. It focuses diffuse rage away from the perpetrators and onto the society that allows such torments to happen with complete impunity. "You wanna know what 'hate' meant to me?" asks Frankie. "It meant love. It meant loving myself and my people so much that I hated everything they are not. Hate was a way of showing love for myself." For others, the movement provided the family they never had. The movement was about "support, protection," Angela said. "It was a *family*—the family they needed."[18]

On the other hand, in some cases, the feeling of belonging means not feeling one-down all the time, invisible, a lonely target. Perhaps it's the ultrahigh self-esteem coupled with the low self-worth that often predicts that one will become a bully. (Self-esteem is based more on an existential sense of self that has little to nothing to do with one's actual accomplishments. Self-worth, by contrast, is based on an individual's assessment of what he or she has achieved. Bullies often have high self-esteem, but low self-worth.) That high self-esteem leads some guys to enter feeling high already. Arno Michaels, for example, described himself as a "cocky jerk who knew he was exceptional" as a young boy and who didn't need anything from anybody. Or so he thought.[19] After all, he grew up in a middle-class family that wanted for nothing—"a nice house in a nice neighborhood and never went hungry or took a beating," he writes in his memoir. But that just made his dad's drinking and his parents fighting harder to take. He believed this was as good as it got. Perhaps there was trouble in paradise after all.[20]

As in Sweden and Germany, one way into the movement in the United States is not through politics, but through culture. The Internet is a major way that guys who feel lonely and alienated, and are beginning to feel that loneliness and sadness bubbling up into political rage, find out that they are not alone, that there are a lot of them out there, and that they all share the same experiences and the same feelings. Guys consistently spoke of either a local group or the Internet as their first step into the world. Trey, a Southern California skinhead, said: "It's really cool how you can get all this shit off the Net now. Ten years ago there really wasn't that much, but now you've got all the music, the clothes. I bought my daughter a toy figure of Hitler from a website. I mean you're not going to find that at Walmart."[21]

THE ROLE OF MUSIC

But at heart, it's really the music that pulls young men in. "The music was the main driving force in the recruitment of young people," admits Tony.[22] You might think the American extreme-right guys would get turned on by country music, especially those uber-patriotic "God and flag and country" anthems that everyone sings along with at NASCAR races and hometown rodeos. A little "Thank God I'm a Country Boy" here, a little Lynyrd Skynyrd "Sweet Home Alabama" there.

And that association is partly true: many still love to sing along with Merle Haggard's "I'm a White Boy," especially when he sings, "I'm proud and white and I've got a song to sing," and the final refrain, "I'm a white boy lookin' for a place to do my thing." But country music is too mainstream for these amped-up adolescents looking for a serious adrenaline rush. True, many male country singers make a career out of men's anguish and pain from hard living, harder drinking, doing tough jobs, and dealing with untrustworthy women. But that music is ultimately too tame, too acceptable, to hold the interest of these young men for very long. Those country singers have award shows, for heaven's sake. The guys in the movement aren't whining about being Okies from Muskogee. They're furious saviors of the white race. They know the 14 Words.

By the way, in case *you* don't know the 14 Words, here they are: "We must secure the existence of our people and a future for white children." Coined originally by David Lane, the late head of The Order, a white supremacist group, the 14 Words have become the most famous slogan for the extreme right wing all over the world.

You certainly can't go looking for today's right-wing extremists among the fans of what *real* Nazis might have liked: Wagnerian opera, Bruckner's derivative style, and Schubert's song cycles. Neo-Nazis are rougher around the edges. And one can just imagine the scions of those older, establishment extreme-right organizations in the United States, such as the Klan and the American Nazi Party, covering their ears as their young disciples mosh to the sound of White Power bands. Far more decorous in their cultural tastes and attire, the most radical that the old guard right would probably get is Ted Nugent.

Today's American white nationalists invariably find their way to "hatecore" (aka "hate metal," "hate punk," and "White Power music"), that combination of hardcore punk, thrash metal, and driving, raging rhythms with shouted hateful lyrics. It's intoxicating to those it attracts. Some bands, especially German and Scandinavian ones, like to overlay their Herderesque evocations of the Fatherland with traditional instruments and vaguely neopagan spiritual lyrics. Groups like Morgenstern and In Extremo are examples. But it's often hard to tell if they are just fusing medieval and metal for self-mythologizing purposes. And of course, as chapters 2 and 3 show, there are fiercely nationalist hatecore bands and neo-Nazi rappers in Sweden and German as well.

SCREWDRIVER AND AMERICAN HATECORE

The American hatecore bands tend to follow the British "Oi!" tradition set by the seminal Lancaster-based group Skrewdriver: driving thrash-punk rhythms and explicitly political lyrics that nobody—*nobody*—could mistake for anything but racist anthems. Or, as the band itself puts it, "marching music, fighting music, spirit-scaring white power rock and roll music from the finest white nationalist band in the West."[23] Andy, a skinhead in Vancouver, Washington, told sociologists Pete Simi and Robert Futrell: "The first white power song I ever heard was 'White Power' from Skrewdriver in high school on a shitty fifth- or sixth-generation cassette copy. It totally floored me. Once I heard that, it took over me. That was the attitude and feeling I had been looking for. I was already racially aware, but Skrewdriver motivated me."[24]

Biggie, a Colorado skinhead, also credited hearing White Power music for the first time as a defining moment in his racial awakening. "I had some racist views before I started listening to music but once I heard that first Skrewdriver song, I was sold. It really did change my life," he told Simi and Futrell. "It connected me to other people who were willing to say, 'You know, I'm a racist. So what? I'm proud of who I am.'"[25]

Most of the guys I interviewed also found their way to racism through racist bands. T.J. recalled how punk rock music in the mid-1980s "spoke to me in a language I understood—the fear, rage, and chaos that was so familiar."[26] Arno Michaels remembers the first time he heard Skrewdriver through headphones on a Walkman: "I had this feeling of, '. . . yeah.' It was like a light bulb went off and from that moment I was really really into it." He found the Chicago group Romantic Violence, which was importing Skrewdriver CDs, and he became hooked. (Romantic Violence was Christian Picciolini's record label.)[27] Arno eventually became the lead singer of Centurion, a hate metal band that did quite well by movement standards, selling some twenty thousand records.

While virtually everyone I spoke with had a history of moshing and partying to hatecore, only a few expressed even a sheepish affection for Prussian Blue, a folk-pop duo of twin prepubescent blond girls originally from Bakersfield, California, who strum an acoustic guitar and sing songs like "Skinhead Boy" (he is "standing fast, not afraid to kick some ass," their "oi boy"). They admonish adults to wake up to the racial holy war in "Aryan Man Awake." In the music video for "Skinhead Boy" they prance in their kitchen around a swastika drawn on the floor.[28] (In 2016 the two girls, Lynx and Lamb Gaede, now high school graduates living in Montana, claimed they'd renounced many of their earlier views and embraced medical marijuana and multiculturalism. Their mother, an unapologetic white nationalist, thinks they're just trying to fit in and be popular.[29])

Wade Michael Page, who massacred six worshippers at a Sikh temple in Wisconsin in 2012, was the bassist in two hatecore bands, Definite Hate and End Apathy, and also sat in on sessions with more than a dozen other

Figure 14. Prussian Blue, 2006. Lamb *(left)* and
Lynx Gaede were a white nationalist singing-group
phenomenon, promoted by their white supremacist
mother. The Gaede sisters have since renounced
their earlier politics and embraced campaigns for
medical marijuana. Their mother remains
unreconstructed. Photo courtesy of Polaris Images.

bands when they needed someone to fill in. Actually, Page had been active
with the punk scene in his hometown of Denver and was radicalized and
"racialized" in the military. "If you don't go into the military as a racist," he
told Peter Simi, "you definitely leave as one." He recalled the National
Alliance actively recruiting at Fort Bragg while was stationed there. After
he was discharged, he went to a music show for the band Youngland, and
he was hooked. He ended up as Youngland's bassist.[30]

T.J. also served in the military, where he met several guys who were
active in the movement. They gave him a purpose within the army, and

Skrewdriver

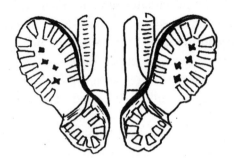

BOOTS AND BRACES / VOICE OF BRITAIN

Figure 15. Skrewdriver was the first and most famous of the White Power bands in Britain, the touchstone for contemporary hatecore bands. This is the cover from their *Boots and Braces/Voice of Britain* album. Photo courtesy of Rock-o-Rama Records (www.rock-o-rama.net).

when he got out, he "joined the largest neo-Nazi skinhead organization in the country as a street soldier."

Christian also came in through the music scene and moved up gradually, starting at age fourteen. The son of middle-class Italian immigrants in Chicago who were fervent believers in the American Dream, he was raised in a good home; his parents had a stable, happy marriage. Despite this unusual profile, he was still lonely and was bullied as a young teen. "I wasn't political at all, just didn't know where I fit in," he tells me. "I was just searching for something to belong to." Kids, he explains to me, "want to do something that matters, you know, like to *be* someone who matters."

In his case, he found hardcore music. It was a whole scene—clothes, ink, and most of all, a posture, a way of carrying himself. He felt powerful; people were actually scared of him. And then he met Clark, a charismatic leader of the Northern Hammer Skinheads, a group known as much for their violence as for their ultraright politics. Christian was hooked. By the mid-1990s he was a leader. "It was so empowering to go from nothing, to go from not having any friends and not having any influence at all, to all of a sudden being part of an organization," he told a journalist. "I remember just feeling very empowered and almost drunk with power because I felt like I could do anything."[31]

Christian's experience parallels that of many adolescent guys. He wore the uniform, cultivating "a look that intimidated without my needing to do a damn thing," and he spruced up his room into a neo-Nazi man cave or, as he calls it, a "Nazi frat-boy dorm room." There was something awe-inspiring about the group walking down the street, fostering the same kind of bonding as members of a collegiate Greek-letter fraternity experience. "We were gentlemen thugs intent on having a good time while on duty protecting our race."[32]

His ascent within the movement was phenomenal. The biggest fish in a smallish pond was all that Christian and his best friend needed to feel like real men, big men, men who were feared and respected: "Every teenager in our neighborhood either looked up to us or feared us. Sometimes both. For the first time I felt completely in control of my own life. I'd yearned for so long to fit in with my peers and now they'd begun to vie for my attention. The ones that had once ignored me now revered me."[33]

For Tony also, the music scene was critical, as an escape from both the unhappiness he felt as a child and the "fortress intellect" he had built up as another way to shield himself. He credits two precipitating experiences as decisive. When he was ten or eleven, he walked in on his father having sex with a woman who was not Tony's mother. Also, he was bullied in his Catholic private school, where the priests used corporal punishment that was as random and cruel as the bullying he got from other students. "It was hard to tell which was worse, being bullied by classmates or being caned by the priests," he recalled. He retreated behind his fortress. His grades suffered.

The punk rock scene in Vancouver saved him. In Vancouver, the punk and skinhead scenes overlapped, which is uncommon; the punk scene is often anarchist and ultraleft, while skinheads are fascist and ultraright. By the time he went to high school in the United Kingdom, he was already deep into the culture, and at a Black Flag concert in Vancouver in 1983, he felt an adrenaline rush while hanging out with a couple of skinheads. Tony had made his choice. This is somewhat ironic since Black Flag was known more for its leftist-anarchist politics, coming out of the SoCal punk scene, with Henry Rollins as its lead singer for several years. But the band's posture was embraced by both right and left—a defiant, nonconformist, raging critique of the complacent status quo.

By the late 1980s, Tony was recognized as a leader of the white nationalist movement in the United States. He had become the manager of Odin's Law, a racist hatecore band, and a dedicated recruiter for the movement. He directed the first Aryan Nations Youth campaign in 1987, and then joined up with Tom Metzger as the National Youth Campaign chair for Metzger's WAR. In 1991 they organized the first racist protest in British Columbian history. Tony operated the telephone hotline Canadian Liberty Net, which used growing Internet platforms to bring people into the movement. Robert Matthews, head of the Aryan Nations, and Tom Metzger were his new father figures, the accepting dads he'd never had. And he prepared himself for the "inevitable" race war. "I believed I would either be dead or in jail by the age of 30 and I was OK about that," he writes.[34]

It's intoxicating, that feeling of power, brotherhood, community, family. You feel as if you matter, as if your life has purpose, namely, saving your race. You feel like a man. "People join because there's something missing from their lives," says Christian. But they stay because they are validated in ways they never expected. "There's an element of fantasy to it," Tony told a journalist. "It was as bad as it could get and there was an excitement that came from that."[35]

Feeling like a real man works only if other people see you as a real man. It's as much what you do as who you are. Gender is a performance as much as it is a property. You "do" gender, perform it—for an audience. Your performance must be credited by others; otherwise, you can feel as manly as you want, but if other people see you as a wuss, then that's what you are. You may have to fight to prove them wrong—now *there's* a performance that can lend credibility. You have to wear the uniform of masculinity, whether it's a pinstripe suit, an army uniform, a team jersey, or a green M-1 bomber flight jacket with Doc Martens, a white T-shirt, and red suspenders. And then other people have to look at you and say, "Yeah, that dude is a real man." Masculinity is relational, performed before the evaluative eyes of others. More than that, it's homosocial; those evaluative eyes are men's.

THE WOMEN OF THE RIGHT

That the narrative arc of entry and experience in the extremist movement is gendered doesn't mean that it's a boys-only club. Women are a crucial part of the white supremacist movement, both corporeally and symbolically. Indeed, one could even say that they're pivotal; they're what these guys are fighting for. Yet there are contradictions, which form fissures that divide white supremacists on the role of women.

Women compose about a quarter of the white supremacist movement. Their motives for joining are similar to the men's, or at least run a parallel course. Sociologist Kathleen Blee interviewed nearly three dozen women on the extreme right, and their narratives provide a fascinating comparison to the narratives of the men I interviewed. Of the neo-Nazis, Klanswomen, white power skinheads, and Christian Identity or other cult members she interviewed, Blee found that virtually all were of the same class background as the men I interviewed—indeed, as the men profiled in virtually every study of the extreme right. They were all lower middle and middle class; the overwhelming majority were educated (more than a third had some sort of post-secondary degree or were currently in college). Yet there are some significant differences as well. For example, none had been subject to abuse as girls.[36]

What brings the women in? The same mundane reasons that bring most people to all sorts of intense identity-oriented politics: a need to belong to something larger than themselves, the collapse of traditional familial or communal forms of identity. By contrast with the Swedes, only a handful of the American women followed a man into the racist world. Many were not especially racist when they entered, and developed their ideology after they joined. Others simply drifted into the deviant subculture. One's friend liked skinhead fashion; another thought it would be fun to hang out with the fringe groups.

Ideologically, many embrace the same traditionalist gender ideals as the men, suggesting that they see their greatest contribution to the cause as bearing and raising white babies. "We were put on this earth to bare [*sic*] the pure white children and if we don't do something to help fight for our White Race, then there won't be a future for our Pure White Children," according to the Ladies of the Invisible Empire (a women's auxiliary of the

KKK). Women "should nurture the family as well as keep the household in order," chimes in the Aryan Confederations.[37]

That's surely the model of older, established organizations such as the Klan. They've been men-only organizations since their founding. So has Hammerskin Nation, the contemporary skinhead organization. Most of the time, women are venerated as "the single greatest treasure of the White Race, the heart of our people, the center of our homes, of our lives," and therefore excluded from most of group activities. A slightly different form of this ideology of male supremacy is voiced by Jack Rader of the Aryan Nations: Women "are not land developers, farmers, ranchers, miners, construction workers, or lumberjacks etc. Women have been put in the armed forces and they have been made so-called cops, but the truth is that they just don't have what it takes to do these things." "Can you think," he demands, "of anything more demeaning to masculinity than a woman as the so-called commander-in-chief over the armed forces?"[38]

On the other side of this thinking is Tom Metzger, who proposes letting the women decide what they want to do. "If they are capable and are able to show that ability, then forget all of the artificial barriers," he writes. WAR welcomes women as equals, says Metzger.[39]

To the men, women are the prize, both symbolically and literally. White men who feel thoroughly emasculated by the multicultural society restore their manhood through joining the movement—and many of them expect to instantly become magnets for blue-eyed babes. Surely reclaiming their manhood will restore the interest of the opposite sex. The women seem to know this. One woman wrote on a white supremacist dating site: "There are PLENTY of us proud white women out here looking for just that—a strong white man that adores us for our values and the way we believe in raising our children. . . . All I see here is a bunch of sniveling teenage boys. . . . Call me when the real white men arrive someone please!!!!"[40]

Several white nationalist websites offer dating services in order to match Aryan men and women. Organizations such as Aryanist Assignations (which sounds like a Nazi escort service) and websites such as allwhitedating.com and wherewhitepeoplemeet.com, as well as dating and relationships sections on portals such as Stormfront.org (white singles), attract thousands of members looking to hook up. (The photos they post look indistinguishable from the photos on Match.com, except that the white supremacists generally pose in front of Confederate flags.) Man up, white guys, and get a date with a real white woman!

It was the coequal, kick-ass skinhead aspect of the movement, not the dating service and certainly not the exalted white motherhood part, that first attracted Angela King, one of the founders of Life After Hate.[41] Angela drifted into the movement from a childhood of casual racism and isolation. Raised in rural southern Florida, away from the glitz and multiculturalism of Miami, she was initially enrolled in a private Baptist school because her parents thought "it would 'keep me safe'—meaning there were no black people around." When her family moved to a more racially mixed suburb, she was stunned by the diversity, and stunned also by her lack of any core center of self. Her parents remained strict, though, which meant no nail polish and no shaving her legs, "which in middle school, you know, is death. I was bullied a lot." Pudgy, with glasses and braces, and an utterly unfashionable mullet perm haircut, she was an easily identifiable target.

Until seventh grade, that is. Bullied relentlessly by a much bigger and far more popular girl, Angela felt she'd had enough. "My mother always told me two things: first, don't ever start a fight. But if you are attacked and you don't fight back and beat her, then you'll get it worse at home."

"And what was the second thing?" I ask.

"I'll love you no matter what you do, but if you ever bring home a black person—or another woman—you're done."

"Well, one day," she continues, "this girl was picking on me again, and I just had it, you know; I just pushed her back and she fell down and was hurt, and I saw myself change, right then. If I was the one picking on others, then I couldn't be humiliated like that again."

By high school, she'd gone "down the rabbit hole" of acting out. Her parents had split up, and she stayed with her mother. She thought "there must be something wrong with me because my father didn't want me." A few years of drugs, alcohol, and promiscuity followed. Her self-esteem plummeted, she got a "bad reputation," and she self-harmed, cutting and burning herself. She hung out with the punk kids in school, without any ideological commitment at all; together they drifted into skinhead culture, suddenly donning Confederate flag do-rags, swastikas, and other neo-Nazi swag. "People were paying attention to us now," she recalls, "and I saw it as respect, not disgust. We were feared!"

And she felt connected. "I finally found a place where I belonged and was accepted." So she went all-in, adorning herself with racist and Nazi tattoos and a Celtic cross and falling for an older skinhead. He was abusive, and when she got pregnant, he kicked her in the stomach, more out of disgust with her for withdrawing her affection than because he didn't want a baby. She miscarried, then left him, but stayed in the movement. She was arrested on her nineteenth birthday for disorderly conduct. "Every crime I've ever been charged with, I've been guilty."

GETTING OUT

We know, then, how young people get in. They're adrift, aimless, and anomic in a world that treats them with contempt and violence. They feel insignificant. They feel alone. They feel small. And along come these guys who seem to have it all together, who bring the comradeship and connectedness that staves off the anomic loneliness. They appear strong, powerful. Big. Menacing. Intimidating. Charismatic. Their lives are animated, fun, and have serious meaning and purpose. They count. They have a mission. If you've ever been a teenage boy and felt marginalized, like a loser or an outcast, you can understand exactly this attraction.

The racism comes later, slowly, until you believe the things they say, because, well, because they say them, and they're your brothers and they seem so smart and know what the score is. They dazzle you as they roll out their lunatic conspiracy theories about a secret cabal of Jewish bankers that has colonized the political institutions of the Western world and uses minorities and immigrants as its front lines to achieve world domination. Conspiracy theories are attractive because they connect random events into a coherent, meaningful narrative. You're not small by nature, they say; you're made small because those forces are determined to keep you weak so that they can get stronger. *They* are actually afraid of *you*—that's how big and important you are.

Given these heady and intoxicating experiences and ideas, leaving the movement is rarely a simple or all-at-once event. As I spoke to the formers, I got a sense that disengagement is a gradual process, just as it's a gradual process to get in. One takes tiny steps away from the life, and

gradually the group's visceral immediacy begins to wane. Gradual disillusionment can be unreliable, and you can be as easily pulled back in as you
can continue to ease yourself away. Several members talked about
moments of intervention, when certain people said something, did something, at a critical time. Tony says you "fade to black." You gradually begin
to slip away, or some thing or things begin to drive a wedge between you
and that life.

Three distinct paths out emerged from my conversations with formers.
To be sure, these are not distinct and categorical; they overlap so that a
cathartic social or political crisis often dovetails with a more personal
moment of self-confrontation. All three paths require a serious confrontation with yourself, a moment of looking in the mirror and not recognizing
who you've become. Or perhaps recognizing *exactly* who you've become
and not liking what you see.

In a sense, all three paths ultimately led to the same end, if the person
was brave enough to follow it. That end was the experience of a cognitive
dissonance so loud and profound that it had to be reckoned with. And
because all three paths led to this end, the stories more commonly evidence a combination of the three paths. Although they may be analytically
distinct, the paths often cross, and it is the junctures, the places of
convergence, that may provide the moment of real disengagement. It's not
enough just to get out. You have to turn things around.

Men and women experienced this dissonance differently. For men, it
was often a contrast between their beliefs and their interactions, often
with people they were supposed to hate. The ideology grew thin; they
could no longer fit their beliefs side by side with the lives they were living.
Christian, for example, found he liked talking to the African Americans
and nonskinheads who were coming into Chaos Records, the small record
store he'd opened in Alsip, Illinois, an exurb equidistant between Gary,
Indiana, and Chicago. They seemed nothing like they were described by
the ideology he believed in. "They were black people and Jewish people
and gay people and Hispanic people," he told a journalist. "I couldn't deny
the fact that I started to bond with them over things like music and the
neighborhood."

But even for him, the process of disengagement came with a powerful
flash of recognition about who he had become:

So I was 18 years old, I believe. And some skinhead friends and I were drinking. And late one night around midnight, we walked into a McDonald's. And there were some black teenagers in this McDonald's being drunk. I screamed that it was my McDonald's and that they had to leave. They ran across the street. We chased after them.

When we caught one of the black teenagers, we beat him viciously. And you couldn't see or recognize him as a human being his face was so swollen. And . . . he managed to open his eyes at one point as I was kicking him. And I connected with his eyes. And for the first time in those eight years that I was involved, the reality and the consequences of my actions came into focus for a split second.[42]

A split second. That was all it took for Christian to experience a momentary flash of recognition of the distorted, contorted person he had become.

Frankie recalls the same dissonance. Here was a "movement that promised us we would be proud white warriors," he told a journalist, but "it wasn't panning out the way they told us it would."[43] There were too many holes in the argument, too many times when your comrades didn't have your back, too many times when it all seemed like play-Nazi.

By contrast, women usually experienced that dissonance in their relationships, trying to reconcile the fact that their boyfriends or husbands exalted white women as the mothers of the race and the sacred bearers of white babies, yet also hit, abused them, and treated them, well, like shit. The men are "incapable of actually relating to another human being like another human being," says Sue, a former I interviewed. "Brothers are brothers—until they're not. Women are not even that, really."

Several women told Kathleen Blee that they had had abortions despite their group's adamant opposition to it. And several had close Jewish, black, or gay friends, even though their political ideology demanded that they shun "mud people" and deviants. At least one-third of the women had mixed-race or homosexual family members, and one Aryan supremacist in New England confessed she was also part of a lesbian-dominated goddess-worship group, while another embeds her white supremacy in a sort of neohippie back-to the-land mentality of "natural family planning, ecological breastfeeding, and home schooling."[44] Lucy, a young Klanswoman, resolved these contradictions in a typical American fashion: "In school my best friend was black. . . . I've got a family member that's bisexual, and the

Klan's supposed to be against that. So you know it's just the person, not the race, not the religion. If I'm gonna like you, I like you for *who* you are, not *what* you are."[45] Well, that's one way to resolve cognitive dissonance!

My guess is that Lucy's route is fairly common, actually. Think of a stereotypical notion you've held of a particular group, in the abstract. And then how you deal with becoming friends or colleagues with a member of that group who doesn't conform to the stereotype at all. What to do? You could, of course, do what most people do: grant the exception. Your friend isn't like other blacks, Jews, women, gays, or whatever. They're different. They're the exception that proves the rule. On the other hand, you could revise the stereotype: I guess "they" don't really fit the description I'd been taught. But that takes enough contact to see the stereotype break down often, and it also takes some support from others who see things as you now do.

Path 1: The External Prod

For some, the catharsis starts outside the self, when the person is confronted with the horrors of what his or her ideology inspires. It's a wake-up call, a reckoning, an existential shock. This is where these guys and these ideas are going—do I really want to go there?

Both Frankie and Angela identify April 19, 1995, as the day they began to wake up from a nightmare of their own creation. That was the day that Timothy McVeigh exploded the truck bombs outside the Alfred P. Murrah Federal Building in Oklahoma City. Frankie begins his autobiography on that day, when he was standing in the deli on his corner, watching on a small-screen TV. Shocked. Horrified. Not in the least celebratory. Angela also was horrified and sad, realizing that Timothy McVeigh "was someone who was like me." Speaking to me, she remembers that day: "There was that picture of the fireman carrying that little girl that just haunted me. That wasn't what I wanted to be doing in the movement."

That flash of recognition is often set up by the most mundane of experiences, like getting older. A lot of the guys find that cognitive dissonance occurs not so much between ideology and behavior as through a slowly building discordance between their youthful selves and their now-adult selves. "I don't know," says Jeff, a former I met through a friend of a friend. "It was cool to be all inked and dressed and Heil Hitler and all when I was sixteen, and I could scare the shit out of everyone else. But now, if I looked at myself in the mirror, I'd scare the shit out of me. I'm a grown-up now, and I have to start acting like it."

Christian describes how, simply with the passage of time, the power of the ideology began to fade. "There are too many things I can't reconcile," he says. Resolving that dissonance meant getting out. He sees his work now as a sort of "penance":

> I did really bad things in my life. I recruited hundreds if not thousands of young men into the movement. My music inspired them to do some really bad things. I need to provide that off-ramp to others, so they don't go down the same path. I need to reach out to the Wade Michael Pages or Dylann Roofs. I don't need to reach out to law enforcement. I need to reach out to my guys.

Arno, too, began to rethink his activism and to look back on what he had done with remorse and a sense of contrition:

> In the absence of love's light, hate can be exciting, seductive. It beckons you and sends torrid, empty power coursing through your veins. At first you think you can dabble. Just for kicks. Just a bit of entertainment to ripple the excruciating monotony of your disdain for the world. You blink, and you're covered in blood. Another blink and the doors of your cell are slamming shut. A blink later and the image of your best friend's mannequin-looking corpse as cold and wooden and wrong as the open casket it sits in is seared into your brain forever. You rub your eyes in response to the blinks and the tears of your family run down your face. The tears of the parents of the people you battered beyond recognition. The tears of survivors who feel their children torn from their arms and their parents murdered all over again at the sight of you.[46]

T.J. also began to age out, as the ideology just felt increasingly hollow. One night at a party, he recalled, the guys were just talking about all the different "others" who would soon be exterminated. What then? T.J. asked. "What happens when we've killed off all the Jews and the blacks and the Hispanics, and it's just us?" he asked. The group scoffed and one said, "We'll start to get rid of freakin' redheads like you!" They all laughed, he recalls: "But somewhere within the laughter the lack of answers made me realize that the Movement wasn't really about white power. It was simply about *hatred.* Once we'd annihilated everyone else, once there were only whites, we would turn on ourselves."[47] A few days later, he left the movement.

Path 2: Encountering the Self through Encountering the Other

A second pathway to that confrontation with self begins inside. Not necessarily provoked by an external event, the process begins, rather, with just a slow dawning realization that what has seemed so normal is suddenly not so normal anymore. "Who am I? What am I doing here? Who is this person who is doing these things?"

Often, this realization is triggered by a confrontation with the objects of one's hatred in a new set of circumstances. For Angela, Frankie, and Tony, this process came about when they actually interacted with the people whose very existence they took to be an existential threat to the survival of the white race. Their experiences of unlearning prejudice by interacting with the "other" offer additional examples of Pettigrew's "contact hypothesis," introduced in the previous chapter. Whether in prison, at work, or even in casual social settings, stereotypes can break down when one actually interacts with the "other." The members of LAH discovered that when they met a member of the despised group, one singular individual whose very existence eroded all their categorical group stereotypes, they began to unlearn the dehumanization the movement had taught them.

In the summer of 2013, the news broke that Derek Black had abandoned the movement. Derek was hardly just another white racist who'd had enough; he was the closest thing to royalty in the White Nationalist movement. His father, Donald Black, founded Stormfront.org. His mother, Chloe, was once the vice president of the Louisiana Ku Klux Klan, and she'd been married to former KKK grand wizard David Duke. At age twelve, Derek was featured in the documentary *Hate.com* after he'd created a site for young people on his father's website. By age 14, he was hosting his own radio program.

But late in the summer of 2013, he renounced it all, and, following the lead of guys like T.J. Leyden, he contacted his old enemies. In a letter to the Southern Poverty Law Center, he described his growing disillusionment. A recent graduate of the liberal New College of Florida, Derek had experienced a series of small epiphanies in classes and in his interactions with other students on that diverse multicultural campus. Derek's letter explaining his motivations suggests the same dissonance that others have described: "A critical juncture was when I'd realized that some individual was considered an outsider by the philosophy I supported. It is a huge contradiction to share your summer plans with someone whom you completely respect only to realize that your ideology doesn't consider them a full member of society. I couldn't resolve that."[48]

Derek's former comrades thought the school had brainwashed him with liberal multicultural crap; his father considered his son's change a sort of Stockholm syndrome and thought he was identifying with his captors. I think it's the "contact hypothesis" in action—the contact triggering the cognitive dissonance. You hate what you don't know, and it's pretty likely that Derek had never met any of the people he hated, having been home-schooled and brought up in a racist bubble. "They" were always "them"—distant, stereotypic.

Path 3: Relationships as a Pathway Out

The confrontation with self is also often the result of the third pathway, which has to do with relationships. Sometimes it's a new romantic relationship, or a new understanding reached with a parent, but most often it's the experience of suddenly becoming a parent and realizing the sort of life you are setting up for your children to follow.

For several of the men, a relationship with a woman was the pathway out. As we've seen in previous chapters, women play a large role in the lives of white nationalist men, both in terms of ideology and as real presences. The white nationalist's view of women is deeply contradictory, but it is only an exaggerated version of the twin visions of women that you can find anywhere on the political spectrum in America, the pendulum simply swinging more dramatically between the "Madonna" (the angelic white woman who will produce, raise, and educate white babies and is therefore the savior of the race) and the "whore" (weaker and less worthy receptacles for men's sexual needs, and little else). "Machismo, control and order were on a higher list of priorities than respecting girls," T.J. writes.[49]

In her analysis of white supremacist literature, sociologist Jessie Daniels found these contradictory images often enabled women to be decisive elements of deradicalization. "Women"—the ideal as much as the reality—play important ideological roles in the lives of white nationalists. They are "glorious mothers" who are naturally maternal; "good whores," the objects of sexual desire; fragile damsels in distress, in need of protection from black rapists, Jewish feminists, and other predators who would do them harm; "bad whores," the race traitors who date black or Jewish men or who become feminists; and finally, "racial warriors," fighting alongside of, but always in support of, their men.[50]

Sociologist Randy Blazak's interviews with formers bear out these categories. He found that many women in different roles—mothers, wives, girlfriends, daughters—influenced guys' ability to get out and stay out. For some it was the women forcing the choice ("the movement or me") that pushed the guy to initiate the process of leaving. Some women addressed the psychological fallacy of racism; others provided a way back to long-suppressed feelings of compassion and empathy for the victims of skinhead hate. In other cases it was women's steadfast support and love that enabled the men to stay away long enough to put distance between themselves and the intoxicating high that belonging to a skinhead group gave them—creating a support system for a cold-turkey withdrawal.[51]

Two of Blazak's interviewees credit their mothers. One of them, Stan, said: "It was easy. She [his mother] gave me unconditional love. I had never experienced that before. Before that I was always angry and looking for someone to blame, someone to beat. Being a skin gave me an outlet. She loved the hate right out of me."[52] Ken, another interviewee, says it was first his wife, who just wouldn't put up with it any longer. In the beginning, she thought it was a joke, "like a bunch of macho guys getting drunk and shouting, 'white power!'" But when she gave him an ultimatum, they broke up—for a while. Then, he realized she was right and he left the movement for her. "Besides, I'd rather be with her than them any day," he told Blazak. When his daughter was born, that sealed the deal. "Like do I want her to be a breeder to some bonehead or do I want her to have her own life?"

Another of Blazak's interviewees credits his girlfriend, an Asian woman in the punk scene, for straightening him out: "Yeah, she kicked my ass. She was like, 'this shit is so bullshit!' I got the whole story about how she has to deal with racism and sexism every single day. All kinds of little things

I never even thought about. I thought whites had it so rough, but I had no idea. It's like I couldn't even see what was so obvious."[53] His girlfriend so turned him around that he actually went over to the other side and became an anti-racist skinhead, a SHARP (Skinhead Against Racial Prejudice).

Family can be crucial. Of course, many of the men had suffered terrible trauma at the hands of family members and so looked elsewhere for validation. But consistently, men credited their parents—especially their mothers—and siblings with leading them to reconsider extremist views. One former mentioned that his younger brother had always looked up to and modeled himself after him, and seeing the disillusionment in his younger brother's eyes when he started spouting racist and anti-Semitic rhetoric pushed him to rethink the road he was headed down.[54]

The key relationship can even range outside the family. One fifteen-year-old high school student who had become a skinhead talked about how a student teacher "saw" him, understood him: "It's too easy to just blame someone instead of looking at yourself. The conspiracy was like a drug. The hate definitely was a drug. It just kept building and building and she was the first person to say, 'look in the mirror at what you're doing to yourself.'"[55]

For Duke Schneider, the Brooklyn-based ex-neo-Nazi, the change began with the slow-dawning realization that the woman he loved and wanted to marry would not exactly fit within the confines of his ideology. That woman, Catherine Boone, you see, was black. They'd been friends for years, and when he faced a serious health problem, she was the one who was there for him. Catherine brought Duke to meet her pastor at a black church. There, Duke publicly confessed and renounced his former beliefs, and even went as far as posting wedding photos on his Facebook page. His former comrades were not pleased. Today he works as a security guard—at Jewish yeshiva schools and temples.[56]

For TJ, Frankie, Tony, and Christian, becoming a parent was also galvanizing. TJ writes:

> Like my father before me, I had a double standard about my behavior. My involvement in the Movement was perfectly acceptable, but I didn't want my children to do this. I wanted my children to be something more than what I was. I didn't want them to be ignorant tattooed racists. I wanted them to be presidents and senators and everything else caring parents genuinely

want for their kids. If they followed my path, there was no way they would ever be successful. They would end up dead, in jail, or bombing Federal buildings.[57]

(Reading this, I couldn't help but remember Don Vito Corleone in *The Godfather* saying the same thing about his son, Michael, how all he ever had wanted was for Michael to be the legitimate one, the one who wouldn't control the family, but rather be "Senator Corleone" or "President Corleone." History, however, often has other plans for those of us who continue to do what we do even while hoping that our children will somehow magically do it differently. It turns out that modeling often counts for more than hoping.)

Tony is a single dad of a son and a daughter, born fifteen months apart. "Having a child was a real pivot," he tells me. "As I was holding my beautiful newborn baby daughter her eyes opened and for the first time since my own childhood I felt connected to another human being," he wrote. Seeing his own children, and then trying to be a good parent, began a process of "heart thawing," as words like *love* and *compassion* were not directed at abstractions like "white people" or "my people," but toward two small, dependent beings who loved him and trusted him. "Being a parent changes your priorities, you know," he adds. "I needed to be present for them, which meant disengaging from the rest."[58]

Frankie, too, found that after a series of relationships were wrecked because of his activities, having kids pushed him to leave. His son is now twelve and his daughter is seven. "She makes my heart melt," he says.

Convergence

Often these paths converge. In fact, convergence is pretty much necessary if you're going to stay out of the movement. You need to have a precipitating moment to catalyze the choice to leave, and then you need all sorts of support to stay out.

Angela's pathway out of the movement began by following the first path, the external prod, as the Oklahoma City Bombing in 1995 pushed her to look in the mirror and begin that confrontation with self. She pulled back, pulled inward. She stopped calling friends, stopped hanging out with them. She thought she was getting out.

But she was wrong. She started getting threatening calls, and her apartment was strafed with bullets. Anti-racist skinheads were given her home address so they could beat her up. One of her former skinhead friends called her and said, "Hey, I just drove by your house and saw your baby brother." She stayed.

Finally, three years later, when she was involved in another abusive relationship, this time with a guy who was in the World Church of the Creator, her relationship facilitated another attempt at exiting. "It was equally abusive this time," she assures me. "I gave as good as I got." A night of partying got way out of hand, and she and four others ended up trashing a bar, beating a young woman senseless, and robbing an adult video store. "It seemed the perfect place," she says. "Debauchery and filth, probably owned by a Jew."

As she sat in jail after her arrest, she started to see things a bit differently. Prison, she tells me, "changed my life."

"First, I knew I had to get out if I wanted to live to see my next birthday," she says. "Second, I had to finally admit to myself that I was gay, and that all the abuse in my relationships was because I was really trying to be somewhere, someone, else."

But mostly, it was the other women in the prison. She met the people she was supposed to hate. Separated from her other skinhead friends, she had no choice but to interact with the largely minority prison population. For one thing, there was the woman in the cell next to Angela's in solitary confinement. (When Angela arrived at the federal detention center in Miami, she was placed immediately in solitary confinement for her first month.) She and the woman in that next cell talked through their air vents. The other woman was older, Hispanic. "What could she possibly have done [to deserve prison]?" Angela asked herself.

Ready to enter the general prison population, her neighbor asked her to deliver a message to someone named Heidi. "Just tell her I'm in here," she asked. Which she did, and was promptly welcomed by some of the toughest Latinas she'd ever met. Angela didn't know it, but her neighbor and friend in solitary was Griselda Blanco, the matriarch of perhaps the largest Colombian drug cartel, the woman also known as "La Madrina" (the Black Widow), "the Cocaine Godmother," and the "Queen of Narco-trafficking." (The biopic *The Godmother,* starring Catherine Zeta-Jones, offers a screen version of Blanco's life.)

Angela now felt accepted by women whom she had dedicated her life to hating. The feeling was unsettling, and never more so than with some of the black women in the prison yard. Jamaican women, they too had been drug runners and dealers. One woman in particular asked Angela if she knew how to play cribbage, and suddenly Angela had a new group of friends. Well, half a group. It turned out that all the women there knew that Angela had been arrested for hate crimes, and a few wouldn't talk to her. (Her new friend had spotted a newspaper floating around the day room featuring an article describing Angela's crime spree, and had hidden it so that others wouldn't see.)

She was more than a little surprised at how well she was treated by people she had spent most of her life hating. "They held me accountable for what I'd done, what I'd thought. They pushed me to see that my actions had real consequences. But they did it with such love and compassion. Really, they were the most forgiving and understanding people I'd ever met. They changed my life."

The cognitive dissonance made her feel as though her head was going to explode. Latina drug cartel members! Jamaican drug-running cribbage players!

One woman presented the mirror image of Angela's race hatred. She was "very, very dark-skinned," Angela says, "and she was, well, 'gorgeous.'" She admitted to Angela that she hated white people. "One day she told me that she had always hated white people because most of the white people she knew in Jamaica were people that came as tourists and treated the land and the people there like shit and like they were property," Angela told a journalist. "That was the majority of her experience with white peo-ple. I never, up to that point, had considered another side of it."[59] Like middle-school girls, they passed notes to each other. And when they were transferred to the federal correction center in Tallahassee, they arranged to be cellmates, which is where they became lovers.

It was Angela's mother's worst nightmare fantasy come true. A black person! And a woman! And it blew Angela's mind as well. Had her racism covered up her lesbianism? Was her lesbianism a way to expiate her former racism? Who knows. What Angela knows is that what she thought she believed was diametrically different from what she knew she felt now. And if these people were not her enemies, her old ideology was unsustainable. Now, what to do with all those tattoos?

Interestingly, it was that same healing confrontation with those T.J. Leyden had formerly victimized that began to turn his life around as well. That and his family. T.J.'s is also a story of convergence. Sure, he was getting older and the ideology just didn't have the same power anymore. And he'd begun to meet some of those very people he had always hated. But what started it was his relationship with his mother and his sons.

His first epiphany, that first click of self-confrontation, came when he was sitting on the sofa watching a multicultural children's TV show with his sons, and his younger son, then three years old, said "Daddy! We don't watch TV with niggers on it in the house!" At first, T.J. writes, he felt proud that his son was turning into a racist like his dad. But suddenly it started to unravel. "I hadn't been raised a racist and I turned out the way I was," he thought. "How much worse would my children be?" And then the penny dropped. "If I didn't want my children to grow up to be like me, there must be something fundamentally wrong with the whole premise and purpose of my life."[60]

First, T.J. went to his mother's home and apologized for the vicious, hateful words and actions he had brought into their home. She suggested— or, rather, insisted—that T.J. do this publicly. And so he gathered up his entire cache of racist materials, documents, and pamphlets and contacted the Simon Wiesenthal Center at the Museum of Tolerance in Los Angeles. They were "flabbergasted," but the rabbi agreed to meet with him, and made a simple proposition. The center would accept his "donation" if he agreed to go public and speak out, under its auspices, about the movement. "What was amazing was that for the first time in my life here was a group of individuals who honestly believed I could do good in the world. For the first time I experienced real compassion. In fact, the greatest compassion I've ever experienced is when I spoke at a synagogue and a Jewish Holocaust survivor came up to me and said they forgave me."[61]

These stories of convergence are important because they illustrate just how difficult it is to get out and to stay out. It requires some serious confrontation with some unusually painful truths. And your former friends aren't especially "understanding." T.J., for example, describes several failed attempts before he finally solidified his departure. He still gets death threats all the time. Entire websites are devoted to his demise. One of his former best friends, a singer in the racist band Extreme Hatred, even wrote a song about T.J. called "Race Traitor."

Tony realized that he needed something more than just comradely moral support. A friend talked him into going to a workshop run by Dov Baron, the famous psychologist whose best sellers combine quantum physics with spiritual enlightenment and psychological self-help to enable people to live more authentically engaged lives. Tony was skeptical, but intrigued.

Something in the workshop spoke to him, in the gut, powerfully. He went to meet Dov, and they bonded over quirky British humor and music. Lots of music. They both loved Monty Python. That was enough for Tony to reveal himself as a skinhead and a member of WAR.

"You know I was born Jewish, right?" said Dov.

"Uh, no," said Tony. He was still in Baron's thrall.

"Dov became my mentor," Tony told me. "He forced me to tell, publicly, my most shameful story. In a way, until you say it, you're going to be haunted by the fear that other people will find it out, and so you build a wall of defenses so no one can see you. And that's your armor."

Tony's exodus from the movement wasn't an overnight thing. Recently, Dov and Tony appeared together on stage for the first time in a United Nations–sponsored conversation about deradicalization and the power of spiritual and psychological reflection. In the Q&A, Dov was asked, "Who was this guy who walked into your office that day?"

"Well," Dov replied, "Tony had left the movement, but the movement hadn't yet left Tony."

He had more work to do. In retrospect, Tony remembers a series of painful conversations with himself. "Why, I asked myself," he recalls, "should I be like Don Quixote, fighting at windmills for white people who actually don't really give a shit about me?" Tony felt burnt out, exhausted, filled with a dark energy that brought him no joy. He began to drift away from the movement, relying on Baron's mentorship for both empathic support and to support implacable challenges. "The further away I got, the easier it got," Tony says.

There were some pivotal moments, too. Tony describes a scene in the powerful film *American History X* as Derek, played by Ed Norton, is starting to get out. In the scene, Derek is getting stitched up after a particularly nasty fight. Lying on his bed in prison, he's visited by Dr. Bob Sweeney (Avery Brooks) who is the principal of Derek's high school. "Derek," Dr. Sweeney asks, "has anything you've ever done made your life better?"

In the film, Derek starts to cry. "I cried the first time I saw that scene too," says Tony. Tony and Derek had the same answer.

LIFE WITH LIFE AFTER HATE

Many of the formers with whom I spoke lamented the lack of an organization they could turn to. It was easy to connect with the Aryan Brotherhood in most maximum security prisons, and drifting into the movement may even have been part of a survival strategy for young white inmates. Getting out is hard enough. What's really difficult is to do it alone. Where will you land? How will you survive, especially after the intense comradeship and community you've experienced, with brothers constantly validating your masculinity as a soldier for the race? What you will need is an alternative band of brothers.

What he needed was Life After Hate—the organization run by formers that helps people get out of the movement. Life After Hate doesn't have a building somewhere, nor is it part of an elaborate youth center like EXIT Sweden. It's not hidden in the backroom of an auto parts store like EXIT Deutschland. LAH lives on social media, as an idea, as a place in cyberspace where people can go for help and support without coercion, and without judgment about what they've done. Its motto, "No Judgment, Just Help," fits perfectly. Come to us, the staff say invitingly. We know what you're going through. We've been there ourselves.

Because white nationalists are scattered all over the place—in big cities and small towns, in densely crowded, impoverished worlds and in remote rural hamlets—they connect virtually, electronically. Life After Hate is the kind of organization the Internet was made for. After all, it's through the

Net that a lot of kids begin their journey into the movement: scared, lonely, and angry, they surf the Web, looking at all the cool pictures of guys just like them, feeling the intense brotherhood of the white gang. Why shouldn't the Internet be a vehicle to get guys out?

Sometimes the support community provides serious counseling. On their closed Facebook page, LAH members offer advice and support: how to stay safe, where to go for help, how to apologize to parents and friends whom you've hurt.

Sometimes the advice is really mundane. Where can I go to get some of these tattoos removed? "Christ," says Bob, a former from Oakland. "I had a fucking swastika on my forehead! OK, yeah, what was I thinking, right? I was thinking that this would make me the scariest motherfucker around. I was thinking that everyone would notice me now. I wasn't invisible!" Except now he wanted to shed his skin and blend back into the crowd.

"We want to create a community of formers," Christian tells me. The idea is that, having gone in lonely and found brotherhood, now they're scared that if they leave, they'll be lonely again. "We offer a 'benevolent gang,' a community, a new brotherhood. They're not alone. They're supported. They're still somebody—in fact, they're somebody better."

Institutional and structural changes in the broader society would go a long way toward helping men leave extremist movements, to the extent that they would undergird the emotional and psychological support that the guys get from formers in LAH. To be sure, enacting more liberal political and economic policies would be a good start: reducing the gigantic differential between the haves, the have-nots, and the have-mores would prevent many men from entering the movement and would incentivize those inside to leave. Jump-starting infrastructure redevelopment, putting contractors and construction crews to work building bridges and roads rather than McMansions, would also go a long way. Yes, fuller employment, health care, and higher-quality education are also vital steps toward bringing these guys back from the paranoid precipice. And former president Barack Obama's plan to make community college free for everyone might have provided another possible off-ramp from the hollow "purpose" of saving one's race—and opened up opportunities to make a living, support a family, and buy into the system.

But economic policies don't automatically trickle down to the individual psyche. Each man must find his own way out, and that often means finding alternate ways to feel like a man. One doesn't return from gendered humiliations through academic lessons in global political economy.

If men feel insignificant, they have to find an alternative way of feeling like they matter, like they are somebody—through a job, education, family, relationships. Much of the sense of one's personal significance has to do with making personal connections of the sort that each of the founders described to me. A connection with a former victim or with a member of a formerly hated group. For example, Frankie and the Jewish antique dealer who gave him a job, trusted him, and shared a love of hockey and especially the Flyers. Angela and those Jamaican women in prison who showed her more compassion than she had ever shown herself.

So LAH has to be creative in coming up with ways they can help others make that connection that they were given. Some guy will call Frankie up, he tells me, and he'll ask what the guy still hates, "because like no one jumps, like, completely clean. So they'll still use the N-word or *kike* or whatever. And I'll think of a way to challenge that." Frankie has developed a gradual-intervention strategy for helping guys get out. He brings people together who share some common interest, lets them bond for a while, and then intervenes to make them uncomfortable, forcing them into a situation of cognitive dissonance they have to resolve.

He tells me, for example, about the "day of interventions" he planned for Donald. Donald was a young guy, only about sixteen, who saw being a neo-Nazi skinhead as being a rebel—a way to express his nonconformity. He'd drawn swastikas on his schoolbooks. Frankie decided to make that particularly uncomfortable for him. Donald was into video games, and the first thing Frankie did was take him to visit a local rabbi, who also happened to be a gamer. "They talked about games for like twenty minutes," Frankie tells me. They got along great, loosened up, developed some rapport. Then Frankie interrupted them. "I asked the rabbi what he thought about the swastikas," he tells me.

There was a silence. They both looked really uncomfortable. "They remind me of when everything in the world was taken away from us, my identity, my life," the rabbi said. "They're not a joke, not a fashion statement." Donald listened.

Next stop was a tattoo parlor where the books of patterns all had "sold out" on the images of swastikas. "Not really," the parlor owner told them. "We just won't do them."

And the final stop was a nursing home where Donald met two Holocaust survivors. It was the same process: Donald and the two octogenarians sat talking quietly, having a good time, bonding like grandparent and grandson. "He really liked these two old people," Frankie recalls. Then he jumped in. "When I asked one of the survivors how he felt about those swastikas, he got so angry, he was literally violently shaking with rage. 'What do the swastikas mean?' the old man said. 'They mean that they took everything, destroyed everything, took my sister, my family,'" he stammered with rage.

Two months later, Frankie ran into Donald in the stands at a hockey game. He was out of the movement, with new notebooks and schoolbooks and a repainted car. No swastikas to be found. A few days later, Frankie ran into Donald's mom. "Those survivors, they had a real impact on Donald," she told Frankie. "He was really shaken by how angry they were still, how much the pain never goes away."

In another intervention, a local white man told Frankie that he is completely racist and hates black people. But he also loves a particular sports team. Frankie introduces the white man to a black friend of his who also happens to be a rabid fan of the same team. Frankie lets them talk. Then he springs his question on them, makes them uncomfortable after they've forged some human connection, some rapport. His strategy is to always ask the marginalized person—the black guy, the Jew—how the racist statement or symbol makes *them* feel. In other words, the experience of the marginalized person is prioritized, given a voice. The LAH client has to listen, has to take in how this *person*, this human being, not some abstraction or statistic, feels.

Frankie tells me of an older white guy he knew, a stone-cold racist. "His sixteen-year-old daughter was giving him all kinds of grief," Frankie says. She was drinking and partying, hanging up on him when he called to check up on her, staying out way too late. The man was worried, angry, anxious. Frankie decided to introduce him to another father with a fifteen-year-old daughter who was giving her father the same sort of grief. This dad was black.

"These two guys start talking about their daughters, how they are impossible," Frankie recalls. "The two of them start bonding about how it's all their daughters' fault, how they were good dads, and how 'kids these days' are just so irresponsible and sassy." The conversation continued, "and they actually became friends. Completely bonded over their shared parental misery." At this point, the story gets even better. It turns out that the white father's racism was one of the causes of his daughter's acting out. She was so embarrassed by her father, and so angry at him for his racist views, that her teenage rebellion became fused with political defiance, and his racism gave him no credibility to reach out to her. "It turned out really well," Frankie tells me. "The white guy and his daughter began to get a bit closer because the father wasn't so racist anymore, and in her eyes that gave her all the more reason to listen to him."

Frankie's process is organic, and it develops over time, replicating his own and others' experiences. Hatred most often arises from, or is at least abetted by, ignorance. How can you say that Jews are not money-grubbing, power-hungry, insidious manipulators if you've never met one? How can you say that black men are not violent animals keen on raping white women if you've never even talked to a black man? Without concrete evidence to contradict the prevailing stereotype, hatred can swell.

Perhaps most important, organizations like LAH have to provide an alternate route to manhood. "These guys felt like nothing, like they'd been kicked to the curb and left for dead—insignificant," explained Joey, one of the actives I met while researching *Angry White Men*. He was active in the movement then, he told me, but not for much longer. "Then suddenly they are men, real men, you know, 'a man among men' type of thing. They— well, I guess I mean 'we'—suddenly feel like we matter, like we are somebody, and we mistake fear and disgust for admiration and respect."

If LAH is going to succeed with its exit program, it has to offer a new way to prove masculinity, a way for these guys to reproduce the feelings they had in the movement while remaining out of it.

Successfully leaving the movement also requires the cultivation of emotions that these guys have spent so much time trying to suppress. Most of them never saw those emotions modeled while they were growing up,

Figure 16. The founders of Life After Hate relax in a hotel room in Seattle, 2016.
Clockwise from left: Sammy Rangel (seated on bed), Frankie Meeink, (lying on bed),
Tony McAleer (seated in chair), Angela King (seated at desk), and Christian Picciolini
(seated on floor, leaning against bed). Photo courtesy of Life After Hate.

and they also were not recipients of actions like forgiveness. The hardest
thing, Tony tells me, is that "we have to forgive ourselves for what we've
done."

"Sounds a little like you're avoiding accountability," I say, "like a TRC
[truth and reconciliation commission] that puts the forgiveness before
the confession."

"I know it sounds self-serving," he says, "but I have to have compassion
and forgiveness for myself if I am to reduce my capacity to do violence in
the world."

That's what Frankie said as well, that every day he makes a choice not
to do harm. For him now, it's a matter of empathy—not empathy as a qual-
ity you can acquire one time and then possess—but empathy as a process,
something that you renew every single day. "I had compassion for others

when I was little," he says. "But I let it go. I gave up my compassion for acceptance. But that acceptance was a fraud, a front. There's really no such thing as acceptance without compassion. The foundation is always empathy. Always."

Compassion. Empathy. The foundations of a new way to be a man, as well. Frankie shares with me how his views of what makes a man a man have changed:

> When I was younger, hanging out in my dad's bar, those were hard guys, you know. Hard guys were guys who knew how to punch and take a punch, and they drank hard, played hard. Some of my friends' dads, though, they were the guys who like were always there to pick up the kids, talk to them, ask them how their day was going, go to their sports games and shit like that. We thought those dads were like the lamest guys in the neighborhood.

He pauses for a few seconds. Long enough. It's happening here, in our conversation, right this moment, the revisioning of what makes a man. "But actually," he says, somewhat quietly, "those are the *real* 'hard guys,' the guys who do the boring business of being a man."

POSTSCRIPT, SUMMER 2017

In September 2016, Life After Hate received a $400,000 grant from the Countering Violent Extremism grant program, sponsored by the U.S. Department of Homeland Security. LAH proposed to develop and implement a program in the United States modeled after the EXIT program in Sweden. EXIT USA would provide psychological services as well as outreach to extremists using a tool developed by a software company. (Potential clients would have included ISIS-inspired jihadists as well as violent white supremacists.) More than that, the program was going to provide a physical, face-to-face community to go along with the virtual community created online. In June 2017, as this book was going to press, Life After Hate received word that the grant had been canceled because the Trump administration had decided that all government funding would be used exclusively for addressing "radical Islamic fundamentalism," and that domestic terrorism was simply not a threat worth combatting. This ideological rigidity to xenophobic nationalism has actually blinded the administration to the significant danger posed by domestic terror from the extreme right. Indeed, one is far more likely to be attacked or killed by a right-wing extremist than by an Islamic terrorist. Life After Hate is currently attempting to appeal this decision.

◆

Mubin

UNDERCOVER JIHADIST

•

The plan was elaborate. The holy month of Ramadan, 2006. Several cars, loaded with fertilizer bombs, would explode simultaneously in downtown Toronto, killing as many shoppers, office workers, and pedestrians as possible, and drawing the police from all over the city. The distraction would mobilize the national police, who would rush to Toronto. On those streets the police might be met by several suicide bombers who would martyr themselves as they killed the police.

Meanwhile, three hundred miles away in Ottawa, bombs would explode at the headquarters of the Canadian Broadcasting Service, the Canadian Security Intelligence Service (CSIS), and the Parliamentary Peace Tower. Then the assault on Parliament Hill would begin, as the jihadists entered the Parliament building and captured the prime minister and as many MPs as possible. They'd behead them right there, on camera, the video to be posted on the Internet, as gruesome inspiration to young Muslim men all over the world. Canada would suffer its worst terrorist attack in its history, perhaps the worst terrorist attack ever in any OECD country. Canada would thus be made to pay for its support of the American-led war against Afghanistan.

Grandiose, yes, and ambitious—but the plans were in place. Except it didn't quite come off as planned. On June 2, 2006, just four months before the planned attack, more than four hundred members of the Royal Canadian Mounted Police (RCMP), Canadian security forces, and local police fanned across the city of Toronto and arrested fifteen young Muslim men on suspicion of terrorism. Two others were already in jail awaiting trial on gun-smuggling charges, and another was arrested a month later, after the police sorted out his identity.

The elaborate plans of the cell that became known as the Toronto 18 were foiled because they'd been infiltrated by a police informant named Mubin Shaikh. Just five years earlier, on the morning of September 11, 2001, Mubin had been sitting in his apartment in Toronto when the news of the terrorist attack came over the television. "Allah Akhbar!" he said to himself. God is great. "Finally the U.S. gets what it deserves!"[1]

How did this man, trained as a jihadist in Syria and Afghanistan, come to thwart Canada's most dangerous terrorist plot? What roads did he travel down to get to that world of messianic jihadism? And what roads did he travel back to transform his Manichean worldview into one that embraced peace and holiness?

One road seems fairly straightforward: the road in. Mubin came from a stable religious family in Toronto. His father, an immigrant from India, was an electronics engineer for the Canadian Telecommunications Company. His family was close, affectionate, but his parents were very strict. He was pulled in two directions, as are so many children of immigrants: between adapting to the carefree, secular world of sex and drugs and non-Muslim friends in an utterly modern Western society, and sticking with the traditional values of one's family. Often this is expressed in language: the child speaks slang English with his friends on the street, and the language of the old country (Italian, Hindi, Yiddish) with his family and relatives. Secular versus religious: girls to dance with, to hang out with, to have sex with, versus the abstinent sex segregation of the mosque or temple.

For a time, Mubin excelled at both, navigating with strategic efficiency the boundaries of each world, attending the mosque and madras, and also going to public school and partying with his friends (who nicknamed him "Moonbeam.") But Mubin also hid a shameful secret—and there was no one to whom he could turn to talk about it. As a young boy, his uncle had sexually abused him. Confused, upset, traumatized, he confessed to his mother. She refused to listen. "You must forget it ever happened," she told him. Both of his mother's brothers, both uncles, also sexually abused Mubin's younger sister, Fatima, and Mubin's shame was doubled that he was unable to protect her.[2]

Why did his uncle abuse them? Was this common among Muslims, in which case he could just repudiate Islam and immerse himself in the secular world? Or was this an aberration, or, even worse, had he done anything to invite it, in which case perhaps he could be cleansed and the horror forgotten if he just redoubled his religious commitment, prayed harder, longer, and with more fervor. He studied hard, committed the Qur'an to memory in Arabic (though he didn't understand what the words meant), and became devout.

(It turns out such within-family abuse is far more common than one might think. There's widespread rape of boys by warlords, members of the Afghan National Army, and by the Afghan police—so common, in fact, that it has its own name. Thursday is colloquially known as "man-loving day" because such rapes and sexual abuse are so common on Thursdays; Friday prayers are believed to absolve sinners of all their sins.)

At the same time, Mubin also continued to hang out with his friends from school. They drank, took drugs, partied. He worked out a lot, built his body, and was known around town as a "scrapper," someone not to be messed with. While in high school, he joined the Royal Canadian Army Cadets. He took to the camping, hiking, and drills with gusto. And it was on one of the cadets' camping retreats that a young woman snuck into his tent and he had sex for the first time. (He was disciplined for it, but not kicked out, because he was such an otherwise exemplary cadet.) He also came to really love cocaine. It made him feel "confident and empowered," as if he was king.[3]

He went a bit too far. His parents' departure on a trip provided the occasion for a wild party at Mubin's house, which was largely trashed by the drunk and stoned revelers. His uncles arrived and shut it down, and Mubin was disciplined by his enraged and disappointed father. It was then that he decided that if he were ever going to be "good," he had to forsake his secular world entirely and immerse himself in Islam. He signed up to travel with Tablighi Jamaat, a religious society designed to connect Muslims with traditional Islamic cultures and religious teachings. While unaffiliated with any particular sect (Mubin himself is Sunni), the group sponsors trips to the Middle East and elsewhere to enable young Muslims to meet and interact with other young Muslim men in a search for a grounded religious identity. "They will be my conduit to rehabilitation!" he thought. "They will fix me! And that will make my parents happy—because I am clearly broken."[4]

Mubin came to the United States and Britain and traveled with the group to Pakistan and India. In Quetta, the capital of Balochistan Province in Pakistan, he met with Taliban leaders just before they crossed the border into Afghanistan and began their reconquest of that formerly occupied country. These were the men he came to admire, who fused their faith with a militaristic ferocity as freedom fighters. "Look at these guys! They are warriors!" he thought to himself as the mujahideen came into the mosque with their guns slung over their shoulders, laid them down, and began their prayers. They were everything Mubin had always wanted to be: "prayerful, prepared, and fierce warriors walking in the path of Allah." They were, he thought, "the pinnacles of male religious fulfillment." What perfect role models for this "naïve, brown, Muslim man, searching for his way out of shame into honor." He was hooked on political Islam.[5]

After a two-year stint in Syria training in religious law, Mubin moved back to Canada and became active with an organization trying to insert traditional Muslim religious and cultural practices into the Muslim community. He became a conflict mediator, attempting to use Sharia law as a method of conflict resolution in the Muslim community. When public exposure shut that practice down, Mubin was further radicalized.

Radicalization is a process, a process of exposing humiliations and seeking to heal from the trauma of those humiliations. Mubin's earlier sexual abuse was humiliating, and his "failure" as a man to stop the abuse of his younger sister was even more humiliating. He tried to swallow the pain, exacerbated by his mother's denial, and submerge himself in prayer and in increasingly radical Islam. And that radical version of Islam is itself based on humiliation: the theft of land by the West, the invasion by the Russians, the invasions by the Americans, the Israeli land grab in the settlements. All these are cast within the radical Islamic community not simply as culturally humiliating, which they are, but also as a specifically gendered type of humiliation, the emasculation of Muslim men. "Muslims are persecuted here and the world over," said one his future coconspirators in the Toronto 18.

Radicalized, yes, but he was also growing disenchanted with the militant faux-jihadists living in Toronto. He now read Arabic fluently, and read all of the Qur'an, not just the decontextualized parts about infidels and jihad. He realized that many of the most militant jihadists knew little of the holy book, save for a few snippets taken out of context. He saw that the leaders would "cherry-pick scriptures in order to justify and brainwash their students into their worldview and dedication to militant jihad."[6]

And he was quite sure that life for Muslims in Canada was actually a whole lot better than life in Syria, where people could be snatched off the street in front of a mosque never to be seen again. He began to feel that the West might not be the enemy after all, and to be convinced that tolerance and freedom were values worth living for.

Increasingly radical and also increasingly disillusioned with the deliberate distortions of the actual scripture, Mubin felt himself stuck again. But when he heard of the arrest of a childhood friend in 2004, his world came unglued. He saw where this path was heading and he wanted no part of the violent extremism espoused by others. He jumped—into the arms of the Canadian Security Intelligence Service.

He knew that something big was in the works, that a bunch of young guys from the mosque were planning a jihadi strike in Toronto and elsewhere in Canada. They were a motley group, young boys who were in shock and pain from family trauma, along with slightly older men in their mid-twenties who felt they needed to do something, something big, to be seen in the world. It was planned for Ramadan, between September and October 2006. "I'll be sitting in the Speaker's Chair in the Commons Chamber and demand that Canadians embrace Islam," mused Fahim, one of the conspirators. "With all that publicity, it will spark an uprising of Muslims and result in guerilla warfare here—just like in Chechnya! I can see it now!" The Toronto 18 is the largest anti-government terrorist conspiracy in Canadian history to date. But, little did the conspirators know, Mubin had already agreed to infiltrate the cell and inform on its activities, first to the CSIS and later to the RCMP, the force that took over the investigation after the group had secured weapons and enough fertilizer to blow up most of downtown Toronto (a few tons more than Timothy McVeigh used in Oklahoma City). He had real experience with guns, and so Mubin trained them in munitions in the middle of the Ontario woods, and even arranged for the delivery of the fertilizer for the bombs. (The fertilizer was fake, and there was no chance that anything would ever explode.) The conspirators also prepared by watching clandestine videos of jihadists beheading captured enemies, cheering when blood spurted from the victim's necks. "It was like watching jihadi porn," Mubin remembers. "It was a visceral thrill."

The ruse worked long enough for the group to become activated and to begin its countdown to the actual event. That's when Mubin told the RCMP and combined security forces about the plot.

The trials of the Toronto 18 began in June 2010. Mubin was the government's primary fact witness. Sentences were handed down that December. Seven pleaded guilty, including the two ringleaders, Fahim Ahmad (sentenced to six years) and Zakaria Amara (who received a life sentence and revocation of citizenship). Five received sentences of up to twenty years. Three adults and one youth who pleaded not guilty were also convicted and sentenced to between six and a half years to life. (The youth was sentenced to two and a half years.) Six had their sentences stayed or were found not guilty. It was the single largest terrorist trial in Canadian history.

Today, Mubin and his father have developed some strategies to help young impressionable jihadi wannabes get out of the movement, or to prevent them from joining in the first place. Much of this program consists of helping them understand the meaning of those canonical texts that are misquoted or decontextualized by the jihadist recruiters. And some parts consist of a sort of Islamic pastoral counseling, differentiating between the anger or pain that has arisen from family trauma or personal issues, and the larger political contexts of Islamic victimization. Mubin is often engaged with young men in the Arab world, offering support and a knowledge that there is an alternative. He's been there; he knows. He knows that picking up a gun and becoming a martyr is not a route to resolving your pain; it's only a path to denying the pain and thereby disconnecting from yourself. It is a sign of weakness to pick up a gun to defend the faith. It takes far more strength to look in the mirror and acknowledge your pain, and more courage still to forgive yourself.

5 Britain: The Ex-jihadists Next Door

> What America is tasting now, is something insignificant
> compared to what we have tasted for scores of years. Our
> nation [the Islamic world] has been tasting this humilia-
> tion and this degradation for more than 80 years. Its sons
> are killed, its blood is shed, its sanctuaries are attacked, and
> no one hears and no one heeds.
>
> Osama bin Laden, October 7, 2001[1]

The suburbs of Antwerp, Belgium, hardly seem a breeding ground for jihad. Yet, since the outbreak of the Syrian Civil War in 2011, more than four thousand Europeans have gone to Syria to join ISIS or Al Qaeda: 400 from Belgium alone, more than 850 from the United Kingdom, more than 135 from Denmark, and 220 from the Netherlands; and more than one hundred Americans.[2]

They're largely disaffected Muslim teenagers, living, for example, in the *banlieux* of Paris, where they are likely to be unemployed youth cast off by an indifferent French state; or living in the impoverished inner-city neighborhoods of Molenbeek in Brussels or Borgerhout in Antwerp; or living in dank and depressed urban enclaves in Bradford or Manchester, the brackish eddies of globalization. To the global elite, the free movement of labor mirrors the free movement of capital and goods. Their parents may have been economic migrants coming to work in Europe; their children are seen as economic detritus, ready to return to reclaim their nonnative homelands.

In that respect, they resemble their martyred heroes very little. The actual 9/11 terrorists were their predecessors in martyrdom, yes, but they were about twenty years older and belonged to that first generation, the ones who were well trained in engineering or technology, but found jobs far below their training and sense of entitlement.

That earlier generation of jihadists, from suicide bombers to the 9/11 terrorists, were largely well-educated middle-class sons of upwardly mobile families. When journalist Nasra Hassan interviewed the families of Middle Eastern suicide bombers, she found "none of them were uneducated, desperately poor, simple minded or depressed"—the standard motivations ascribed to those who become suicide bombers.

Although several of the leaders of Al Qaeda were wealthy—Osama bin Laden was a millionaire's son, and Ayman al-Zawahiri was a physician from a fashionable suburb of Cairo—many of the 9/11 hijackers were engineering students, fully one-fourth. Job opportunities had been dwindling dramatically for engineering grads. Kamel Daoudi studied computer science at a university in Paris; Zacarias Moussaoui, who did not hijack one of the planes but was the first man to be formally charged with a crime in the United States for the events of September 11, took a degree at London's South Bank University. Marwan al-Shehhi, a chubby, bespectacled twenty-three-year-old from the United Arab Emirates, was an engineering student, while Ziad Jarrah, a twenty-six-year-old Lebanese, had studied aircraft design.

The same was true for the mujahideen in the Afghan war against the Soviet Union. (The term came originally from that struggle, but now refers to pretty much any Islamist who believes himself to be engaged in jihad.) Marc Sageman's survey found that of the 102 mujahideen he surveyed, 18 were from the upper class, 56 were middle-class, and 28 were lower-class. In a larger sample, only 17 percent had not graduated from high school, while 29 percent had gone to college, another 33 percent had a college degree, and another 9 percent had either the equivalent of a master's degree or a doctorate. It was not poverty—or at least not poverty alone—that drove them to their initial declaration of war against the West. Nor was it an individual traumatic event in their lives; it was, Sageman argues, more a "collective trauma," the sustained humiliation of globalization and secularism. It was choked economic possibilities, coupled with a kind of cultural disdain that these fighters rightly perceived coming from Western nations, a disdain that was the humiliating spark, the insult that required avenging. Imagine these *kuffar* (nonbelievers), these *jahili* [non-Muslim] societies, holding us in contempt! We must make them pay for their arrogance.[3]

Politically, these terrorists opposed globalization and the spread of Western values, and opposed what they perceived as corrupt regimes in several Arab states (notably Saudi Arabia and Egypt), which they claimed were merely puppets of US domination. Central to their political ideology was the recovery of manhood from the devastatingly emasculating politics of globalization. The Taliban saw the Soviet invasion and Westernization as humiliations. Osama bin Laden's October 7 videotape, from which I've drawn the epigraph for this chapter, describes the "humiliation and disgrace" that Islam has suffered for "more than eighty years." And over and over, Nasra Hassan writes, she heard the refrain "The Israelis humiliate us. They occupy our land and deny our history."[4]

Terrorism is fueled by a toxic brew of anti-globalization politics, convoluted Islamic theology, and virulent misogyny—and a need for masculine validation, a need to claim, or reclaim, some legitimate status as a man. According to Barbara Ehrenreich, while these formerly employed or self-employed males "have lost their traditional status as farmers and breadwinners, women have been entering the market economy and gaining the marginal independence conferred even by a paltry wage." As a result, "the man who can no longer make a living, who has to depend on his wife's earnings, can watch Hollywood sexpots on pirated videos and begin to think the world has been turned upside down."[5]

In Afghanistan, the Taliban's policies had two purposes: to remasculinize men and to refeminize women. Journalist Peter Marsden has observed that those policies "could be seen as a desperate attempt to keep out that other world, and to protect Afghan women from influences that could weaken the society from within." The Taliban prohibited women from appearing in public unescorted by men, from revealing any part of their body in public, and from going to school or holding a job. Men were required to grow their beards, in accordance with religious images of Muhammad, yes—but also, perhaps, because wearing beards has always been associated with men's response to women's increased equality in the public sphere, since beards symbolically reaffirm natural biological differences between women and men, while gender equality tends to blur those differences.[6]

The Taliban's policies removed women as competitors and also shored up masculinity, by enabling men to triumph over the humiliations of globalization and to triumph over the savage, predatory, and violent sexual urges they believed would be unleashed in them in the presence of uncovered women.

All across the landscape of what President Donald Trump has insisted be collectively called "radical Islamic terrorism," there are significant differences in tactics and ideology, distinctions that may be too subtle for a blanket nationalist condemnation. But on gender issues, these disparate groups appear pretty similar: global economic conditions produce a "crisis" of masculinity, a new anxiety among men about their ability to claim their entitlement to be productive and respected workers in public and unquestioned patriarchs at home. With employment more precarious, their children gradually escaping complete parental control in schools, and their wives entering the marketplace, where they develop alternative poles around which their social lives might revolve, a sense of "aggrieved entitlement" grows within them, a sense of humiliation at not being enough of a "real man."

This dynamic can be seen in perfect microcosmic detail in the life and death of Mohamed Atta, the presumed leader of the 9/11 hijackers. He was slim as a boy, sweet-faced, neat, meticulous, a snazzy dresser. The youngest child of an ambitious lawyer father and pampering mother, Atta grew up shy and polite, a mama's boy. "He was so gentle," his father said. "I used to tell him, 'Toughen up, boy!'"[7]

He didn't. While his two sisters both became doctors—one a physician and the other a university professor—it was Mohamed who got the attention of his punitive father, who constantly reminded him that he wanted "to hear the word 'doctor' in front of his name. We told him your sisters are doctors and their husbands are doctors and you are the man of the family." The humiliation.

Atta decided to become an engineer, but his "degree meant little in a country where thousands of college graduates were unable to find good jobs." After he failed to find employment in Egypt, he went to Hamburg, Germany, to study architecture. He was "meticulous, disciplined and highly intelligent," an "ordinary student, a quiet friendly guy who was totally focused on his studies," according to another student in Hamburg.

But his ambitions were constantly undone. His only hope for a good job in Egypt was to be hired by an international firm. He applied but was rejected every time. He finally found work as a draftsman—humiliating work for someone with engineering and architectural credentials and an imperious and demanding father—at a German firm involved with razing lower-income Cairo neighborhoods to provide more scenic vistas for luxury tourist hotels perched on the tops of nearby hills.

Defeated, humiliated, emasculated, a disappointment to his father and a failed rival to his sisters, Atta retreated into increasingly militant Islamic theology. By the time he assumed controls of American Airlines Flight 11, he evinced genuine hysteria about women. In the message he left in his abandoned rental car, he made clear what mattered to him in the end. "I don't want pregnant women or a person who is not clean to come and say good-bye to me," he wrote. "I don't want women to go to my funeral or later to my grave." Interesting fantasy, since Atta's body was instantly incinerated in the crash, and no burial would be likely.

The terrors of emasculation experienced by lower-middle-class men all over the world will no doubt continue as they struggle to make a place for themselves in shrinking economies and shifting cultures. They may continue to feel a seething resentment against women, whom they perceive as stealing their rightful place at the head of the table, and against the governments that displace them. Globalization to them feels like a game of musical chairs in which, when the music stops, all the seats are handed to others by nursemaid governments. Today, every major city in Europe and many in the United States have become breeding grounds for Islamism because extremist theologies allow these young men to reconcile the contradictory experiences of being a young Muslim man in a strange and inhospitable land.

Yet, if this were simply a problem of disaffected youth, you'd expect there to be millions of jihadists, not just hundreds or perhaps a few thousand. The reality is that most young British Muslims find a way to manage despite the racism they face, much the way that African Americans and other people of color do in the United States. They don't pick up arms; they pick up a university degree and try to make a life.

In an interestingly counterintuitive study, sociologist Charles Kurzman asks the apposite question: not why are there so many disaffected youth who become jihadists—that's pretty evident—but rather, in a world with more than a billion Muslims, why so few actually sign up.[8] Kurzman argues that the vision of the Islamists is not, as they proclaim, to replace modernity with an eighth-century caliphate, but rather to "Islamicize modernity," that is, to amend modernity with Islamic ideas. They do not want to do away with modernity, not at all. They want to infuse it with traditional Islamist values.

For example, he observes, Islamists believe in many modern ideas. They do not embrace the fine-tuned differentiation among social strata of bygone Islamic eras, but rather assert the entirely modernist idea of global equality among all Muslims. They say they hate democracy, but they embrace one of democracy's core values: equality of citizens. No great historical Islamic figure, Kurzman reminds us, would ever have endorsed the notion that kings and commoners were all equal souls. This is an entirely modern idea into which Islamists inject a traditional erasure of class before God. Actually, he argues, what the jihadists fear most is the converse: modernizing Islam. They cannot abide the idea that Islam and modernity are compatible, or that Islamic ideas can easily coexist within a multicultural, gender-integrated society.

The route to Islamism is somewhat different from the route to neo-Nazism among Swedish youth or among white nationalists in the United States. As this chapter shows, young Muslims don't get into extremism because of awesome parties, drinking, or sex. In fact, they get in so that they can *avoid* parties and drinking—and especially sex. They seek spiritual solace from Western amorality, and find it in scripture and in spiritual devotion. They are the only group on the extremist landscape for whom cognitive encounters with texts is an entry point. This is a key difference—and it implies that efforts to deradicalize them should take a different form among jihadists than it does among white nationalists and neo-Nazis in Germany, Sweden, and the United States. On the other hand, there is a signal commonality: just as surely as the white nationalists and neo-Nazis, jihadists are set up for a religious and cognitive deepening of their faith by a series of specifically gendered experiences of shame and humiliation—that is, like the other groups profiled in this book, they seek redemption *as men* in a world that denies them their manhood.

Who are these everyday neighborhood jihadists? How do they get in? What attracts them to violent jihad against the very countries in which they are living? And how can they get out? *Can* they even get out? There are stories of parents rescuing their errant sons in Turkish towns that line the border with Syria, extracting their impressionable sons from training camps run by ISIS or Al Qaeda. And there are horrific stories of their sons fighting back, even killing their parents. There are so many anguished mothers whose sons have left their comfortable middle-class homes in Britain, Canada, and Continental European countries that they have formed a global support group. This chapter travels to London, with a brief stop in Toronto, to talk with ex-jihadists, many of whom are getting out through the work of an organization that, like EXIT and LAH, mobilizes formers to extricate themselves from Islamism.

GETTING IN

At first glance, European jihadists may look identical to the guys who get into extremist right-wing politics in the United States or Europe. They're young—the average age for those who are exiting the movement is about twenty-five—and they're male, about 90 percent. Virtually all have stories of feeling isolated, and some add on being bullied in school. Central to their experience is that they feel they don't belong.

In many respects, they're right. They don't belong. They don't belong in a country where they are constantly reminded that they're different. Ed Husain says he was "British by birth, Asian by descent, and Muslim by conviction." He certainly did not to fit in anywhere.[9] At least the neo-Nazis feel that their country is "their country," even if they also feel it is going down the toilet or that all the goodies are being given to "others." The young Muslims in Europe feel as if they've landed in that toilet, or worse, that others think that they *are* that toilet.

At the same time, most grow up in stable, middle-class families, in which they are pressured by their families and extended communities to hold fast to all the traditions imported from their home country. Most of the ex-jihadists I spoke with did not come from violent or abusive families.

Some did, to be sure. But their stable, middle-class immigrant families also were extremely controlling, anti-assimilationist, families caught between the cosmopolitan hedonism of the West and the strict traditionalism of their former countries. The boys, especially, found their parents overcontrolling, insisting that their sons pray five times a day and go to mosque, and forbidding them to hang out with girls, or even meet with them in public. In fact, if they entered a place where there were girls, they had to leave immediately. Sex was out of the question. They could not smoke, drink, or violate tradition in any way. And they were expressly prohibited from listening to any of "that" music, which is to say, any music that might be popular among other British teenagers.

"Perhaps my relatives back home were doing the same thing," says Ali, now twenty-seven, who was radicalized and ready to fly from London to Istanbul, there to continue by van, car, and foot into Iraq. (His family, with the Quilliam Foundation's help, got him to delay the trip, and eventually changed his mind about going. Quilliam is the organization that works with jihadists to get out of the movement, the Islamist counterpart of EXIT and Life After Hate.) "But here in London it just seemed ridiculous. We were British now, and we guys wanted to bust out and be British, you know. We wanted to party, and listen to music and, well, can I say it? Get laid! We were teenage boys, and we wanted to act like teenage boys, not like clerics or monks!"

"These guys just want girls," says Alyas Karmani, a former jihadist, now an imam in Bradford in West Yorkshire. He was filmed by Deeyah Khan for her stunning documentary film, *Jihad: A British Story*. "But they feel like they are nothing, not good looking, not rich, have nothing to offer. But then they join up and they carry around a big rifle and they feel proud and they say, 'look at me!' And the girls look."

The young Muslim men feel trapped between tradition and modernity. Their families prohibit them from assimilating, from acting like "normal" teenagers where they are living now. And even if their families did allow it, the natives of those countries wouldn't let them assimilate. They're just teenagers, you know? But acting like "just teenagers" means they'll be hated by both white people—who want them gone—and by other brown people, who want them to remain true to their families. "It was a triple whammy," says Usama Hasan, a former Islamist and one of the founders of Quilliam. "We'd moved from East to West, from rural to urban, and from religious to secular. We had no idea where we fit."

"We were young, Muslim, studious and London-born," writes Ed Husain, who drifted into Islamism as a way to reconcile these tensions. "We were not immigrants and [did not understand] the mentality of our peers who reminisced about their villages in Bangladesh." Husain continues: "The mainstream British lifestyle of dating, premarital sex, living together, and dissolution of partnerships with comparatively little fuss was not something that appealed to us. Simultaneously, the customs of our parents' generation—arranged marriages with cousins—were equally abhorred."[10] Faced with this impossible situation, constantly sliding between deliberately being "other" and being forced by racism to be "othered"—trying to be the same as everyone from whom they're racially different and being told they *cannot,* or trying to be different from those who share their background and being told they *may* not—they don't know where they fit, or even if they'll ever fit anywhere.

Some young Muslim teens risk becoming alienated from their families by becoming more assimilated, by becoming proper British teenagers. Others retreat into the study groups and youth groups sponsored by the mosques, and become avid readers of scripture as a way to gain coherence in an incoherent world. And some become enraged that they do not fit in, enraged by the racism they encounter daily and the prohibitions of their families. They politicize that rage. They become political. It is hard to feel that you have a home in the world when you declare war on the very country that welcomed your parents as refugees.

In a sense, though, the dictatorial overparenting of their traditional Muslim families actually compounds the daily racist bullying and discrimination, conspiring to prevent these young guys from feeling like men. In *Jihad: A British Story,* Deeyah Khan reveals several young jihadists for whom radicalism was "a form of machismo, a way to get women." Despite coming from intact families, few former jihadists could remember their families being happy. They felt so isolated, alone, and insignificant. They fit in nowhere. These are young men who feel emasculated, Deeyah Khan explained to a journalist. They feel "small, pathetic, weak."[11]

And it is those sorts of feelings, as seen in many cases in previous chapters, that lead to anger: anger to ward off the feelings of shame; anger to make someone else pay for making you feel so small; anger as a way to feel bigger by making other people feel small. Shame and humiliation are deeply gendered feelings, and the code of masculinity decrees that men do not, cannot, let themselves feel such feelings. Those feelings must be avenged, denied, destroyed. Real men do not feel shame; they punish others for making them feel that way.

"I just had so much hate in me," says Muniz, one of the ex-jihadists in Khan's film. Disabled at birth (one arm and hand were totally atrophied), he was constantly hated and bullied, and his family did nothing to support him. Another ex-jihadist in the film, Alya, was angry because of the discrimination he experienced. "I'd be constantly stopped and searched by the police because I was brown [skinned]," he tells Deeyah Khan. At the end of her film, Khan concludes: "Radicalization is about pain. It's the pain of young people facing racism, exclusion from society, isolation from the opposite sex, overwhelming pressure from families and communities, a crisis of identity and feeling powerless and insignificant." While it's true, she adds, that many people who become radicalized have had material comforts, they live in a desperate "emotional poverty."

This shame turning to rage, this emotional poverty and pain, is a political aphrodisiac for the jihadi recruiters. For so many jihadists, as for so many European and American skinheads, the immersion is gradual, beginning with emotions of belonging (in a community), friendship, and trust and only gradually becoming mingled with ideology to form an elixir both visceral and cognitive, both emotional and seemingly analytic. The recruiters let the young man—usually around age thirteen or fourteen— know that they totally accept him, that they think he is important, that he matters. They are strong, brave, fighting for a cause. Their lives matter. The recruiters are the new family, simultaneously fatherly and fraternal, strong and dedicated to the authority of the scriptural word, warm and embracing of their new brothers.

Another point of entry is a path for slightly older and somewhat more financially stable young men. Most of the movement leaders, and those who left the movement to form Quilliam Foundation, for example, were recruited in university. They'd believed that the university was a way to navigate the chasm between being British and being Muslim: their parents had staked their entire lives on making a place for their children to experience upward mobility and a secure financial foundation for future generations. At the large, sprawling new universities that sprang up across the country in the education boom of the 1970s and 1980s—including London Metropolitan University and London South Bank University—they resemble other first-generation college students, like my parents' generation of Jewish students at City College and Brooklyn College or the children of Chinese and Korean immigrants at my own university today. First-generation sons, they are poised between two worlds but feel as if they belong in neither, embodying the bridge from the old world to the new, yet carrying with them the critique of the new that the old world inevitably harbors. We welcome these immigrants into our society with some ambivalence, and they enter with both ambition and wariness.

Islamic State recruiters play on that ambivalence, those discomforts. They work carefully to recruit each fighter, spending hours with him on the Internet, nurturing him, finding out his dreams, his yearnings. "It's like grooming," says filmmaker Deeyah Khan. Recruiters "played on their sensitivities of guilt, shame, and humiliation," Husain observes.[12] "They find out," Khan says, "what all your needs are; they build that loyalty and love."[13] ISIS is the "band of brothers," the brothers you never had but always wanted, the older brothers who will intercede for you, who will protect you, their vulnerable little brother. With that protection, that dismissal of vulnerability and humiliation, you're suddenly a big man. "Someone who is otherwise invisible now feels like a rock star."[14] They even become hypermasculine. "They can put on this persona: 'I'm a holy warrior. You don't respect me, but you're afraid of me.'"[15]

In fact, the crafty recruiters take that sense of shame, humiliation, and emasculation that brings guys into the movement in the first place and turn it around into a deepening of their commitment by playing on exactly those same feelings. Islamism is seen as a way out of that cycle of shame and emasculation. One Danish recruit to Islamism, who left Denmark to go fight in Syria, put it this way: "*Kuffar* [nonbelievers] have always tried to take our faith away from us. They want to tell us that we should not be proud of being Muslims. This [establishing a caliphate] is like telling them: 'We are proud of who we are. No matter what you do, you cannot take away our pride.' I am telling you the *khilafah* [caliphate] makes us proud."[16] By the end of the process, the recruit feels, as this young

Danish jihadi told his journalist friend, that "it seemed shameful to stay behind."[17]

The key to recruitment is to link these two strands together—the experiential and the cognitive, the sense of emasculation with the sense of spiritual mission. In other words, according to Maajid Nawaz, one of Quilliam's founders, recruiters make Islam "cool." Islamism is, to these young men, what gangsta rap and hatecore music is to their racist cousins in Britain and elsewhere. It's cool, it's hip, it's manly.[18]

If this is your story, you have many options to choose from. In Sweden and Germany, there are only a few, as the Muslim extremist cells and cults tend to cluster around a handful of political organizations that have enough numbers to create anything more than a tiny cult. But in the United States, and across the Muslim world, which counts more than a billion adherents, there is a veritable smorgasbord of options, some more religious than others, others more political, some messianic and others more proselytizing.

The Quilliam Foundation finds that most of its contacts in Britain come from three moments on the Islamist ideological spectrum. First, there are the *Saudi Salafists*. Salafists are the Muslim equivalent of biblical literalists; they take the Qur'an as the literal blueprint for society. They are uninterested in interpretation or nuance. The holy book is a literal rule book for how to do things. Think Mike Pence in a keffiyeh. The second source of clients is *Al-Muhajiroun*. Less literalist, this terrorist organization is determined to use its interpretation of Islam to create the Caliphate. As a violent terrorist group, it is currently banned in the United Kingdom. Third, there is *Hizb-ut-Tahrir*. This group originated in the Palestinian territories in 1953 and was influenced by the Muslim Brotherhood. It seeks to establish a global caliphate that would be sustained around the world by a network based on a franchise model of governance and controlled and run centrally from the Middle East. Although Hizb-ut-Tahrir is not opposed to violence, that is not its primary reason for existence.

Salafism seems to have been the most common way for Muslim men to burrow deeper into Islam in Britain in the 1980s, as a way to cope with the experience of virulent racism. This is a significant point: the deepening of commitment to the sacred texts is the response to, not the cause of, British racism. Today, it's difficult for many to remember just how virulent that racism was. In the 1970s and 1980s, waves of "Paki-bashing" incidents flowed through northern industrial mill towns such as Bradford and southern manufacturing centers such as Slough and Luton, and just as the violence would die down in one area, a group of skinheads would revive it somewhere else. The extreme right in Britain fed off the resentment toward immigrants, fusing its nihilistic loathing of the "other" with contempt for an incompetently "inclusive" government.

Salafism eschewed political engagement, at least initially. Its followers stressed "purification and education" within the Muslim community in Britain, focusing on community organizations and remaining "activist while being (mostly) quietist." To purify the community, they urged prayer, fasting, and sex segregation, avoiding alcohol and non-Muslims. And they opposed indulging in Western cultural forms, including music, especially hip-hop. To protect the community, they delivered services in Birmingham, Luton and other cities, and confronted drug dealers and far-right groups like the English Defence League and the National Front.[19] As Michael Privot, a historian and director of the Brussels-based European Network Against Racism, told writer Hisham Aidi: "The Salafis are culturally disruptive. For the fragile youth, Salafism offers an easy alternative, a rupture with the past. Yesterday they were listening to rap and dealing drugs, today they're against music, calling people infidels, passing out leaflets telling Muslims not to wish Merry Christmas to the *kuffar*, telling their mothers not to shake hands with non-Muslims, to not cook for Christians."[20]

The other two groups saw their mission as more proactive. Many went to Afghanistan to join the mujahideen in the struggle against the Soviet army. In the civil war that followed the withdrawal of the Soviets, intra-Islamic tribalism disillusioned many of the fighters, who returned to Britain dispirited and angry. All of these themes are evident in the stories of the founders of Quilliam and other ex-jihadist leaders. Noman Benotman, the current president of Quilliam, fought the Soviets in Afghanistan and worked with Osama bin Laden and Ayman al-Zawahiri in Sudan.[21]

Manwar Ali has a fascinating story. He was raised mostly in England; his father, a Bangladeshi academic, was imprisoned after the War of Independence in 1971. After more than two years, during which Manwar visited his father every week, the family applied for refugee status to England and fled. Manwar was seventeen. He felt a strong desire "to right wrongs and help the victims of oppression."[22]

Like so many others, including his friends Ed Husain and Maajid Nawaz, it was in university that Manwar began his radicalization. His first stop was Afghanistan, where he joined the mujahideen in defending the Muslim Afghan population against the Soviet army. On his return he became an imam, "one of the pioneers of violent jihad in the UK." Manwar was entirely convinced by what he now calls "fascist Islamists"—"people who use the idea of jihad to justify their lust for power, authority and control on earth."[23] He also fought in Kashmir and in Burma, always to protect Muslims and establish an Islamic state.

It was in Burma that the tight knot of violence, overcoming oppression and humiliation, and jihad began to unravel. Manwar met two Rohingya fighters, barely thirteen years old, who were carrying grenade launchers and machine guns—his allies in those jungle fights. They were not ideological, he recalls now; they were children. "Looking at me, they begged me to take them away to England. They simply wanted to go to school—that was their dream," he notes in his powerful TEDx speech. Manwar thought of his own family, his own children, who were the same age as these boys. These *children*. And for what were these children's lives being risked? Their leaders were all corrupt, and their faction spent more time fighting other factions than they did fighting outsiders in order to achieve an Islamic state. What hypocrisy! What a colossal lie. Everywhere Manwar looked it was the same: "Petty warlords got the young and vulnerable to kill one another in the name of jihad. Muslims against Muslims. Not protecting anyone against invaders or occupiers; not bringing relief to the oppressed."[24]

Maajid Nawaz is the cofounder of Quilliam. Born to a stable middle-class Pakistani family in Southend-on-Sea, England, in 1977 (his father was an electrical engineer who worked for maritime companies), he is well educated, with degrees from the London School of Economics and the School of Overseas Advanced Studies. He's also largely self-taught. As a young teenager, he felt torn between his British and Pakistani identities. But the local gangs were pretty sure where he fit, and he experienced the brutal racism of the street gangs who were out Paki-bashing; the contemptuous racism of the police, who saw all Pakistanis as potential threats (much the way American police officers, white and black, often see young black males as threats, not as teenagers); and the casual, if serious, racism of school bullies. "When you're that age," Nawaz writes in his autobiography, "already angry and disenfranchised, you're very susceptible to absolutes. This globalization of our grievance was what many would later come to know as the powerful Islamist narrative. It would go on to stir the hearts of thousands of young Muslims around the world, leading to the creation of groups who would commit many atrocities in its name."[25]

Maajid's older brother was recruited first, and eventually Nawaz joined the Islamist group Hizb-ut-Tahrir (HT), mentioned above, the extremist group proposing the establishment of the *khilafah*, or "superstate," which would be the answer to the global injustices suffered by Muslims. His recruitment consisted of watching videos of Serbian forces undertaking ethnic cleansing by massacring Bosnian Muslims. He joined.

By age seventeen he was recruiting students at Cambridge, and by nineteen he had joined the leadership of HT for the entire United Kingdom, traveling to Pakistan and to Denmark to establish HT cells. Eventually, he ended up in Egypt for a year abroad as part of his studies. He arrived in Cairo on September 10, 2001, where he was arrested (Islamist political organizations were prohibited) and imprisoned for five years. Along with several other foreigners, he was declared a "prisoner of conscience" by Amnesty International. He was released in 2006. While in prison, he met with jihadists, Islamists, and more liberal Muslims; he committed half the Qur'an to memory and began to rethink his ideas. Particularly crucial was the growing sense that Islam and Islamism were very different ideals, and that, in fact, Islamism was a perversion of Islam. It was this distinction between Islam and Islamism that became the guiding principle of the Quilliam Foundation, which Nawaz cofounded in 2007, just after his return to Britain from the Egyptian prison.

Usama Hasan, another cofounder of Quilliam, experienced a similar drift into Islamism; indeed he was one of the young men inspired by Manwar Ali's story. A trained scientist, he was, like many other movement leaders, radicalized in university. Usama saw no real contradiction between his faith and his work as a scientist; indeed, he says, many of his beliefs are expressed well in the book *Engineers of Jihad*.[26] (However, that book uses sociological explanations, not textual ones, to explain the high number of jihadists who are also engineers; the authors, Gambetta and Herzog, argue that choked mobility for engineers in the Muslim world leads many to continue their studies in the developed West, where discrimination and racism restrict their mobility yet again.) Usama is more cognitive: he sees little contradiction between scientific facts and religious faith. He remains devout in his religious practice, and equally committed to the wonder of science.

As with many others, it was at university that Usama began his radicalization. As a student at Cambridge, he would bicycle around town in a full turban and robes to attract attention to the Salafi form of Islam he was practicing. The war in Afghanistan was also his wake-up moment, and he, too, went to repel the Soviet invaders. "There were different training camps for different language groups," he remembers. "Pashtun, Urdu, and Arabic camps. The Salafi ideal was that it was not enough to preach. One must act. We each got one week of training, both spiritual and military. Hardly enough to understand how to hold a rifle!" But the trainees got a lot more than that. "It was both spiritual and emotional for me. I got power, belonging, and adventure. That was itself really powerful."

As with Quilliam, many of the Canadian jihadists, including the conspirators of the Toronto 18, followed a similar pattern. Unlike the British jihadists, a few of the Canadian jihadists' parents were divorced. Another couple faced family tragedy. The wife of one man (not Mubin Shaikh) suffered serious, near-suicidal postpartum depression after the birth of their child, and he felt "inadequate" to address her needs.[27] Since the conspiracy of the Toronto 18 was the single most extensive terrorist conspiracy in Canadian history to date, it's useful to add the profiles of those men to the mix as we try to understand the radicalization of young Muslim men

Saad Khalid, one of the Toronto 18, came home one afternoon when he was sixteen and found paramedics trying to revive his mother, who had died in the bathtub at home. "Poor guy," says one of his friends. "After that he became ultra-religious." Mubin Shaikh notes that becoming more militant enabled Saad to give "voice to the anger of his traumatic grief over [his mother's] senseless death and permission to act out his anger for what he came to believe were righteous causes."[28]

For Dave (a pseudonym), a Canadian-based former, it was likely just plain loneliness that started him on his path to convert to Islam and move further and further toward extremism. Now forty-four, Dave has been a Muslim for nearly twenty years. He converted because he found Islam's theology "more precise" and the lifestyle more "structured," which is what he was looking for. Raised a generic Christian—Protestant, and not especially religious—in Winnipeg in a modest middle-class family, he was a reasonably happy kid, doing all those things that Canadian boys do—playing hockey and golf, watching *Hockey Night* on TV. From the outside, at least.

But he "lacked direction," he tells me. Without ambition, he drifted out of high school after graduation and went to work for the railroad, where his father worked as an electrician. He taught English in Taiwan and dreamed of being a professional golfer, but knew better than to try, given his skills. "I'd managed to get through my entire life without ever having to, you know, 'decide' on a career," he tells me.

By his mid-twenties, he hit bottom. Making decent money, he was also in debt, spending more than 100 percent of the borrowed funds at the casinos. Searching for a way out, he looked to religion. He got some Bible study cassettes at a local Goodwill store and tried to implement Christian values. It didn't really stick. One night in July 1998, he walked into a convenience store with a friend and struck up a conversation with another man who was there. This man was Muslim, and he and Dave started to debate theology. It was intriguing, so they kept at it. For three days and nights straight they debated, talked, discussed. On the third night, his new friend taught him to pray as a Muslim.

Dave became a believer. He started going to the local mosque, where he felt he was accepted and embraced. At least at first. He worked around the mosque, performing menial tasks. His "handler," for lack of a better term, introduced him to people in the mosque who would, he promised, help Dave pay off his $35,000 gambling debt. Not only did that turn out to be untrue, but he was actually denounced by the imam for being a "Muslim only for the money." This is quite often the case, says Australian researcher Scott Flowers, who has studied Canadian converts to Islam. Many are lonely, depressed, and searching for community. But they are not accepted by the local mosques, because the Turkish or Pakistani immigrants are distrustful of outsiders.[29]

Still searching for the perfect spiritual fit, Dave changed mosques and fell into an arranged marriage. (The entire courtship was over in an hour, he remembers. "I went to her house and sat with her parents. She was not in the room. After an hour, her mother said, 'Well, do you want to marry my daughter?' We were married two weeks later.") A friend he met at the new mosque was highly political and brought Dave further and further into a more militant sect. "I really needed a friend," he tells me, "and this guy, Ali, seemed to really care about me. He told me that 'we were the chosen, the saved ones,' and that there were only 100,000 of us chosen to die for Islam." It cut through the loneliness, the isolation. Dave felt that he mattered after all.

But when he traveled to Egypt with the group Ali had introduced him to, for training and indoctrination, something clicked, or rather, something clicked off. "There was something false about it, something surreal." But still, he was committed. "My first thought on 9/11 was that America is finally getting back what it has been dishing out to everyone else," he remembers. But when the group was in Syria, during the "shock and awe" campaign of 2003, he went to provide humanitarian aid to the Iraqis. Many in the group left Syria to join ISIS, but Dave couldn't pull that trigger, so to speak. He returned home, confused by the way politics and religion seemed to be mixing. "People were going to fight, but they didn't know how to pray," he says. "How can they do that? How can they not pray? It is the single thing every Muslim must do." All of those friends he first traveled with are dead, or so he suspects.

MUSIC TO THEIR EARS

In both Canada and Britain, music was another entry point. Some had the terrible sense that they were excluded from both sides of the musical divide, prohibited by their parents from listening to the hip-hop or punk music that others in their schools could listen to, and at the same time entirely uninterested in the music of the mosque or the traditional music of the countries not of their origin, but of their *parents'* origins. Neither was right, neither spoke to them, neither felt particularly theirs. While some felt that music of any kind—except that sung in mosques—was forbidden, others engaged in the creation of an Islamic counterculture, embracing the musical forms and turning the content inside out.

And so some of these guys found their way to Islamic rap music and then an even harder-core jihadi rap. It's ironic, I suppose, that the Islamic State, which wants to take us forward into the past and establish a seventh-century caliphate in the twenty-first century, would embrace not only the technologies of the twenty-first century—show me an IS fighter without several mobile phones, a website, and a large Internet footprint—but also the musical iterations of the Great Satan: gangsta rap and hip-hop. But just as with their American and European counterparts, their hardcore music scene brings young guys in and begins to help them build community with others. "As much as these are guys who go into IS saying they want to return the world to a seventh-century state, they are actually creatures of their own society and their own cultures," says London-based political scientist Peter Neumann. "They cannot stop using the internet and they cannot bring themselves to stop expressing themselves in twenty-first-century Western forms of expression, which, of course, hip-hop and rap are."[30] This fusion of medieval religious purity and modern technology is the place where jihadi rap is born. It is ironic. You see guys in a nightclub listening to this music, "rather than fighting in the desert for an organization that would, traditionally, whip you for listening to music."[31]

Sometimes I imagine a London neighborhood in transition, early on a damp Sunday morning, say, 1 A.M. Some skinheads are staggering out of one club after a night of hardcore Oi and hatecore music, having moshed themselves into a drunken frenzy. Around several corners, another club is emptying of young Muslim boys, having been raging at the "dirty *kuffars*" in jihadi rap for the past several hours. Perhaps not drunk (since observant Muslims do not drink), but high on the adrenaline rush of collectively induced hatred, they stream onto the street. One hopes both groups make the turns in the street that lead them away from each other. Were they to turn onto the same street, the result might not be pretty. (Yeah, I know that neither group is likely to go clubbing like that—it's an image. But maybe the skinheads have just left a pub on Brick Lane and they walk toward Whitechapel Road just as a group of Muslim guys, equally juiced on anger and resentment, come teeming out of a kebab shop at that moment. You get the picture.)

Just as hatecore does for their white neighbors, jihadi rap fuses musical urgency with lyrical protest. "The key to understanding this is the idea of a counterculture," explains Peter Neumann. "[People] often start engaging in hip-hop as a form of protest and rebellion against a situation where they feel they are marginalized in society, and that, of course, is exactly the same sort of feeling that the jihadists are also exploiting. They are trying to recruit people who are feeling lost. Who are feeling marginalized. Who feel that society doesn't accept them."[32]

Perhaps the most famous practitioner of the genre is British musician Sheikh Terra, whose song "Dirty Kuffar" basically runs through a list of enemies (Tony Blair, George W. Bush, Ronald Reagan, the National Front) and rhythmically calls each a dirty *kuffar* while bouncing to a charging rhythm with a revolver in one hand and a Qur'an in the other.[33] Denis Mamadou Cuspert, who rapped under the names Abou Maleeq and Abu Talha Al-Almani, was actually a well-known German rapper using the name Deso Dogg, who gave up his career when he converted to Islam. The same is true for L Jinny, a London-based rapper who converted and rapped as Abdel Majed Abdel-Bary (his father is an Islamist extremist currently held by the United States on terrorism charges).

Some jihadi rappers are American. Omar Hammami, who came from Alabama (without the banjo on his knee) rapped under the name Abu Mansoor al-Amriki; he released "Blow by Blow" in 2009, whose lyrics include the lines:

> Bomb by bomb
> Blast by blast,
> Only going to bring back the glorious past.[34]

His other songs include "Make Jihad with Me" and "First Stop Addis." The stateside duo Sons of Hagar feature two African American converts to Islam from Washington State. (Hagar, you may recall, is Sarah's maid in the Bible, and she bears Abraham's first child, Ishmael, the father of Islam.) In their song "Motive Transportation," one raps about how "trials and tribulations had me feeling less than a man," so he decides to leave and join the struggle in the Middle East.[35]

Here, however, is a significant difference between jihadi rappers and the hatecore bands that so captivate and inspire white nationalists in Europe and the United States. White supremacist music is just that, entertainment for those in the movement, a vehicle to engage young guys already in the movement. But few bands decide to pick up guns and start shooting. (Wade Michael Page, of course, is the exception.) But for jihadi rappers, their songs are an expression of their intentions, not just their feelings. Many have gone to fight for the Islamic State. Abdel-Bary was reportedly videotaped beheading the journalist James Foley. Hammami joined al-Shabaab and is believed to have been killed in 2013 in southern Somalia by members of a rival Islamic group. Abu Talha Al-Almani was also killed in 2013, in a Syrian airstrike.

THE WOMEN OF JIHAD

As they enter the movement, young recruits to white nationalist groups in Europe and the United States typically find themselves in the presence of women—women who hang out with them, party with them, and even have sex with them. (So many have felt like losers around girls before joining the movement that this is quite a boost to their self-esteem.) Access to women, while not a primary motivation for joining, is often seen as a perk.

For the young men and boys attracted to jihad, in contrast, the rewards are a little more distant and treacherous. Since Islamism requires strict dietary regimens, abstinence from alcohol and drugs, and most important, separation of the sexes and abstention from all forms of sexual contact, including masturbation, there are a lot of horny boys, testosterone surging through their limbs, being urged to remain pure for their God. That's not to say that there aren't some lapses; there are. But sexual frustration is probably saturating the air in many a jihadi cell. It is, let's face it, a pretty horny feeling of humiliation. The rewards promised had better be pretty persuasive.

And they are. According to Islamist interpretations of the Qur'an, the martyr ascends to Jannah (paradise), where he is awaited by seventy-two virgins with "full grown," "swelling," or "pear-shaped" breasts. (By contrast, female martyrs are awaited by only one man, but, they are assured, "they will be satisfied with him.") Unlike the Christian heaven, which is a rather sedate and seemingly chaste affair, Jannah is a garden of sensual delights, and Islamic scholars have long debated just how awesome it will be for these believers. One early cleric saw paradise as a kind of free brothel, where you could have sex with any woman you fancied. My personal favorite is a sixteenth-century cleric who declared that the seventy-two virgins will be "perpetual" virgins (that is, they will return to being virgins immediately after sex), will have "appetizing vaginas," and so "the penis of the Elected never softens" and "the erection is eternal."[36] (Paradise is clearly different from this mortal coil, where, as the Viagra ads tell us, you should seek immediate medical attention for erections lasting over four hours. Eternity? Ouch.)

For those who have lapsed and had sex, it'll still be OK. One seventeen-year-old boy told Deeyah Khan that "once the martyr's blood hits the ground, all his sins are forgiven." (That practically encourages you to sin now, so it can all be wiped away later.) Martyrdom is a win-win: expiation for all one's sins and—finally!—access to some hot women.

Although sex with women in the present is not offered as a direct tool of recruitment, women still play an active role in enlisting members and maintaining the community. Some women's militant sacrificial jihadi activities are used as a motivator for young potential recruits. Tashfeen Malik, for example, one of the two perpetrators of the attack in San Bernardino, California, in December 2015, is held up as a martyr and as a recruitment tool to shame men into participation. Recruits read, for example: "The brother's blessed wife [Malik] accompanied him despite the fact that combat is not even obligatory upon her, but she did not want to lose the opportunity for *shahadah* [martyrdom] at a time when many 'men' of the *Ummah* [global Muslim community] have turned away from the obligation of jihad."[37] You'll note, of course, the quotation marks around the word *men*.

Women can be used as tools for recruitment, both as emasculators or rewards for martyrdom, true. But the real women currently in these young men's lives are also very much on their minds. According to Nelly Lahoud, jihadist organizations depend on women to "advance jihad in the domestic sphere and also in the public sphere through raising money for jihadis and preaching the merit of jihad to others in mosques, print, and online publications."[38]

Recall that many of these young men have distant or overly demanding fathers, and they idealize their relationships with their mothers. They wanted their father's approval, yes, but they were comforted only by their mother's love. Forget the virgins in paradise. "The Mother is extremely important in jihadist Islam," says deradicalization expert Daniel Koehler. "Mohammed said, 'Paradise lies at the feet of mothers.' You have to ask her permission to go on jihad or to say goodbye." Koehler, you may recall, was my guide in my initial meetings with members of EXIT Deutschland, and he now runs the German Institute for Radicalization and De-radicalization Studies (GIRDS) in Berlin, where he specializes in working with Islamic radicalization. In working on these issues, he's met dozens of mothers who have lost their sons to jihad.

It's a significant group, what one journalist has called the "mothers of ISIS." When we say that more than four thousand young men from Western countries have made their way to Syria and Iraq to fight for Al Qaeda or the Islamic State, we overlook the experiences of those left behind—their parents, their siblings. Their stories are poignant, and the mothers of these jihadists have found their way to one another online. These stories are heartbreaking, precisely because the women lost their sons to a progressive radicalization; they could sense their sons drifting away but felt powerless to pull them back from the brink. A story in *Huffington Post* tells the stories of several of these mothers, and it is wrenching for me to watch as a parent now, but also as a man, remembering my own forays into independence and a community separate from my family.[39]

To help families understand what is happening, Koehler identifies the stages that the young Islamist recruit goes through. Usually, by the time a parent realizes what is happening, their son may have already slid into the world of jihad. At first, Koehler explains, the recruit is euphoric "because he has finally found a way to make sense of the world." The emotions of loneliness and isolation begin to dissolve, leaving him energized and outgoing. He wants to convert the world. Families are eagerly seduced by the change, delighted that their sons are staying away from drugs and crime. "I just felt they were so positive," one woman told a journalist about her sons. "They showed respect with heads held high."[40]

But then, things begin to sour. The young man "realizes that his loved ones aren't receptive to his message," and a chasm opens between him and his family. They start to argue over everything: music, clothing, ideas. And that's when the young recruit is told by his handlers that "perhaps the only way to be true to his beliefs is to leave home for a Muslim country." He begins to work out at the gym and sells his clothing and worldly possessions. And then one day he's just gone.[41]

One of the stories is particularly illustrative of this process. Thom Alexander, a Norwegian, converted to Islam. When Thom Alexander was

seven, his father died of a heroin overdose. Thom himself had been diagnosed with ADHD at fourteen. He was not destined for a happy adolescence. By his early twenties, he was in and out of prison for petty crimes
and in rehab for his addiction to increasingly harder drugs. But then he
discovered a copy of the *shahadah,* the Muslim declaration of faith, in the
locker room of the local gym. He read it. It made sense. He followed it. He
became a new man. He kicked heroin. He called his mother. He got a job
at a kindergarten, and met a nice Moroccan girl. "It was like getting a new
son, a good son," his mother remembers.

Thom Alexander also converted his seventeen-year-old half-sister,
Sabeen. He was suddenly stable and happy, it seemed, until he started a
clothing drive for refugees from the war in Syria. This seemed to deepen
his convictions—and set him on course for jihad. Thom divorced his first
wife and married a Somali, who insisted that they move to a Muslim country. He sold all his belongings. It was then that Torill, Thom's mother, realized she was losing him. The last time she saw him was when he came to
the house to make pizza. He was clean-shaven and dressed in Western
clothes. She interpreted this as a hopeful sign that he was coming back to
his old life. In fact, young jihadists often do this so they can get through
security at airports more easily. One recent study of Dutch jihadists found
that virtually all those who were close to the individual who radicalized
and prepared to travel to Syria was "caught by surprise" when they realized the young man had gone. That last cleaning up and returning home
is not about reconnecting, but about saying goodbye.[42]

And that's what happened with Thom Alexander. Immediately after
that pizza dinner, he was driven to the airport by his handlers and gone. He
had come to say goodbye, without his family knowing. Though he continued to write messages on Facebook, he was increasingly distant and cold,
affectless about the death and destruction around him. Finally, he was sent
on a mission destined to fail. Even though ISIS had lost control of Kobani,
in northern Syria, several months earlier, ISIS kept sending waves of foreign fighters to harass the Kurds, and to face certain death. Resisting the
command to go resulted in execution. Either way, you were dead.[43]

Could his mother have stopped Thom Alexander? Perhaps, but not for
long. He was determined to salvage his dignity, his honor, to demonstrate
his newfound faith by dying. And it is extremely difficult to prevent

someone who really wants to die from eventually succeeding, as anyone knows who has suffered through trying to prevent a friend or a family member from committing suicide, only to have the person kill him- or herself in the end. Still, a mother can intervene at strategic times. She can, perhaps, keep her son tethered to this world before he hurls himself headlong into the next. She can try to bring her son back from the precipice of martyrdom. She—and her husband and other relatives if she has them— can recognize the signs that their son is getting ready to leave: it's the moment he cleans up his act, shaves, and seeks to reintegrate.[44] Magnus Ranstorp, a Swedish expert at the Radicalization Awareness Network, notes that since so many Muslim men feel emasculated by Western society, and this emasculation is transmitted to their sons, the father fades into the background. "The mother is the pivot," he says.[45]

STRATEGIES OF DISENGAGEMENT

For each of the groups discussed in previous chapters, there are several different routes toward radicalization, but all seem to lead through questions of identity more than questions of ideology. The ex-jihadists are somewhat different, since their recruitment fuses ideology and identity quests, but even recruiters refer back to identity questions as initial strategies. Some of those who join simply age out, a pattern previously observed, particularly among the Americans in Life After Hate. The movement doesn't quite square any longer with the imperatives of grown-up life. As one former Islamist told an interviewer:

> I always think of these Islamic groups and it could probably apply to others as well, [as] sort of these revolving doors. You're in high school, you're a freshman in college, you come into contact with these guys. You haven't read a whole lot, and your knowledge base is not where you can distinguish between what they are saying, and the rhetoric and reality. By the time you graduate, you're out of that revolving door. You're out the other way, so you move on. You go find a job, get married, get a mortgage, have kids, and whatnot. So there's a lot of turnover, if you will.[46]

The efforts to help jihadists out of the movement, though, do tend to emphasize ideological concerns alongside identity concerns. Important textual references must be examined, references to holy scripture. Neo-Nazis do not parse *Mein Kampf* as though it were the Talmud, debating the finer points of genocide as prophesy; thus, their path out is centered far more around identity and community. But for the jihadists, identity and community are deeply interwoven with the textual and the ideological. As a result, many deradicalization programs use the same tools that engaged the young guys in the first place. For example, some Saudi programs use the Internet to counter the jihadist narrative, developing university-based curricula and also using the testimony of "repentant terrorists and extremists who negotiate and argue with potential recruits on relevant websites and in other media."[47]

The most successful and visible organization currently working to help young jihadists disengage is the Quilliam Foundation. Based in London (its official headquarters is secret for security reasons), Quilliam was named after William Henry Quilliam, a nineteenth-century British convert to Islam who founded Britain's first mosque, in Liverpool, and then went on to argue for a caliphate. He supported the Ottoman Empire during the First World War, which hardly endeared him to British authorities (some denounced him as a traitor). Established in 2007 by three former members of Hizb-ut-Tahrir—Maajid Nawaz, Ed Husain, and Rashad Zaman Ali—Quilliam has as its prime mission to take the Islam out of Islamism, that is, to disentangle the incorrect politicization of Islam by Islamist groups. Islam, they argue, is a religion, nothing more and nothing less. Political claims made in the name of Islam—jihads, holy wars, caliphates, and the like—are anathema to the religion, they argue. Like LAH and EXIT, Quilliam has one arm devoted to helping young men leave the movement.

In an internal study, the Quilliam Foundation found a pattern among the ex-jihadists they have worked similar to that among the other groups discussed in this book. Even though the staff engage the ideological, their clients' profiles require that they also engage their identity issues. As with the other groups, the most important emotional motivations for joining were shame and guilt, which opened these young boys up to searching for answers, for a way to fit in. That usually brought them to the Internet, the chief site of initial recruitment. And as with the white nationalists in the United States and Sweden, their recruitment had far less to do with ideology than it did with emotions—feeling as if they belonged, as if they mattered. The former jihadists in the Quilliam study were able "to consume and regurgitate extremist material," but they were unable to critically engage with its content. They could mouth all the slogans, but they really had no idea what they meant.[48]

It is perhaps ironic, then, that Quilliam and so many of the other organizations involved in deradicalization of Islamists and jihadists are so concerned with textual and cognitive approaches. Despite similar pathways into the movement, efforts to help young men get out of the jihadist movement look strikingly different from those made to help neo-Nazis and white nationalists leave the movement in Europe and the United States. In the Muslim world, there's far less emotional support for former jihadists; there are fewer efforts to help young men feel like men, help them repair a sense of damaged manhood—and there's a lot more textual confrontation. Even though Quilliam acknowledges that "events which induce feelings of shame, guilt and vulnerability can often become the catalyst towards radicalization," they choose to focus on challenging the young men's understanding of sacred texts.[49]

In their self-study, former extremists acknowledged that it was the scholars and activists with whom they spoke who had the ability to undermine the foundations of the extremist narrative through a theological lens, and that this discussion encouraged them to reflect and challenge their extremist ideology. "The ability of Quilliam to provide nuanced arguments which highlight the political and religious errors of modern Islamist movements have been highly important," because it helps the jihadi "deconstruct the foundations which underpins [sic] the jihadist narrative."[50] That is, the jihadist begins to detach from the movement because of a cognitive confrontation with the error of his political views.

Still, Quilliam acknowledges that mere scholastic confrontation is insufficient; the counselors also have to be "engaging, inspiring, and articulate."[51] And in that sense, Quilliam depends on the erudition and charisma of its two principals, Maajid Nawaz and Usama Hasan. Even they had a difficult time getting out. Usama Hasan was sure deradicalization was the right move when one of his four children was diagnosed with cancer at age two. "Watching the NHS [National Health Service] doctors and nurses work so heroically—working together, all of different faiths, different backgrounds—really reminded me of the strengths of diversity. There is no way she would be alive today, thanks be to God, if she were in the hands of fundamentalists." Yet, no sooner did he begin to drift away, than he was threatened and attacked. While attending a local festival with his family, he was assaulted by two guys from ISIS who shouted Islamist slogans and personal threats. Hasan and his friends at the festival—and even his wife—joined in to drive their assailants away. Vigilant now, he does not reveal the foundation's address (we met in the lobby of my hotel).

At the end of our interview, Hasan tells me that he thought he had it bad getting out—the assault, the threats, the constant looking over his shoulder—until he was on a panel at a conference in 2012 with T.J. Leyden, from Life Against Hate. T.J. said there were websites with his photograph on them, like a wanted poster, that said, "Shoot him!" across the top. "OK, I said to myself," Hasan tells me, "it's not so bad here. God had prepared us for these trials with my daughter's illness. We can continue, God willing."

Quilliam counselors attempt to engage with young jihadists. About one-third of the jihadists Quilliam works with are in prison already when they are first contacted. (In this sense, the British ex-jihadists share a prison background with the German ex-neo-Nazis; they were either radicalized in prison or their incipient radicalization was deepened there and their level of commitment rose.[52]) The majority are in schools and university. A few contact Quilliam directly and ask for help. The foundation spends a lot of time on university campuses, distributing pamphlets and leaflets that refute the pamphlets of the Islamist recruiters, and the particular interpretations of radical *dawa* (conversion) efforts.

In their internal self-study, Quilliam's "clients" evince stories of entry strikingly similar to those of the former neo-Nazis, skinheads, and other white nationalists described earlier. Take, for example, Sohail (he used only his first name). Sohail came from a "pretty standard" Muslim family in London that began a friendship with a neighboring family whose members were quite a bit more radical. Sohail's family increasingly embraced Salafi fundamentalism, and both families spent their time listening to more extremist fundamentalist preachers, who were "championing hatred for all non-Muslims." The family became stricter in its Islamist authoritarianism. Sohail was prohibited from listening to music or watching TV. He was prohibited from attending school assemblies—he was even removed once by his parents in the middle of the assembly. Why? There were girls in the room.

In college, Sohail became a leader of Islamism, and preached himself. He began to think about carrying out an attack in the United Kingdom. But gradually he began to wonder, to question his beliefs. One of his friends introduced him to the writings of Usama Hasan, and Sohail found his positions shifting. Old truths were shaky; new truths felt more stable. He began a serious internal self-questioning, examining the "apparent contradictions between Islamic scripture and the Theory of Evolution."[53]

Finally, he admitted some other truths to himself. He was gay. Ever since he was seven or eight, he had known he was attracted to boys. This had deeply confused him and made him terribly ashamed. He knew what he felt was "wrong," and he knew he couldn't tell anyone. In fact, Sohail had hoped his religious observances would help him, would save him. He had tried to use Islam and extremism "as means to cure his homosexuality."[54]

Abdul, another Quilliam client, grew up in a close-knit Pakistani community in London, and in a family that wasn't especially religious. He would fast during Ramadan, for example, but he didn't pray. And he enjoyed living in the multicultural neighborhood and hanging out with different sorts of people. Unfortunately, there was a group of young, anti-immigrant guys in the neighborhood who would engage in Paki-bashing, targeting Asians in the area, and constantly mugging them as they walked down the street.

This made Abdul feel small and vulnerable, in part because he did not "have brothers or cousins who could protect him." He needed a posse. Al-Muhajiroun, a violent splinter group of Hizb-ut-Tahrir, now banned in Britain, came to the neighborhood and offered protection. "A group of thuggish boys from Al-Muhajiroun would regularly go to local schools and colleges" and terrorize the non-Muslim students, Abdul recalled. And he was attracted to it; he liked the gang mentality. He felt safer, and started to go to the group's mosque and gradually became part of the group; listening to speakers who preached a literalist and militant interpretation of Islam. Eventually, he was indoctrinated.

In fact, he became a recruiter. He was especially adept at using as a recruiting tactic the promise of the seventy-two beautiful virgins waiting for the martyr. His pitch was clever—and disingenuous: he would evoke the very guilt that martyrdom could then expiate. He knew that young Muslim boys had the same experience he did: virtually no knowledge of the opposite sex, no outlet for healthy sexual inquisitiveness and exploration. So he encouraged the young boys to do what boys all over the wired-world do: he suggested they watch online porn. (Not, mind you, Islamist porn, with burqas and veils and no body parts. No way. These guys wanted hardcore action.)

Naturally, the boys felt sheepish and confused, and more than a little guilty, as most adolescent boys feel when they first encounter online porn. They'd feel aroused, masturbate, have orgasms to the writhing of beautiful women, and then feel that immediate rush of post-orgasmic shame. Feeling guilty, the boys would go to the mosque to seek forgiveness for their sins. At the mosque, they would be met with stern imams who suggested, in increasingly severe terms, that the only way to purge oneself completely of such sinful urges and pleasures was to renounce all secularist ideas and feelings and make jihad. In that way, Abdul actually produced in potential recruits the feelings that were sinful, and "seduced" the boys into a feeling of guilt that only radical extremist violence could purge.[55]

Quilliam has helped young men all over England. Javed grew up in a modest second-generation Pakistani family in the west of England. He got radicalized in university, where Islamists mingle with Muslim students and gently push the latter toward greater separation from their non-Muslim classmates. At eighteen, Javed was arrested on terrorism charges for trying to detonate a bomb in London. Prison psychiatrists found him to be "naïve and immature," and thus susceptible to extremist ideas. It was in prison that he encountered Usama Hasan's writings from a fellow prisoner and began to question his own beliefs.

Mohammed was a young violent extremist with "all sorts of crazy ideas about Jihad this, bomb that," as he remembers. But he read Maajid Nawaz's story and began to change his views, eventually becoming a counterterrorism operative.[56]

And finally, there is Aamir, who dove headfirst into Islamism. "I was a fanatic who desperately needed to believe in a cause," he says, so he worked toward what he thought would be a paradise on earth, the full imposition of Sharia law across the entire globe. He grew unhappy with the manipulation and coercion used to recruit. A true believer, he thought the ideas themselves should be enough. Since his whole identity was wrapped up in Islamism—his entire social network, all his professional, social, and familial contacts—he was afraid to get out. Again, it was initially Maajid Nawaz's writing that began to help him unravel this tightly wound knot, and eventually he made personal contact with Nawaz, who counseled him through his entire process of deradicalization.[57]

And it's not only Quilliam that uses such a cognitive, text-based strategy. Other organizations throughout the Middle East rely on textual confrontation to help guys get out. For example, Yemen's Committee for Dialogue challenges the jihadists' ideas. "People will revise their ideas when they listen to rational debates which are well reasoned and articulate," says Nabil al-Sofee, a former member of the Islamic Party and the Muslim Brotherhood, now chief editor of *The New Yemen*.[58]

Similarly, the Saudi Counseling Program, which works with prisoners in their rehabilitation, focuses on the "war of ideas," rather than paying any attention to the embodied gendered experiences of the former jihadis.[59] The centerpiece of the Saudi strategy is the counseling program that "is intended to assist those individuals that have espoused *takfiri* [apostate] beliefs to 'repent and abandon terrorist ideologies.'"[60] It assumes that the terrorists were "abused, lied to and misled by extremists into straying away from true Islam," and now the program seeks to help them "return to the correct path"[61] I guess it must work. Of roughly 3,000 prisoners who have gone through the program, half have renounced their former beliefs.

This strategy is quite different from that adopted by EXIT and LAH, where the emphasis is on emotional support leading to the client's accountability for his actions. Quilliam's strategy would surely have been ineffective with the actives I interviewed while researching *Angry White Men*. Most had barely finished high school, and, if they read anything other than *The Turner Diaries*, it was online blogs. And rarely, if ever, the Bible. A conversation about exiting extremism would not have sounded anything like the evening's premise at the Oxford Debating Society. For the Americans on the extreme right, there's scant reference to the Bible, especially the New Testament, which is really about forgiveness and mercy, not about vengeance and wrath against those unlike us. As a result, the spiritualist side of the extreme right usually has to invent its own church, its own religious cult, in order to make the case for a God who hates immigrants and people of color.

I suspect, however, Quilliam's is not simply a cognitive process of textual reinterpretation. That would be the *content*. But the *form*—the characteristics of the one who delivers the content—is equally important, though in the case of the ex-jihadi radicalization projects, more subtle and nuanced than EXIT. Consider, for a moment, if *I* were to say the exact same words to a young jihadist sitting in jail as a member of Quilliam might say to that young jihadist. I am an older, American social scientist—Jewish, no less!—and so I would have little to no credibility. What's in the package is just as important as the packaging. Form is also content. Usama Hasan, with his kindly, soft-spoken avuncular style, and Maajid Nawaz, with his emotional expressiveness and piercing eyes—they and their colleagues become the father figures these young guys need. They are the approving elder men—remember, Usama Hasan and Manwar Ali are imams themselves—whom these young men need to help them get out. They've already repudiated their biological fathers—often emotionally absent, inept authoritarians—and embraced the intense brotherhood of the terrorist cell. Now, they meet a new, authentic father figure, one who has gone into the Islamist world and returned, one who has been there, who can guide the young men back without any loss of their sense of purpose or meaning, without any loss of face, of manhood.

CROSSING OVER

Quilliam's work has spilled over into the British skinhead and racist scene as well. The organization tells the story of Dan, who swung wildly between extremes, being at times an Islamist extremist and at other times a member of the far-right racist and anti-immigrant English Defence League (EDL). Such wild careening between racist poles isn't as uncommon as you might think. After all, as seen throughout this book, young guys get into these movements for similar psychological reasons (feeling humiliated, scared, lonely, emasculated) and through similar means (friendship networks, family networks, the Internet, and the music and party scene). Initially it surprised me that so many of the clients of EXIT Sweden described leaving their neo-Nazi organizations only to become radical environmentalists or, at least, Social Democrats. Middle-of-the-road politics may be more steadying and pragmatic, but mainstream life just doesn't offer the emotional connection, the visceral camaraderie, and the validation of manhood that these young men crave. Ironically perhaps, it is the authoritarian groups that expend the most effort in validating your masculinity. Subordinate yourself to the leader, the hierarchy, and your manhood is simultaneously validated.

Psychoanalysts would have no trouble explaining this trajectory, since it is a foundational to Freud's description of the pathology of group life. To Freud, especially in his later works, such as *Group Psychology and the Analysis of the Ego* and *Totem and Taboo*, all groups are characterized by two fundamental characteristics: intense bonding among the members and complete subordination to the leader. Each tendency indicates a certain weakness of the autonomous ego, the inability of the ego to stand apart from reliance on group ties. Freud's paradigmatic groups were, of course, the church and the army, where such intense bonding among equals and the subordination to authority were most intense. But these groups also reproduce the idealized family: the mother's love for her children provides the ecstasies of connection with siblings and emotional merging; the father's strict discipline means that no one can live outside the hierarchies of rules and roles.

When family life is weak, when the boy, in particular, does not have these maternal and paternal principles in his life—or when they are damaged, dysfunctional, unsafe, or violent—he must seek them elsewhere. And some of the boys find them in the paramilitary skinhead and National Socialist bands of brothers, and others in religious extremist cults. These two sorts of groups have much more in common with each other than either of them might believe. They just have a different ideology. Form is similar; content different.

And thus we begin to understand Dave's story. White and middle class, Dave came from a multicultural community in Birmingham. As he tells it, he hung out with a mixed group of "skinheads and rude boys" who were mostly into ska music, reggae, and hip-hop. Moderately adrift, he found his first community with an organized group of soccer hooligans that was centered on the Birmingham Football Club, but they had no ideology except drinking and fighting, and after a few fights and a few arrests, he drifted away.

When he moved to Southwest England, he started dating a girl who was Palestinian and whose Palestinian stepfather invited him into the family on the condition that he accept Islam and covert. So he did. But like many converts to Islam, he still did not feel accepted. His girlfriend, Laura, also confided that she, too, had been forced to convert and had been sent to a mosque where she had been sexually abused and forced into an arranged marriage at seventeen. What hypocrisy! Dave grew angry about the hate preachers, "that they were allowed to do and say anything about gays, Jews, and anyone who didn't fit into their supremacist ideology." They were just full of it.

So from Muslim convert, it was but a short step to anti-Muslim, anti-immigrant activist. He'd seen Islam up close, and it looked hypocritical, abusive toward women, and filled with authoritarian intolerance. Hardly the religion of peace and love. He started hanging with the EDL as a way to fight against Islamist extremism. The group, he understood, was only against "political Islam" (Islamism), not against the religion itself.

That didn't last long. Pretty soon, EDL members were marching in the streets shouting "No more mosques! No more halal!" Dave and others drifted away; he was political, not racist. He and a few others found their way to a new little group called Nice Ones UK, which had been founded by an ex-EDL member. And through them, he heard about Quilliam and read Maajid Nawaz's life story. He came to understand that the "only way to counter extremism is to hit it head-on with a counternarrative." As Maajid always insists, Islam is not the problem; Islamism is the problem.

Sometimes the collision of these two ideologies doesn't end so well. Maajid Nawaz played a role when Tommy Robinson, the founder of the EDL, jumped out of the extreme right wing. Nawaz and Robinson had met in 2013, during the filming of the BBC documentary *When Tommy Met Mo*. Through Robinson, Nawaz also met Kevin Carroll, the other leader of the EDL. Both credited Nawaz with helping them leave the EDL, which they had founded. However, in 2015 Robinson joined with PEGIDA in Dresden (see chapter 2) and was visibly back in the extreme-right scene. Robinson now claims that Quilliam was paying him 2,000 British pounds per month to enable it to take credit for his jumping out of the movement, a claim Quilliam denies.

Of course, what is interesting to us now is not the truth or falsity of these claims, but the fluidity of political positions, the ease of movement between two seemingly diametrically opposed poles, the simple possibility that such fluctuations are possible. We believe it because we know that though they are such polar opposites ideologically, the two groups look very much like each other organizationally.

One more story. Adam Deen, a young British man of Turkish descent, grew up in North London. His family bore no particularly notable signs of dysfunction, nor did he have much of a history of being bullied or otherwise targeted. Just a "normal" guy. When he encountered a young man distributing pamphlets outside a mosque, he thought the analysis was thin, "pseudo-intellectual." Nothing really compelling. Then, at Westminster University, he encountered someone from Al-Muhajiroun who invited him to the 2003 conference "The Magnificent 19," celebrating the lives of the martyrs who killed themselves in the terrorist attacks of September 11.

Something about it touched him. Maybe it was their dedication to a cause, that unquestioning sense of purpose, the certainty about life and death and life after death. After the conference, he was recruited to join. It felt, he says, "amazing, actually." He felt seen, important. "Someone had a purpose for me."

Alongside this sense of purpose was also a sense of guilt "that I wasn't doing enough to develop the Islamic State." That was a pretty potent mix, and Adam spent, he tells me now, "my twenties as an Islamic extremist, and my thirties trying to figure out what went wrong." He'd cut his ties with his family, broken away from all is friends, immersed himself in an Islamist world. "They all thought I was becoming more religious. Actually, I was becoming more Islamist."

But the discipline and authoritarianism began to grate against his sense of purpose and meaning. There was enforced unity on all ideas, all thoughts. You couldn't question anyone in the group. If you asked a question of the speaker, you were really questioning God. It was impossible.

He was part of the group as it began to outline plans for a terrorist attack in London, to plant a bomb at the Tower Bridge tube station. Interestingly, he says now, alarm bells didn't go off. He didn't say (or think), for example, "What do you mean you want to put a bomb in a public place and kill people?" It all just seemed perfectly reasonable.

"I can't understand why I didn't feel that way," he tells me. "The only question I had was whether I was going to be trained properly."[62] But something still felt not quite right, something that kept nagging at him. It was strange—he couldn't just accept his mission. "I can't really describe it," he says, "but something just felt, well, 'off.'" He started to pull away, becoming withdrawn, nonresponsive, sullen. This wasn't easy, as the movement had become his entire life, his entire social network. Having cut himself off from his family, he now had to find a way back to them. He began to read outside of Islam, and over two years began to question the basic tenets of the Islamist interpretations of the holy texts.

Even in retrospect, his efforts to keep out now, to maintain his distance, is as much textual as it is emotional. He reads the Qur'an daily and is still a believer. He just believes differently from those he used to plot with. "Islam is about connecting to God to be a better human being. It's about mercy, compassion, justice." The extremists pervert that message; his goal is not to renounce the faith, but to renounce the perversion of the faith for political ends.[63]

And remember Dave, the Canadian convert who really was just looking for a friend? "I was lonely, and I needed to feel connected to a community." Since his own motivation to join radical Islam had been to combat loneliness, he understood what was motivating those other Christian Anglo-Canadian guys who were converting to Islam. So Dave started an organization for them, to offer them a very different kind of social, moral, and spiritual support. So far, nearly two hundred young Canadians have connected with Dave through his organization, Paradise Forever. They're searching for something, something they cannot find in their Canadian homes and Christian religion. Which means, he finishes the thought, "that they all come with baggage. They need a friend, a mentor, a job, some financial support. Just like I did."

He helps in any way he can. Jobs? He's found about a dozen, all in framing and drywall, through the union he works in himself. Support? That's provided through groups that meet regularly so these guys can talk about their journeys to Islam. "I don't want them to leave Islam," Dave tells me. One of a Muslim's duties is to convert others. "That's not what I want to do. I want to help them find support to stay in, but get relief from financial, emotional, or dependency issues. What I really want is for them not to die in jihad."

It's possible, but not easy. After my interviews with the leaders of Quilliam, and with Mubin and his Canadian colleagues, I sensed a contradiction: a heaviness from the burden of the task, but also an optimism that Islamism can be challenged, one jihadist at a time, slowly, patiently. It is a longer process than that for ex-skinheads, partly because, for the skinheads, getting out doesn't require textual unraveling of deeply held beliefs, but rather a jump between different models of manhood.

But the contrast amounts to more than that, more than just the relative ease by which camaraderie, community, and even visceral pleasures can be transferred as compared to the ideas of the true believer. It's not just the jihadist or skinhead himself. It's the world he is about to re-enter.

After all, the ex-neo-Nazis in Sweden or Germany and the ex–white nationalists in the United States, can return to a world that still welcomes them, that still offers them a chance to get a job, raise a family, and feel like stakeholders. The ex-jihadist, on the other hand, has to return to a Western world that still doesn't recognize his humanity, that would denigrate his culture, would discriminate against his ethnicity and nationality, and even as I write this book, would tell him that he is formally, legally, unwelcome in Great Britain and even the United States, once the land of opportunity to which millions of "others" sought refuge and a new chance. It is a far tougher route, and the end is uncertain.

Still, the formers who work so diligently to help young jihadists leave that world behind remain optimistic. "What have I learned?" asks Manwar Ali. "That people who engage in violent jihadism, that people who are drawn to these types of extremisms, are not that different to everyone else. But I believe such people can change. They can regain their hearts and restore them by filling them with human values that heal."[64] Once those new seeds are planted, however, it is up to the rest of us to help them germinate and grow.

Epilogue

REDEMPTION SONG

If the young are not initiated into the village, they will burn it down just to feel its warmth.

African proverb[1]

All through the research and writing of this book, I keep coming back to something Deeyah Khan said in an interview about her film focusing on the ex-jihadists. These are "damaged people," she says. These are "broken men." So many young children have been "broken"—abused, physically, sexually, by those who say they love them. So many are bullied and tormented in schools. So many feel they matter not at all to those in charge, feel as though their lives have no purpose, no meaning.

Yet we pay so little attention to them, especially as men. We fail to see their pain or anguish or rage or disaffection as a specifically gendered rage, a rage designed to mollify that anguish, to transform that reality of pain into the illusion of power, to transmute the feeling of being totally ignored and unvalued by the society into a feeling that theirs is a sacred mission, that they have been chosen for it. I make the case in this book that we need to add gender to this analysis. These are broken *men*, broken by wounds both seen and unseen.

That there are so many such men suggests that this is not simply the problem of a few bad apples—the victims of some rare combination of abusive parents, indifferent school officials, callous community leaders, corrupt politicians ignorant of what the lives of their own citizens actually look like. When the problem gets this big, this widespread, it's serious.

If there is a "boy crisis" in the United States and Europe, it is not because boys' educational achievements are being surpassed by girls', or that young women now outnumber men at our nations' colleges and universities. This is not an issue of numbers. It's a crisis of meaning. More broadly, it is a crisis of connection, in which we have come to value autonomy and independence to the exclusion of our equally crucial need for community and connectedness. And now too many young men feel that the future they felt they were promised, and to which they feel entitled, has been stolen from them. They've been good boys, good men even, and now they are not getting the rewards for that goodness they were promised. They feel betrayed, as though they are the victims. And they're half right.

Through much of my work over the past two decades, I've argued that white men in Europe and the United States were the beneficiaries of invisible privilege—well, at least it was invisible to them. I've often used a metaphor from my days as a runner. When you run with the wind at your back, you feel like a great runner, as if you can run forever, effortlessly. It's only when you turn around that you realize the strength of the wind that has been propelling you—propelling you so that you could feel your running was so effortless. So many people in the world are running into that wind, and when they are less successful, we with more privilege often tell ourselves that somehow they didn't try hard enough, that we are simply the better runners.

There are still many privileges that white men get that others simply don't. White men rarely have to fear that if a taillight on their car is broken and a police officer pulls them over, that encounter might be their last moment on earth. I'd probably get a friendly warning, at most a ticket. The privileges white men get are so numerous, but we white people typically don't see them. They just look like life.

I once had a conversation with an elegantly dressed African American attorney who worked for a large corporate law firm in downtown Chicago. He said that when he leaves his office, in his Brioni suit, he cannot get a taxi to stop for him heading south on Michigan Avenue. But when his equally well dressed white colleagues put out their hand, taxis screech to a stop. "That's what racism looks like," he said. "The white guys don't see it. They just think, 'Hand out, taxi comes.' They just don't see the discrimination, because it doesn't happen to them."[2]

On the other hand, that story, while certainly true for middle-class and affluent men, doesn't really capture the experience of many of the men and boys I talked with in the research for this book. White privilege means different things in a country like the United States than it does, perhaps, in Sweden or even Germany. Class complicates race—and so does religion, immigrant status, sexuality, and a host of other aspects of our identity. Many of the men I've spoken with for this book have significant obstacles thrown in their way on that running path: for some it was the overt discrimination and racist hatred that led many sons of Muslim immigrant parents in Britain to feel suspended between two worlds, neither of which was their "home." For others, it was the class-based feeling that their way of life—the skilled worker, the small shopkeeper, the independent farmer—was being undermined and was gradually eroding because of indifferent politicians and craven bankers and bureaucrats.

And do you know what? They're also right. They *have* been passed by, discarded, brushed aside like so many mosquitos. If there is a speed ramp to get on the Information Superhighway to new jobs in the new global economy, they have not been able to get off the surface roads. If white male privilege were a banquet, these guys haven't even tasted the appetizer. They have certainly not tasted the fruits of their privilege.

To be sure, the guys described in this book have been angry, and they politicized that anger, however justified it might have been, by lashing out in all the wrong directions. It's hardly immigrants who seduced them with predatory loans and credit default swaps. It's not feminist women, or LGBT people, or Jews who caused climate change, who outsourced their jobs, and who have been the indifferent observers of their plight. Yes, these guys are right to have been angry, but they have been delivering their mail to the wrong address.

And yet, I feel a certain optimism in finishing this book. Most of the men I've met are the guys who got out. These are the people who realized that the path they were on would not ultimately give them what they needed. And that's because most of them realized that what they needed was to form stable family relationships, to get a decent job that can provide at least half a family income, and to feel they are participants in the political process as citizens. In short, they became stakeholders in the system they had once pledged to destroy in a racial holy war.

Make no mistake: while the answer for the individual may be to become a stakeholder, a participant, and not a marginalized outsider, for the whole society the answer is not simply to adapt to a system that perpetuates the racism that Muslims in Britain experience, or the choked economic opportunities that global economic concentration and dramatic wealth disparities produce. The extremist solutions discussed here are always regressive, looking back nostalgically to a lost world of economic autonomy. That world is not coming back, no matter how many times you shout slogans about making some country or other "great again." So while individual former extremists find their way back in to the system, that is but a first step. To change society, they must join with others who are trying to change the underlying conditions that result in such marginalization in the first place.

My central argument, though, is that we cannot generate policies or programs that enable young men to get out without recognizing gender, without enabling them to make that gendered transition to being a stakeholder. Part of the story of their entry concerned gender—proving their manhood, feeling like successful men, feeling validated and "seen" as men by other men, feeling that spirit of community and camaraderie. We cannot help them get out or support their own processes of exit unless we pay attention to both how they got in and what they found through their participation. All of which is wrapped up in proving and restoring their sense of themselves as men.

Let me be clear, once again, about what I am not saying: I am not suggesting that we sweep aside all the political and economic theory about extremism, all the analysis of ideology, all examination of the many elements leading to entry into extremist movements, and replace all of that with an equally monocausal focus on gender as the single predictor of participation in extremist politics. What I am saying is that we cannot adequately address the problem *unless* we also include gender. The participants understand this; it's just we analysts who seem to be chronically unable or unwilling to listen to them when they tell us. We cannot help young men and boys get out unless we fully understand what brings them in.

In this book, I call for a *gendered political psychology of extremism*. The stories of these young men illuminate how deeply gendered their motivations for entry are and how gendered their experiences in the movement are. They do not enter because they are committed to an ideology. They become committed to the ideology because they are embraced in gendered community and gendered comradeship by others who hold these ideas.

It is a gender problem, and also a generational problem. How do we enable a larger portion of our young people to feel like stakeholders in the system, to buy into the same value system that animated their grandparents—the ideals of Western democracies, the belief that by your own hard work and discipline you can make a good, honest, decent, and honorable life for yourself in this society? How is it possible that so many no longer feel this way, that so many feel instead that the system is so hopelessly stacked against them that they have nowhere to stand? You cannot stand for something if you have nowhere to stand in the first place.

I am not for a moment suggesting that the way to assure these extremists of a place in the system as stakeholders is to return nostalgically to the world of their grandfathers, that by somehow restoring their grandfathers' world we might keep these young men from spiraling off into extremist politics. Far from it. That world, a world of stable jobs, single-family male breadwinners with unquestioned domestic authority; a world of high-wage, union-protected, manufacturing jobs in a high-tax economy with a government that would use those revenues to build highways and schools—that world is gone for good. National and global economics have moved on, and these angry white men in the United States, Germany, and everywhere else that extremist politics has raised its head, are going to have to move on with it. Nor will global Islam revert to some anachronistic, seventh-century theocracy; indeed, many of the former Islamists are seeking a way to reconcile Islam with modern political and economic realities—and, surprisingly, finding that one fits with the other without much effort.

That is not to say that our message must be "Get over it." That is clearly a losing strategy. Nor is it an effective strategy to tell people that their feelings are "wrong." Feelings are real, even if they are not "true"—that is, you may feel something even if the information that feeling is based on is not an accurate analysis of your situation. We need to acknowledge those feelings as real, and acknowledge the fundamental humanity of those who feel them.

And then we need to go to work changing the circumstances, the empirical foundations on which those feelings are based. We will need policies that enable these disaffected, disillusioned, disheartened men, who simultaneously feel entitled and victimized, embattled and enraged, to feel that they belong, that they matter—and we need to make all of that possible from within the system, not in opposition to it. If they cannot go backward to that world of their grandfathers, perhaps they can move forward, through policies that make the transition to the new economy easier (such as free tuition in community colleges and technical training programs), and through projects that encourage contact with the vilified "others," so they might be able to recognize their common humanity.

These men may look back nostalgically to a lost past, but they cannot anchor their sense of themselves as men in that world any longer. The global economy and demographic shifts have made that impossible. "Forward into the Past!" is as phantasmagorical as "Back to the Future"— minus the flux capacitor and the 1.21 gigawatts of electricity. Today's angry white men and their Islamist brethren need to find new ways to validate their masculinity. But let's not make the same mistake that our policy makers have made: to pretend that the validation of masculinity is not a central element in the attraction to extremist politics.

The young men depicted in this book—and thousands more just like them all over the world—went to a very dark place to attempt to heal their wounds, to hide their shame, to rectify conditions that they did not create but with which they now have to cope. We need to understand what they went looking for so we can understand how the organizations I profile here can support their movement toward the light.

And so I find myself guardedly optimistic. Many of the stories I recount in this book tell of nihilistic rage turning into purpose, religious fanaticism turning into meditative and thoughtful activism to help communities challenged by racism and economic despair. How can one not be moved by people turning their lives around? Whether it is Manwar Ali's "jihad of forgiveness and compassion" or Christian Picciolini saying that "the only way to show them that there is nothing to hate is to show them that there is something to love," the formers who are working in EXIT, Life After Hate, and Quilliam are filled with compassion for the guys they are helping to get out, and hope that the right combination of support, guidance, and concrete material support (job training, job placement, safe houses) can help more guys leave the movement. They are still true believers, in the sense that they believe—no, they *know*—that change is possible. If the Trojan T-shirt changed, so can they. If they changed, so can others. If many can change, so can the world.

There's even some empirical evidence beyond the individual. Some political programs that have addressed these same issues and made gender part of their process have met with some success. In the 1980s the Green Jackets were a Danish neo-Nazi group widely known in Arhus and Copenhagen as among the more violent political extremists. The Danish national police developed a strategy that split the leaders from the followers and worked from the outside in, concentrating first on the outer group of followers. Youth workers provided extensive counseling, job training, job placement, and help finding apartments. They organized leisure activities, youth clubs, and sports clubs. Quite a few of these guys, once they had jobs and apartments, also found girlfriends, had children, and began to have lives outside the movement. The base dissolved as the outer circle left and as those further inside the group become increasingly alienated and lured by the prospect of becoming a stakeholder. By the beginning of the 1990s, the Green Jackets had largely disintegrated.[3] I believe that the efforts of these formers to offer support, validation, counseling, and material support encompassing job training and placement, safe houses, and enrollment in drug and alcohol abuse programs, taken together, can offer a lifeline of hope to those whom many of us have already written off as lost.

It's true that programs developed and staffed by formers are always vulnerable to a breakdown of trust, backsliding by the staffers, or personal tensions exploding into organizational fissures—so, yes, my optimism is tempered, guarded. In addition to that possibility of corruption or backsliding, there are several other factors that temper my natural inclination toward optimism.

First, although I believe that the politics of nostalgic entitlement will in the long run crash into the present tense, and then the future it also appears that in the short run, the rise of xenophobic, nationalist, anti-immigrant administrations in the United States and Europe will have the dual effect of emboldening the white nationalists in those countries, and then also perhaps lead them to believe that serious organizing in opposition to the government may not be necessary. Perhaps they already *are* the government! Current short-term setbacks may not portend long-term erosion of fundamental freedoms, but the path will be rocky and difficult.

Second, such myopic politics are also reflected in the efforts of extremist groups to become a bit more palatable to mainstream sensibilities. As these groups get closer to the seats of power in the United States, Britain, France, and other countries, they will begin to tailor their messages to appear to be mainstream populists rather than dangerous extremists. In fact, in recent years the neo-Nazi scene has actually become more mainstream. This involves more than the formerly white-robed David Duke now dressed in a jacket and tie and running for political office, or the former scion of the alt-right taking up residence at the right ear of the president of the United States. It also includes movement stalwarts dressing like other young people, fitting in rather than sticking out; at an anti-immigrant rally one might find nearly as many "nipsters" in Timberland boots and hipster beards as skinheads in flight jackets and Doc Martens. Skinny jeans, not skinned heads! In 2014, *Rolling Stone* profiled Patrick Schroeder, a leader of the nipster movement, who decries skinhead thugs as passé: "It's like they're always dressing up for a costume party," he says, as he proclaims a desire to "give the German National Socialist movement a friendlier, hipper face."[4]

This cooler, hipper look articulates with some recent concerns among some European neo-Nazis that would be unthinkable among American right-wing extremists. European National Socialists are concerned about the environment and want to preserve the bucolic German or Swedish countryside from the invading hordes of immigrants. (The American extreme right, meanwhile, finds high-polluting extractive industries just fine and wants to eliminate environmental regulations because they "kill jobs.") Many nipsters are vegetarian, animal rights types. In fact, in one of those bits of cultural ephemera you would not likely predict, there is even a German neo-Nazi vegan cooking show called *Balaclava Kuche*. A neo-Nazi cooking show—on TV! You can't make this stuff up. In each episode, "Tim" and "Kevin," two skinny fast-talking guys from Hannover, wearing T-shirts, tattoos, and balaclavas, earnestly teach their viewers how to make such dishes as tofu scramble. "The left-wing doesn't have a prior

Figure 17. Nipsters: neo-Nazi hipsters make the extreme right more palatable, literally. "Tim" and "Kevin" from Hanover, Germany, who together have created *Balaclava Kuche*, a German neo-Nazi vegan cooking show. Photo courtesy of *Balaclava Kuche.*

claim to veganism," explains Tim. "Industrial meat production is incompatible with our nationalist and socialist world views."[5] Old alignments shift. Neo-Nazi vegan cooking shows. Ex-neo-Nazi hockey leagues.

Finally, I see neither law enforcement nor the policy-making establishment in most countries focusing at all on the similarities among these various groups so that policies can be developed to address several different iterations of violent extremism at the same time. Successful governmental action is unlikely when it cannot fully understand the scope of the problem. For example, the United States has just revised its protocols on "combatting violent extremism" (CVE) to address only Islamism. All references to, and programs designed for, white nationalists have been eliminated, so that the sole focus will be Islamism. And even those policies cannot really combat violent extremism without better understanding the gendered political psychology that brings young guys into the movement and sustains them there. If we ignore gender—masculinity—as a factor in their entry, then we will never be able to help them exit.

Yet I'm guardedly optimistic because there is also a political alternative. As I've argued, populism is an emotion, not an ideology. First comes the emotion of being aggrieved, done badly by and to—the emotional sense of political victimization. Something bad has happened to us. The ideology is added later, mixed into the emotional turmoil of despair and anger.

Populist sentiments need not necessarily turn us to the right, let alone the extreme right. There are populisms of the left (the Spanish anarchists, for example, or the American populists of the late nineteenth century) and populisms of the right (such as the Italian fascists, the current American alt-right, and Hungarian and Polish neofascists). We've seen the rise of a right-wing populism here in the United States in recent years, culminating in the electoral college victory of President Donald Trump.

Populist movements are class-based phenomena, movements of the aggrieved, the downwardly mobile, those pushed aside by larger-scale macroeconomic trends that demolish their traditional ways of life: dominance of too-big-to-fail financial institutions, massive corporations that treat their workers as simple instruments, eroding the dignity of work. These are, of course, deeply gendered experiences, not because women don't work or feel the despair of the downwardly mobile, but because American manhood has, since the country's founding, been inextricably linked to the ability to provide for a family as a breadwinner. One simply does not "prove" one's femininity by working hard and supporting a family. One can prove a lot of other things that way—one's competence, autonomy, self-worth—but female gender is not one of them.

What distinguishes the populisms of the left from those of the right is not class-based grievances. It's race. Populisms of the right see racial difference as the source of their class-based unhappiness. If only "they" went away (deport the immigrants, send the black people "back" to Africa), then our problems would vanish. Our problem is not "us"; it's "them." Populisms of the left privilege class-based grievances over racial differences. Left populists recognize class-based similarities despite racial differences, and link the struggle against racism to the struggle for class-based solutions from below. Left populists understand that as long as racial divisions are fueled by class-based elites, there can be no long-term economic solutions. As Martin Luther King Jr. once put it, "We may have all come on different ships, but we're all in the same boat now."

Right-wing populism is doomed to failure, I believe, because it cannot sustain a vision of the future that seeks only to return us to a more racially pure past, when America was "great." Left populism looks to the future, not the past; toward racial healing, not racial division; toward genuine inclusion based on acknowledging, appreciating, and honoring our various multicultural differences. You can hear that populism of the left in every Woody Guthrie song; in Pete Seeger's exuberant singing of folksongs from around the world; in Ani DiFranco's edgy folk, Tom Morello's searing guitar, Sweet Honey in the Rock's singing the whole world together, and in the Wu-Tang Clan and Public Enemy fighting the power. You can hear it in both Bruce Springsteen's darkest, most anguished cries of the declining white working class, and in his triumphant, transgressive, cross-racial kissing his friend and bandmate Clarence Clemons—on the lips!—at so many of their concerts. You can hear it in Elizabeth Warren's efforts to protect consumers—not just white consumers—or in Bernie Sanders's railing against the corporate banking elites (when he wasn't denigrating the salience of identity politics). Populism of the left must heal the racial divides through class-based coalitions; populisms of the right try to ignore those class-based similarities by exaggerating and polarizing racial divides. A populism that succumbs to racial division only serves those who benefit from middle-class and working-class disunity. But a populism that ignores the specificity of our experiences by race, in favor of some mythic class-based unity, cannot build the coalitions we need to move forward.

That is what makes the optimism of the formers so important an object lesson for us now. Many of these guys have come to acknowledge the humanity of the "other," to see them as fully human, worthy, capable of dignity. By admitting the other, if not always fully embracing them, formers reveal the possibilities open to us all. They express their own humanity by experiencing the humanity of the other. They have returned from a very dark place, but now they can show us the warning signs of our own potential descent. They show us the most essential human needs for connection, to feel that you matter in the world, to feel that life has meaning. And they remind us that it is not too late.

In this book, I argued for that gendered political psychology because all three moments of a young extremists' trajectory—entry, experience, and exit—are deeply gendered processes. Between entry and exit lies the specifically gendered experience of having your masculinity validated by other men; the camaraderie and community that one experiences as being a "man among men"; the feeling of being successful, of having a mission, a duty, a sacred trust, of feeling "called" to that mission, as opposed to feeling coerced by economic hardship to find a dead-end job that will provide something close to resembling a salary to provide for your family. That experience is gendered; masculinity is being expressed, performed, and restored. The world takes manhood away, emasculates the man. Movement participation restores that sense of manhood. It is a powerful narcotic, easily addicting; and asking someone to just give it up without addressing the needs it was meeting is like asking an addict to go cold turkey on his own without any psychological, social, or physical support to address the needs the addiction was meeting.

I believe that our politics must be a politics of possibility, and that we can in effect feed off the optimism of the formers themselves. They are themselves hopeful. Theirs is a politics of hope in a world that gave them no reason to hope. They fought hard against that hopeless despair, looked for community and meaning, that sense that they belonged somewhere, were rooted in a place, that their lives mattered, that they were somebody, somebody who counted. And while they may not be made fully whole after the terrible damage that they and so many others have suffered, they can begin to heal themselves enough to love again or, perhaps, for the first time. More than that, they can heal enough to feel the love that might surround and sustain them from families, children, and a world that values them.

Pelle, one of the workers at EXIT in Stockholm, perhaps put it best. Becoming a skinhead and a neo-Nazi enabled him to express his rage, he tells me and, eventually, to put that rage behind him. In leaving, he was forced to examine who he was and who he wanted to be, to delve into the lineaments of identity and discard those elements that were destructive. Now twenty-seven and ten years out of the movement, Pelle is, like many of the longtime ex-Nazis I met, soft-spoken, thoughtful, and deliberate in speech.

"I'm a better man for having been a Nazi," he says. I am startled when he says this. I blink several times. I'm incredulous, angry, and moved to tears. And yet I think I believe him. I believe I will never need a small suitcase by the door of my home.

Notes

PREFACE

1. "Active Hate Groups in the United States in 2016" (map), Southern Poverty Law Center, https://www.splcenter.org/sites/default/files/ir-162-hate-map-fb.jpg.

2. Peter Bergen, Albert Ford, Alyssa Sims, and David Sterman, "In Depth: Terrorism in America after 9/11," New America (n.d.), https://www.newamerica .org/in-depth/terrorism-in-america/.

3. See Bethany Allen-Ebrahimian, "DHS Strips Funding from Group That Counters Neo-Nazi Violence," *FP* (June 26, 2017), http://foreignpolicy.com /2017/06/26/dhs-strips-funding-from-group-that-counters-neo-nazi-violence/

CHAPTER 1. THE MAKING—AND UNMAKING—OF VIOLENT MEN

1. Cynthia Enloe, *Bananas, Beaches and Bases* (Berkeley: University of California Press, 1989), 44.

2. "Secretary Kerry's Townhall Meeting with Embassy Ottawa Staff," U.S. Embassy and Consulates in Canada, U.S. Department of State, October 28, 2014, https://ca.usembassy.gov/secretary-kerrys-townhall-meeting-with-embassy-ottawa-staff/; "Remarks at the Council of the Americas' 44th

Conference on the Americas," U.S. Department of State, Archived Content, May 7, 2014, https://2009-2017.state.gov/secretary/remarks/2014/05/225729.htm.

3. Jane Huckerby, "When Women Become Terrorists," *New York Times*, January 21, 2015. See also, for example, Kathleen Blee, *Inside Organized Racism: Women in the Hate Movement* (Berkeley: University of California Press, 2003), and Rebecca M. Klatch, *Women of the New Right* (Philadelphia: Temple University Press, 1986).

4. Ben Taub, "Journey to Jihad," *The New Yorker*, June 1, 2015.

5. "Empowering Local Partners to Prevent Violent Extremism in the United States," August 2011, Department of Homeland Security, https://www.dhs.gov/sites/default/files/publications/empowering_local_partners.pdf. See also Erin Miller, "Terrorist Attacks in the U.S. between 1970 and 2013: Data from the Global Terrorism Database (GTD)," START: National Consortium for the Study of Terrorism and Responses to Terrorism, November 2014, https://www.start.umd.edu/pubs/START_IUSSD_GTDTerroristAttacksinUS_ResearchHighlight_Jan2014.pdf.

6. "Empowering Local Partners to Prevent Violent Extremism in the United States."

7. Marc Sageman, *Understanding Terror Networks* (Philadelphia: University of Pennsylvania Press, 2004); Scott Atran, *Talking to the Enemy: Faith, Brotherhood, and the (Un)Making of Terrorists* (New York: Ecco, 2010).

8. Steven Windisch, Pete Simi, Gina Scott Ligon, and Hillary McNeel, "Disengagement from Ideologically-Based and Violent Organizations: A Systematic Review of the Literature," *Journal for Deradicalization* 9 (Winter 2016); Jacob Aasland Ravndal, "Thugs or Terrorists? A Typology of Right-Wing Terrorism and Violence in Western Europe," *Journal for Deradicalization* 3 (Summer 2015); Charles Mink, "It's about the Group, Not God: Social Causes and Cures for Terrorism," *Journal for Deradicalization* 5 (Winter 2015); Afzal Upal, "Alternative Narratives for Preventing the Radicalization of Muslim Youth," *Journal for Deradicalization* 2 (Spring 2015); Alyssa Chassman, "Islamic State, Identity, and the Global Jihadist Movement: How Is Islamic State Successful at Recruiting 'Ordinary People,'" *Journal for Deradicalization* 9 (Winter 2016).

9. Sageman, *Understanding Terror Networks*.

10. Mink, "It's about the Group, Not God," 69, 70.

11. Maleeha Aslam, *Gender-Based Explosions: The Nexus between Muslim Masculinities, Jihadist Islamism and Terrorism* (New York: United Nations University Press, 2012).

12. Ibid., 234, 202, 181, 204–5.

13. Ibid., 268.

14. Ibid., 234.

15. Jared Cohen and Brendan Ballou, "SAVE Supporting Document: Becoming a Former," Council on Foreign Relations, March 22, 2012, http://www.cfr.org/united-states/save-supporting-document-becoming-former/p27056.

16. Daniel Koehler, *Right Wing Terrorism in the 21st Century: The "National Socialist Underground" and the History of Terror from the Far-Right in Germany* (London: Routledge, 2017); Daniel Koehler, *Understanding Deradicalization: Methods, Tools, and Programs for Countering Violent Extremism* (London: Routledge, 2017).

17. Koehler, *Understanding Deradicalization*, 42–43. See also Alessandra L. Gonzalez, Joshua D. Freilich, and Steven M. Chermak, "How Women Engage Homegrown Terrorism," *Feminist Criminology* 9:4 (2014), 344–66.

18. Michael Kimmel and Rachel Kalish, "Suicide by Mass Murder: Masculinity, Aggrieved Entitlement, and Random School Shootings," *Health Sociology Review* 19:4 (2010).

19. Koehler, *Understanding Deradicalization*, 123.

20. Ibid., 192.

21. James Gilligan, *Violence: Reflections on a National Epidemic* (New York: Vintage, 1997).

22. Cohen and Ballou, "SAVE Supporting Document: Becoming a Former."

23. National Center for Health Statistics, "Adolescent Health," Centers for Disease Control and Prevention (last updated May 3, 2017), https://www.cdc.gov/nchs/fastats/adolescent-health.htm.

24. Mark Granovetter, "The Strength of Weak Ties," in *American Journal of Sociology* 78:6 (May 1973), 1360–80.

25. Cohen and Ballou, "SAVE Supporting Document: Becoming a Former."

26. Ruth Manning and Courtney La Bau, *In and Out of Extremism: How Quilliam Helped 10 Former Far Right and Islamists Change* (London: Quilliam Foundation, 2015), 27.

MATTIAS: INTERGENERATIONAL NEO-NAZI

1. *Stolpersteine*, http://www.stolpersteine.eu/en/.

2. Harald Welzer, *Grandpa Wasn't a Nazi: The Holocaust in German Family Remembrance*, International Perspectives No. 54 (New York: American Jewish Committee, 2005), 25, 9–10.

3. Ingo Hasselbach, *Führer-Ex: Memoirs of a Former Neo-Nazi* (New York: Random House, 1996), 149–50.

CHAPTER 2. GERMANY: ANTI-SEMITISM WITHOUT JEWS

1. Joachim Kersten, "The Right-Wing Network and the Role of Extremist Youth Groupings in Unified Germany," in *Fascism and Neofascism: Critical*

Writings on the Radical Right in Europe, ed. A. Fenner and E. D. Weitz (New York: Palgrave, 2004), 185.

2. Jack Sommers, "Holocaust Never Forgotten, but Germany's Jewish Population Has Skyrocketed," *Huffpost, United Kingdom,* January 29, 2015 (updated), http://www.huffingtonpost.co.uk/2015/01/19/german-jewish-renaissance_n_ 6499750.html. The *American Jewish Year Book, 2014* provided the number 250,000, which includes the wider Jewish community and especially the newly arrived Russian Jewish immigrants, in particular to Berlin. Sergio DellaPergola, "World Jewish Population, 2014," in *American Jewish Year Book, 2014,* ed. Arnold Dashefsky and Ira Sheskin (Dordrecht, The Netherlands: Springer, 2015), 301–93.

3. Hasselbach, *Führer-Ex,* 61.

4. Houssain Kettani, "Muslim Population in Europe: 1950–2020," *International Journal of Environmental Science and Development* 1:2 (June 2010).

5. Nicholas Kulish, "Neo-Nazis Suspected in Long Wave of Crimes, Including Murders, in Germany," *New York Times,* November 13, 2011.

6. Ibid.; Helen Pidd, "Germany's Far Right Marches out of the Shadows," *The Guardian,* February 23, 2012, http://www.guardian.co.uk/world/2012/feb/23 /germany-neo-nazis/print.

7. Neal Baker, "New Version of Hitler's 'Mein Kampf' Is a Bestseller in Germany as Sales Near 100,000," *The Sun* (January 3, 2017), https://www.thesun .co.uk/news/2527401/new-version-of-hitlers-mein-kampf-is-a-bestseller-in-germany-as-sales-near-100000/.

8. Pidd, "Germany's Far Right Marches out of the Shadows."

9. Available in English: Bundesamt für Verfassungsschutz, "Figures and Facts," n.d., https://www.verfassungsschutz.de/en/fields-of-work/right-wing-extremism/figures-and-facts-right-wing-extremism. Original German version "Rechtsextremistisches Personenpotenzial (Gesamtübersicht)," Bundesamt für Verfassungsschutz, https://www.verfassungsschutz.de/de /arbeitsfelder/af-rechtsextremismus/zahlen-und-fakten-rechtsextremismus/zuf-re-2015-personenpotenzial.

10. Erik Erikson, *Childhood and Society* (New York: W. W. Norton, 1950), 314–15.

11. Kersten, "The Right-Wing Network and the Role of Extremist Youth Groupings in Unified Germany," 181.

12. Daniela Pisoiu and Daniel Kohler, "Radical Careers: A Theoretical Model for Islamist and Right-Wing Extremist Radicalisation and Deradicalisation," unpublished manuscript, 2013 (in author's files).

13. Hasselbach, *Fuhrer-Ex,* 243. Following particulars and quotations are from the same source (pages 243–44, 245, 328, 92, 316, 320).

14. Kersten, "The Right-Wing Network and the Role of Extremist Youth Groupings in Unified Germany," 186.

15. Daniel Koehler, "Right-Wing Extremist Radicalization Processes: The Formers' Perspective," *Journal EXIT-Deutschland (JEX)* 1 (2014), 336.

16. Ibid., 336.

17. Tore Bjørgo, Jaap van Donselaar, and Sara Gruneberg, "Exit from Right Wing Groups: Lessons from Disengagement Programmes in Norway, Sweden, and Germany," in *Leaving Terrorism Behind: Individual and Collective Disengagement*, ed. Tore Bjørgo and John Horgan (London: Routledge, 2009), 147.

18. Ibid.

19. Ibid., 149.

20. Elena Cresci, "German Town Tricks Neo-Nazis in Raising Thousands of Euros for Anti-extremist Charity," *The Guardian*, November 18, 2014, https://www.theguardian.com/world/2014/nov/18/neo-nazis-tricked-into-raising-10000-for-charity.

CHAPTER 3. SWEDEN: ENTRY AND EXIT

1. *Våldsbejakande extremism i Sverige* (Swedish Justice Ministry, 2015), http://www.regeringen.se/contentassets/a76118e6b4fc49bfba45804f6bb3c956/valdsbejakande-extremism-i-sverige--nulage-och-tendenser-ds-20144.

2. Henning Mankell, *The Return of the Dancing Master*, translated by Laurie Thompson (New York: Vintage, 2003), 158.

3. Allan Pred, *Even in Sweden: Racism, Racialized Spaces and the Popular Geographic Imagination* (Berkeley: University of California, Press, 2000).

4. Katrine Fangen, "Pride and Power: A Sociological Interpretation of the Norwegian Radical Nationalist Underground Movement," PhD diss., Department of Sociology and Human Geography, University of Oslo, 1999. See also "A Death Mask of Masculinity," in *Images of Masculinities: Moulding Masculinities*, ed. Søren Ervø and Thomas Johansson (London: Ashgate, 1999), 184–211; "On the Margins of Life: Life Stories of Radical Nationalists," *Acta Sociologica* 42:4 (1999), 357–73.

5. *EXIT: A Way Through: Facing NeoNazism and Racism among Youth* (Stockholm: EXIT, 2000), 3–4.

6. Quoted in Katja Wahlstrom, *The Way Out of Racism and Nazism* (Stockholm: Save the Children Foundation, 2001), 13–14.

7. Stuart Hughes, "Swedish Neo-Nazis: Moves to De-radicalise amid Far-Right Rise," *BBC News*, December 19, 2014, http://www.bbc.com/news/world-europe-30528918.

8. Jens's story appears in an unpublished paper by Jeppe Lyng, "Masculinities and Right Wing Men in Denmark: Intersections and Core Concepts," 2007 (copy in author's possession).

9. *EXIT: A Way Through,* 6.

10. Jonas Hallen, "Chronicle of a Racist," *Metro,* November 30, 2000.

11. Quoted in in Karl-Olov Arnstberg and Jonas Hallen, *Smaka Kanga: Intervjuer med avhoppade nynazister* (Stockholm, Fryshuset, 2000).

12. Quoted in Les Back, "Wagner and Power Chords: Skinheadism, White Power Music, and the Internet," in *Out of Whiteness: Color, Politics, and Culture,* ed. Vron Ware and Les Back (Chicago: University of Chicago Press, 2002), 114.

13. Quoted in Arnstberg and Hallen, *Smaka Kanga,* 23.

14. Quoted in Tore Bjørgo, *Racist and Right-Wing Violence in Scandinavia: Patterns, Perpetrators, and Responses* (Oslo, Norway: Tano Aschehoug, 1997), 234. See also Tore Bjørgo, "Entry, Bridge-Burning, and Exit Options: What Happens to Young People Who Join Racist Groups—and Want to Leave?" in *Nation and Race,* ed. J. Kaplan and T. Bjorgo (Boston: Northeastern University Press, 1998).

15. Cited in Arnstberg and Hallen, *Smaka Kanga,* 7.

16. *EXIT: A Way Through,* 3.

17. Quoted in Arnstberg and Hallen, *Smaka Kanga,* 31.

18. Quoted in Tina Wilchen Christensen, "Adding a Grey Tone to a Black and White Worldview: How Role Models and Social Encouragement Can Lead Former Right Wing Extremists to Transform Their Identity," unpublished manuscript, Department of Psychology, Roskilde University (copy in author's possession).

19. Quoted in Arnstberg and Hallen, *Smaka Kanga,* 29.

20. Quoted in Wahlstrom, *The Way Out of Racism and Nazism,* 18.

21. Hughes, "Swedish Neo-Nazis."

22. See, for example, Thomas F. Pettigrew and Linda Tropp, "A Meta-Analytic Test of Intergroup Contact Theory," *Journal of Personality and Social Psychology,* 90:5 (2006): 751–83.

23. *EXIT: A Way Through,* 9.

24. Quoted in Arnstberg and Hallen, *Smaka Kanga,* 37.

FRANKIE: "BORN TO BE WILD"

1. Frank Meeink, *Autobiography of a Recovering Skinhead,* as told to Jody M. Roy (Portland, Ore.: Hawthorne Books, 2009), 52. All unattributed quotations are from my interviews with Frankie in 2016 and 2017 and from e-mail correspondence.

2. Ibid., 27.

3. Ibid., 58.

4. Ibid., 166–67.

5. Ibid., 223.

6. Ibid., 224.

7. Ibid., 219.

8. Ibid., 228–29.

9. Ibid., 293.

10. See "Harmony Through Hockey," (news release), *Our Sports Central*, November 29, 2007, http://www.oursportscentral.com/services/releases /harmony-through-hockey/n-3564925.

CHAPTER 4. LIFE AFTER HATE WITH "LIFE AFTER HATE"

Since I wrote about the forty-five active white nationalists I interviewed for *Angry White Men* (2013), I have borrowed from that book here on occasion when talking about how men get into the movement. After all, their recruitment stories are in every way similar to the stories of the formers I've interviewed for this chapter. Their stories begin to diverge, as I show, when we talk about how men get out.

1. "'Reaping the Whirlwind,'" *Intelligence Report* (SPLC), no. 204 (Winter 2001), 13. See also Jim Ridgeway, "Osama's New Recruits," *Village Voice* (November 6, 2001), 41.

2. Christina Couch, "Recovering from Hate," *NOVA Next*, July 29, 2015, http:// www.pbs.org/wgbh/nova/next/body/hatred/.

3. *The Truth at Last*, July 1991, Spencer Library, University of Kansas, accessed July 2013.

4. Cited in Deborah Kaplan, "Republic of Rage: A Look inside the Patriot Movement," paper presented at the annual meeting of the American Sociological Association (August 21–25, 1998), 34.

5. Jeff Coplon, "The Roots of Skinhead Violence: Dim Economic Prospects for Young Men," *Utne Reader* (May–June 1989), 84.

6. Quoted in Abby Ferber, *White Man Falling: Race, Gender, and White Supremacy* (Lanham, MD: Rowman and Littlefield, 1998), 136.

7. Andrew Macdonald, *The Turner Diaries* (New York: Barricade Books, 1978), 33.

8. Randy Duey, "Yahweh, Give Us Men!" *Aryan Nations*, no. 36 (1979), 18.

9. See, for example, "Famous Geraldo Skinhead Brawl" (originally broadcast on *Geraldo* in 1988), on YouTube, https://www.youtube.com/watch?v= i0yN0dGNfwk.

10. Arno Michaels, *My Life after Hate* (Milwaukee: La Prensa de LAH, 2010), 167–68.

11. Christian Picciolini, *Romantic Violence: Memoirs of an American Skinhead* (Chicago: Goldmill Group, 2015), 49, 283.

12. Michaels, *My Life after Hate,* 62–63.

13. "White Supremacist Leader Tries to Make Amends," *Morning Edition,* National Public Radio, April 25, 2017, http://www.npr.org/2017/04/25/525516754 /white-supremacist-tries-to-make-amends.

14. Michaels, *My Life after Hate,* 170.

15. Quoted in Joseph Goldstein, "The Rehabilitation of a Former Wrestler Who Became a Neo-Nazi Leader," *New York Times* (February 3, 2017), A25.

16. See James Gilligan, *Violence* (New York: Vintage, 1997).

17. Jason Wilson, "Life after White Supremacy: The Former Neo-Fascist Now Working to Fight Hate," *The Guardian,* April 4, 2017, https://www.theguardian .com/world/2017/apr/04/life-after-hate-groups-neo-fascism-racism.

18. Couch, "Recovering from Hate."

19. Michaels, *My Life after Hate,* 36.

20. Ibid., 38.

21. See also Pete Simi and Robert Futrell, *American Swastika: Inside the White Power Movement's Hidden Spaces of Hate* (Lanham, MD: Rowman and Littlefield, 2010), 85.

22. Wilson, "Life after White Supremacy."

23. Handbill for Skrewdriver concert, cited in Picciolini, *Romantic Violence,* 46.

24. Andy, quoted in Simi and Futrell, *American Swastika,* 64–65.

25. Biggie, quoted in ibid., 66.

26. TJ Leyden, *Skinhead Confessions: From Hate to Hope* (Springville, UT: Sweetwater Books, 2008), 19.

27. Michaels, *My Life after Hate,* 169.

28. "Prussian Boy ≠ Skinhead Boy," YouTube, published June 29, 2016, https:// www.youtube.com/watch?v=4-YGckxH0gU.

29. ABC News, "Teenage Sisters Singing: Neo-Nazi Beliefs Have Changed as These Two Girls Grew Up," YouTube, published July 20, 2011, https://www .youtube.com/watch?v=ULsTm5VR73c.

30. Brian Levin, "Exclusive: Interview with Professor Who Extensively Studied Alleged Wisconsin Mass Killer," *HuffPost,* October 7, 2012, http://www .huffingtonpost.com/brian-levin-jd/exclusive-interview-with_b_1751181.html.

31. Couch, "Recovering from Hate."

32. Picciolini, *Romantic Violence,* 60, 87, 90.

33. Ibid., 94–95.

34. "Tony McAleer (Canada)," *The Forgiveness Project,* August 24, 2014, http://theforgivenessproject.com/stories/tony-mcaleer-canada/.

35. "Former B.C. Neo-Nazi Abandons Racist Views," *CBC News,* February 7, 2012, http://www.cbc.ca/news/canada/british-columbia/former-b-c-neo-nazi-abandons-racist-views-1.1188498.

36. Blee, *Inside Organized Racism*.

37. "Ladies of the Invisible Empire," Homestead.com, http://swkloties2 .homestead.com/MAIN~ns4.html (accessed August 14, 2012); Aryan Confederations, www.geocities.com.arcon_wp/policies.htm (accessed March 14, 2007).

38. Jack Rader, "The Plot against Aryan Masculinity," *Aryan Nations*, no. 37 (1985), 18, 17.

39. Tom Metzger, "What We Believe as White Racists," in *Extreme Deviance*, ed. Erich Goode and D. Angus Vail (Thousand Oaks, CA: Pine Forge Press, 2008), 131.

40. Memo from Randi Fishman to the author, July 24, 2008.

41. All unattributed quotes in the following discussion are from my interviews with Angela King.

42. "White Supremacist Leader Tries to Make Amends."

43. Caitlin Dickson, "Derek Black, the Reluctant Racist, and His Exit from White Nationalism," *Daily Beast*, July 29, 2013, http://www.thedailybeast.com /derek-black-the-reluctant-racist-and-his-exit-from-white-nationalism.

44. Blee, *Inside Organized Racism*, 93, 114, 143.

45. Ibid., 105.

46. Michaels, *My Life after Hate*, 38.

47. Leyden, *Skinhead Confessions*, 131.

48. Caitlin Dickson, "Renounced Racist Derek Black Speaks Out," *Daily Beast*, July 29, 2013, http://www.thedailybeast.com/articles/2013/07/29 /renounced-racist-derek-black-speaks-out.html. See also Dickson, "Derek Black, Reluctant Racist."

49. Leyden, *Skinhead Confessions*, 57.

50. Jessie Daniels, *White Lies: Race, Class, Gender, and Sexuality in White Supremacist Discourse* (New York: Routledge, 1997).

51. Randy Blazak, "'Getting It': The Role of Women in Male Desistance from Hate Groups," in *Home-Grown Hate: Gender and Organized Racism*, ed. Abby L. Ferber (New York: Routledge, 2004), 161–79.

52. Ibid., 172.

53. Ibid., 174.

54. While several interviewees mentioned the centrality of family, Blazak's research in prisons underscores this dynamic. Randy Blazak, personal interview, May, 2017.

55. Quoted in Blazak, "'Getting It,'" 173.

56. Quoted in Goldstein, "Rehabilitation of a Former Wrestler," A25.

57. Leyden, *Skinhead Confessions*, 122.

58. "Tony McAleer (Canada)."

59. Couch, "Recovering from Hate."

60. Leyden, *Skinhead Confessions*, 121.

61. TJ Leyden (USA), *The Forgiveness Project*, August 3, 2011, http:// theforgivenessproject.com/stories/tj-leyden-usa/.

MUBIN: UNDERCOVER JIHADIST

1. Anne Speckhard and Mubin Shaikh, *Undercover Jihadi* (McLean, VA: Advances Press, 2014), 89. All unattributed quotations are from interviews with Mubin Shaikh in 2015, 2016, and 2017.
2. Ibid., 26.
3. Ibid., 43.
4. Ibid., 51.
5. Ibid., 68.
6. Ibid., 101.

CHAPTER 5. BRITAIN: THE EX-JIHADISTS NEXT DOOR

1. "Text: Bin Laden's Statement," *The Guardian*, October 7, 2001, https:// www.theguardian.com/world/2001/oct/07/afghanistan.terrorism15. See also Jakob Sheikh, "'I Just Said It. The State': Examining the Motivations for Danish Foreign Fighting in Syria," *Perspectives on Terrorism* 10:6 (December 2016).
2. "Who Are Britain's Jihadists?" *BBC News*, July 5, 2017, http://www.bbc .com/news/uk-32026985. See also Edwin Bakker and Roel de Bont, "Belgian and Dutch Jihadist Foreign Fighters (2012–2015): Characteristics, Motivations, and Roles in the War in Syria and Iraq," *Small Wars and Insurgencies* 27:5 (2016), 837–57.
3. Sageman, *Understanding Terror Networks*, 73, 75, 85, 13.
4. Nasra Hassan, "An Arsenal of Believers" *New Yorker*, November 19, 2001, http://www.newyorker.com/magazine/2001/11/19/an-arsenal-of-believers.
5. Barbara Ehrenreich, "A Mystery of Misogyny," *The Progressive*, December 1, 2001, http://progressive.org/magazine/mystery-misogyny/.
6. Peter Marsden, *The Taliban: War, Religion and the New Order in Afghanistan* (London: Zed Books, 1998).
7. This and the following quotations come from Neil MacFarquhar, "A Nation Challenged: Disavowal: A Father Denies His Gentle Son Could Hijack Any Jetliner" *New York Times* (September 19, 2001), http://www.nytimes.com/2001/09/19 /world/a-nation-challenged-disavowal-father-denies-gentle-son-could-hijack-any-jetliner.html?mcubz=0.
8. Charles Kurzman, *The Missing Martyrs: Why There Are So Few Muslim Terrorists* (New York: Oxford University Press, 2011), 69–70.

9. Ed Husain, *The Islamist: Why I Joined Radical Islam in Britain, What I Saw Inside, and Why I Left* (London: Penguin, 2007), 3.

10. Ibid., 23, 69.

11. Rosamund Urwin, "Deeyah Khan: What IS Do Is like Grooming—They Prey on Guilt, Loneliness, and Anger," *Evening Standard*, November 23, 2015, http://www.standard.co.uk/lifestyle/london-life/deeyah-khan-what-is-do-is-like-grooming-they-prey-on-guilt-loneliness-and-anger-a3121011.html.

12. Husain, *The Islamist*, 63.

13. Urwin, "Deeyah Khan."

14. Ibid.

15. Ibid.

16. Sheikh, "'I Just Said It. The State,'" 65.

17. Jakob Sheikh, "My Childhood Friend, the ISIS Jihadist," *Mashable*, October 14, 2014; http://mashable.com/2014/10/15/childhood-friend-isis-jihadist/.

18. Thomas Chatterton Williams, "Radical Ambition," *New York Times Magazine* (April 2, 2017), 27.

19. Hisham Aidi, *Rebel Music: Race, Empire, and the New Muslim Youth Culture* (New York: Pantheon 2014), 49

20. Ibid., 65.

21. Williams, "Radical Ambition," 27.

22. Manwar Ali, "Inside the Mind of a Former Radical Jihadi," TED, April 2016, https://www.ted.com/talks/manwar_ali_inside_the_mind_of_a_former_radical_jihadist/transcript?language=en.

23. Ibid.

24. Ibid.

25. Maajid Nawaz, *Radical: My Journey out of Islamist Extremism* (Guilford, CT: Lyons Press, 2016), 51.

26. Diego Gambetta and Steffen Hertog, *Engineers of Jihad: The Curious Connection between Violent Extremism and Education* (Princeton: Princeton University Press, 2016).

27. Speckhard and Shaikh, *Undercover Jihadi*, 145.

28. Ibid., 247.

29. Chris Cobb, "Canadians Converting to Islam: A Rocky, Complex Road, New Study Finds," *Ottawa Citizen*, July 26, 2015, http://ottawacitizen.com /news/local-news/canadians-converting-to-islam-a-rocky-complex-road-new-study-finds.

30. Neumann quoted in Richard Smirke, "Jihadi Rap: Understanding the Subculture," *Billboard*, October 10, 2014, http://www.billboard.com /articles/news/6273809/jihadi-rap-l-jinny-abdel-majed-abdel-bary. Two recent books amplify the discussion: Raffaello Pantucci, *We Love Death as You Love Life: Britain's Suburban Mujahadeen* (London: Hurst, 2015); and Aidi, *Rebel Music*.

31. Amil Khan, "Al Qaeda's New Front: Jihadi Rap," *Politico Magazine*, August 31, 2014, http://www.politico.com/magazine/story/2014/08/al-qaedas-new-front-jihadi-rap-110481.

32. Smirke, "Jihadi Rap."

33. "Sheikh Terra feat Soul Salah Crew Dirty Kuffar," published April 26, 2015, https://www.youtube.com/watch?v=SWP_95eSLBI.

34. "Rapping American Jihadi Sings 'Blow by Blow,'" published September 12, 2013, https://www.youtube.com/watch?v=MDDYqV9V5kA.

35. Sons of Hagar, "Motive Transportation," published May 16, 2011, https://www.youtube.com/watch?v=p0KuC3oCIlA.

36. I got this information from "72 Virgins," on Wikipedia's WikiIslam, https://wikiislam.net/wiki/72_Virgins.

37. Quoted in Mia Bloom, "Bombshells: Women and Terrorism," *Gender Issues* 28 (2011), 1–21. See also Audrey Alexander, *Cruel Intentions: Female Jihadists in America* (Washington, DC: George Washington University Program on Extremism, 2016), 7–8.

38. Nelly Lahoud, "The Neglected Sex: The Jihadis Exclusion of Women," *Jihad, Terrorism, and Political Violence* 26 (2014), 783.

39. Julia Ioffe, "Mothers of Isis," *Huffington Post*, n.d., http://highline.huffingtonpost.com/articles/en/mothers-of-isis/

40. Richard Watson, "The One True God, Allah" *Granta* (January 2008), 58.

41. Ioffe, "Mothers of Isis."

42. Daan Weggemans, Edwin Bakker, and Peter Grol, "Who Are They and Why Do They Go? The Radicalisation and Preparatory Processes of Dutch Jihadist Fighters," *Perspectives on Terrorism* 8:4 (August 2014), 108.

43. Ioffe, "Mothers of Isis."

44. The short story "My Son the Fanatic," by Hanif Kureishi, in *The New Yorker* (March 28, 1994, pp. 92–96), eloquently describes a parent's continuing confusion over his son's descent into terrorism, until it is too late.

45. Ioffe, "Mothers of Isis."

46. Cohen and Ballou, "SAVE Supporting Document: Becoming a Former."

47. Richard Barrett and Laila Bokhari, "Deradicalization and Rehabilitation Programmes Targeting Religious Terrorists and Extremists in the Muslim World: An Overview," in *Leaving Terrorism Behind*, 179.

48. Manning and La Bau, *In and Out of Extremism*, 25.

49. Ibid., 12.

50. Ibid., 28.

51. Ibid., 32.

52. See, for example, Mark S. Hamm, *The Spectacular Few: Prisoner Radicalization and the Evolving Terrorist Threat* (New York: New York University Press, 2013).

53. Manning and La Bau, *In and Out of Extremism*, 34.

54. Ibid., 36.

55. Ibid., 42–46.

56. Ibid., 55–56.

57. Ibid., 59–61.

58. Christopher Boucek, Shazadi Beg, and John Horgan, "Opening Up the Jihadi Debate: Yemen's Committee for Dialogue," in *Leaving Terrorism Behind*, 192.

59. Christopher Boucek, "Extremist Re-education and Rehabilitation in Saudi Arabia," in *Leaving Terrorism Behind*, 212.

60. Ibid., 213.

61. Ibid., 215.

62. See also "Adam Deen," Extreme Dialogue, http://extremedialogue.org /adam-deen/.

63. Ibid.

64. Manwar Ali, "Inside the Mind of a Former Radical Jihadi."

EPILOGUE

1. "African Proverbs (2011)," JJ Bola (blog), http://www.jjbola.com /african-proverbs-2011/.

2. Such a story was the cause of a major investigation in New York City when David Dinkins, the former mayor, announced that he, too, had been passed by, and when Floyd Flake, a former black congressman from Queens, wrote in an op-ed in the *New York Post*, "I don't know of an African-American who has not endured the shame and anger of having a cab driver lock his doors upon approaching them. An additional indignity usually follows: the cracked window and the question about where the rider is headed—and then the driver pulling off, saying he's not headed in that direction."

3. Tore Bjørgo, "Processes of Disengagement from Violent Groups of the Extreme Right," in *Leaving Terrorism Behind*, 45.

4. Thomas Rogers, "Heil Hipster: The Young Neo-Nazis Trying to Put a Stylish Face on Hate," *Rolling Stone*, June 23, 2014, http://www.rollingstone.com /culture/news/heil-hipster-the-young-neo-nazis-trying-to-put-a-stylish-face-on-hate-20140623.

5. "Balaclava Küche #1," YouTube, posted February 18, 2014, https://www .youtube.com/watch?v=FQd12gFWKb8; Tim quoted in Rogers, "Heil Hipster."

Index